WANNABE IN MY GANG?

WANNABE IN MY GANG?

FROM THE KRAYS TO THE *ESSEX BOYS*

BERNARD O'MAHONEY

MAINSTREAM
PUBLISHING

EDINBURGH AND LONDON

Reprinted, 2006, 2008

First published in Great Britain in 2004 by
MAINSTREAM PUBLISHING COMPANY (EDINBURGH) LTD
7 Albany Street
Edinburgh EH1 3UG

ISBN 978184018767 0

A catalogue record for this book is available from the British Library

Printed in Great Britain by
CPI William Clowes Ltd, Beccles, NR34 7TL

Extracts from *Stop the Ride* by Dave Courtney,
reproduced by permission of Virgin Books Ltd.
© Dave Courtney, 1999, Virgin Books Ltd.

Extracts from *Inside the Firm* by Tony Lambianou,
reproduced by permission of John Blake Publishing.
© Tony Lambrianou, 1991, 2002

This book is dedicated to those who survived those years of madness, mayhem and murder:

My good friend Gavin Spicer, who was always at my side; my good friend Martin Hall and family; Sue Woods; Steve 'Nipper' Ellis; Big Greg from Leytonstone; Ian from Barking; Jeff (stitch my head) Bulman; Larry Johnston; Mark Rothermel; Peter and Tony Simms; Chris Raal; Mark and Carol Shinnik; Roger Mellin; Dave (where's my television) Thomkins; Steve Curtis and Nathan from Bristol; Liam the jogger from Basildon; Maurice (I'm so handsome) Golding; Paul Trehern; Chemical Bob and partner Mark. Special thanks to Martin Moore of Great Barr, Birmingham. Last, but not least, my partner Emma Turner, and my children, Adrian, Vinney and Karis.

Those that have passed cannot change anything.

www.bernardomahoney.com
www.mesh-29.co.uk

CONTENTS

Reg Kray, 'gang boss':
'There are no sex offenders or the like on my wing. We are the so-called hard men of the prison and we simply wouldn't tolerate them. No one likes these monsters.'

David Courtney, 'gang boss':
'One thing that never fails to amaze me is some people's capacity for self-delusion. I can understand trying to con someone else because you might get a reward, but conning yourself? One of the hardest things in life is to be honest with yourself; do that and you're halfway there.'

Leighton Frayne, 'gang boss':
'I was stabbed very bad, through the lung, heart and spleen and seven other wounds. Pretty bad ones, but that's life isn't it?
   'I don't like bullshit, I'm a man of my word.'

Tony Lambrianou, 'gang boss':
'I have regrets about my past, I must admit, but more important than anything else, I'm not ashamed of it. It's important to me as a person that I can hold my head up, knowing that I didn't point the finger at anybody, that I was with the twins and I fell with the twins.'

John 'Gaffer' Rollinson:
'All families are good families. I believe in the family structure; people look after each other. If I could have been born into a Mafia family, I would have loved it.
   'I was what I was. Basically, a violent, selfish, lazy, pig-headed thug, whose idea of domestic bliss was to say goodbye on a Friday evening and turn up again on Monday morning, smashed out of my skull, with a load of drunken mates in tow, waking up the kids.'

Kate Howard (Kray):
(*1993*) Ron Kray: 'I don't like your book. It's too personal . . . no more books about us?'
   Kate: I smiled back. 'No more books about us.'
   Ron: 'Let's forget about it.'
   Kate: 'I couldn't agree more.'
   (*2003, from the official Kate 'Kray' website*) 'When Kate married gangster Ronnie Kray, he introduced her to some of the most feared and deadly criminals Britain has ever known. She persuaded them to open their hearts to her and talk about their crimes, their fears and their dreams. Kate is now an established author and has written three books on the Kray Twins and many more on what she knows best – tough guys.'

INTRODUCTION

I can hear them now in the pubs and clubs around Essex and London: calling me a hypocrite, swearing murderous revenge for showing them disrespect by casting doubt on their prowess.

They will call me a hypocrite because I am a man who, like them, has broken the law, spent time in prison, intimidated, punched, kicked, cut and stabbed others to get what he wanted. They will want their revenge because nobody who thinks they have a reputation likes to hear the truth about themselves.

So, I hear you ask, who are 'they'?

'They' are the men who promote themselves as 'the kings of the underworld', the 'hardest men in Britain', or the 'most evil men on the planet'.

Fucking idiots . . .

To be honest, I couldn't care less what these people say or think because I am my own man and I say what I feel needs to be said. Throughout my life I have been at odds with people who have tried to impose their views or authority on me. I couldn't see eye to eye with my father, school teachers, policemen, probation officers and later in life, prison officers. They didn't seem to realise when they were shouting and screaming at me that I consider nothing more despicable than so-called respect based on fear. I loathed their attempts to intimidate me, make me do their will and agree with their twisted philosophy simply because they thought they could scare or overpower me. I am neither ashamed nor proud of the fact that I have been in trouble all of my life. I would be ashamed if I and those close to me had endured the years of misery it has caused for nothing.

I don't believe we have. Adversity has given us a bond nobody can break. It has also given me the will to try and prevent others from following the same path that I took.

I wish somebody had been there to guide me before I embarked on this nightmare of a journey.

Few in Essex will ever forget 1995 – I certainly won't. Young people, fuelled initially by recreational drugs, embraced and danced at raves across the county. The Summer of Love, as the media called it, soon soured and gave way to the Winter of Discontent. My friends, their minds poisoned with Class 'A' drugs and ideas of gangland grandeur, began murdering one another. As well as the casualties of an undeclared war, others on the fringes were suffering mental-health problems, imprisonment and death because of the drugs the combatants supplied.

Five weeks before Christmas in 1995, an eighteen-year-old girl called Leah Betts died after taking a pill that had been supplied by my associates. Two weeks later, three of my friends had their brains blown out by an assassin as they sat in their Range Rover, parked down a quiet farm track. So much for the season of goodwill.

The death of Leah Betts and the murder of my friends in such a short period of time had a profound effect on me. I knew my time had come, that I had to get out or I too would die an undignified death or be imprisoned. I realised I had to try and shed the criminal make-up I had worn since I was a boy.

I did everything I could to break my criminal bonds. I distanced myself from my associates and I did the unthinkable; I assisted the police. I told myself that I was a reformed character but I soon found out that society never really wants to forgive, because people are not prepared to forget. Why should they, particularly when the debt you owe involves the deaths of others?

Such debts can never really be settled.

In 1996, Leah Betts' father appeared on national television and called me a bastard, saying he held me responsible for the death of his daughter. The public naturally felt for a man who had lost somebody so young and many believed that I had indeed killed her. At school my children were taunted by other children who said that I was a murderer. Life for us all became impossible. In an effort to set the record straight, I wrote *So this is Ecstasy?*, telling the true story of the events which led up to Leah's death.

I have since written three other books. *Essex Boys* highlights the plight of Jack Whomes and Mick Steele, who were convicted of murdering my three friends as they sat in their car. I firmly believe that they are innocent and so felt it was a book that needed to be published. I then wrote *Soldier of the Queen*, an honest account of my time serving as a British soldier in my family's native Ireland. Forget those SAS memoirs, this book tells the true story of what life was really like fighting an everyday war against the IRA. After a three-year legal battle at the High Court in London, I won the right to publish *The Dream Solution*, which tells the story of my involvement with sisters Lisa and Michelle Taylor who butchered 21-year-old bride Alison Shaughnessy and evaded justice.

There is nothing wrong with anybody writing books that are factual and have something worthwhile to say, but I do think that during the last decade publishers and those in the media who serialise and review books have turned misery and murder into a form of light entertainment.

When 'gangster' Dave Courtney wrote his biography (1999), he boasted about getting away with murder, living a life of luxury funded by crime and dealing in drugs. The book was serialised by a national newspaper who printed a photograph of one of Courtney's young children holding a gun. This was an absolutely obscene episode and should have been condemned, but the newspaper concerned paid Courtney for the 'privilege' of promoting him as a successful criminal and showing the offensive photograph. I can now reveal that Courtney has never committed a murder; the book is based on his weird and disturbing fantasies.

Sadly, Courtney is not the only one who has written a 'true crime' biography which is in fact bullshit. Several more are exposed in this book.

Many young kids think that being a gang member is flash or

something to aspire to. That is a disturbing enough thought, but when you consider that gun crime in the UK has risen by 35 per cent in the last few years, promoting such a lifestyle is criminal in itself.

Lying fools like Courtney, to whom the media give oxygen, are not men of respect as they want others to think – they are despicable. They use their books to boast and brag to impressionable young kids about the heinous crimes they have committed, the lavish lifestyle they have enjoyed on the back of a life of crime and the 'useful' time they have spent in prison. I describe them as despicable because they are recommending a lifestyle to kids that they themselves have never experienced or had to endure.

I have endured it and I can assure you if you've bought this book to read about the glamour of being a gangster, you're going to be very disappointed.

1

ABOUT A BOY

As the car came hurtling down the street nobody could have imagined the devastation it was about to cause. The teenager at the wheel was under age, had no licence or insurance and had taken the car without the consent of the owner. Unaware of the approaching car, ten-year-old James Fallon, who had moved from Wolverhampton to South Africa with his parents, was walking across a zebra crossing with his BMX bike. By the time the driver saw James, it was too late. The vehicle struck the boy and dragged him along the road for 30 metres before tossing his body onto the pavement. Ironically, the accident took place close to a nurse's house. By the time James's body had come to rest he was unconscious and had turned blue. The nurse, having heard the collision, ran on to the street and gave James the kiss of life before calling the emergency services.

When he arrived at the hospital, James underwent surgery for seven hours. A steel collar had to be put on his body in order to hold his head in place on his shoulders. James was put on a life-support machine, but nobody thought he would survive the night.

An examination of James revealed that he was paralysed from the neck down. He was unable to breathe without the aid of a respirator and he was unable to swallow or speak. He could hear and see and, crucially, his comprehension was unimpaired. With the help of round-the-clock nursing care, James's heartbroken parents began the slow process of bringing him back to life.

Miraculously, he learned to communicate by eye movement and within six months was ready to return home to his parents. Not only did James continue to improve his communication skills but also managed to pass exams in maths, general knowledge, English and geography with the aid of videotapes. James's terrible accident generated publicity locally, nationally and back home in England.

On Friday, 20 January 1989, I was visiting my mother in Wolverhampton when I read the following article in the local evening newspaper, *The Express and Star*:

UNCLE STARTS FUND TO HELP PARALYSED CRASH BOY, 10

A Codsall man has launched an appeal fund for his nephew who 'died' twice and is now totally paralysed after a road accident in South Africa.

Former Codsall boy James Fallon, aged ten, had his skull detached from his spine in the smash last September. Top surgeons from all over South Africa managed to save his life in a seven-hour operation, which has since featured in medical journals throughout the world. It was the first time it had been carried out in the country and only the fourth time it had been attempted anywhere.

But now James cannot talk, breathe or swallow without the aid of life-support systems. He is still in Johannesburg General Hospital where he has been taught to use a computer, which allows him to communicate, by eye movement.

'We are hoping he will be allowed home some time in May,' said his uncle, Paul Nicholson of Wilkes Road, 'but his parents will have to install very expensive equipment if he is to survive.'

His parents, Elaine, 33, and Roger, 35, who also lived in Wilkes Road, emigrated to South Africa six years ago. The accident happened as James was going back to school for a concert recital. He was hit by a speeding car driven by an under age motorist. The 17-year-old driver, who had taken his father's car without consent, was later fined £50.

James was hurled more than 90 feet along the road and also suffered internal injuries and crushed legs. He stopped breathing once at the roadside and again in the hospital.

'It was a miracle he survived, but now he is a prisoner in his own body,' said Mr Nicholson. His parents need a lot of money to convert their home and he is starting an appeal in James's name at Barclays Bank in Codsall.

I knew all about being a prisoner and the thought of an innocent ten-year-old boy being trapped in his own body really struck a chord with me. I had quite rightly been imprisoned on two occasions for wounding people. I also had convictions for robbery, violent disorder, breach of the peace, affray and assaulting police. Yet here was a ten-year-old boy, with his whole life before him, imprisoned in his own body and he had done nothing. I really felt for him.

His mother, Elaine Fallon, used to live in the same street as me in Codsall, where I was brought up. Even though she had only lived 20 doors away, I had never really spoken to her. I did know Elaine's elder brother, Paul, but only to say hello to. They were a close-knit family, good hard-working people who kept themselves to themselves. James would receive all the love and moral support he needed from them – of that I was certain. All the Fallon family required was financial support to pay for the specialist equipment that James needed. I decided I would 'do my bit' and try to raise a bit of money locally.

At this time I was living in Basildon, Essex, with my partner Debra and our son Vinney. I didn't fancy making endless trips up and down the motorway, so I settled for a one-off event. I decided that the quickest and most efficient way of raising money would be if I could get lots of items off famous or infamous people and hold an auction. I wrote about 150 letters to well-known people and bands such as The Rolling Stones, The Who, Paul McCartney, Madonna and Dire Straits. I also wrote to numerous football clubs including Arsenal, Manchester United and Wolverhampton Wanderers. In fact I wrote to everybody I could think of who had ever been 'a somebody'. Amongst those 'somebodies', I included the infamous Kray twins.

I asked the various people I wrote to if they would donate something of theirs that had been signed and which people would be prepared to pay money for. It didn't matter if it was a book, an album, a T-shirt, a football, photo or item of clothing. The vast majority of people did send something: Dire Straits sent a gold disc, The Rolling Stones sent signed albums, as did The Who. Madonna donated a signed T-shirt and most football clubs sent signed footballs and photographs. Even Great Train Robbers Ronnie Biggs and Buster Edwards sent signed white £5 banknotes – the same type as they had stolen in their infamous heist.

The Kray twins donated a signed photograph and a picture that Ronnie had painted in Broadmoor. The picture looked as if a three-year-old had painted it. It was a house on a hill. The hill was green. The house was orange and red. There was a tree by the side of it that looked more like a stick with a green blob on the top. The sky was black and to me that said more about the state of Ronnie's mind than his obvious lack of artistic talent.

I wasn't sure anybody would want to hang it on a wall in their home, but I was certain somebody would buy it just because 'a Kray had painted it'. I was sitting in the garden one afternoon when the telephone rang. Debra answered it and then called out to me.

'Bernie, there's a man on the phone. He says his name is Reggie Kray and he wants to talk to you.'

'Here we go,' I said. 'Some fucking unemployed fool I've met with nothing better to do than play jokes on people.'

I went in and picked up the receiver. The man on the other end of the line sounded elderly, weak and almost effeminate.

'All right, Bernie? This is Reggie Kray.'

'Oh yes, and what can I do for you, Reggie?' I still thought someone was trying to wind me up so I was being sarcastic.

'I've read the article you sent me about the boy James Fallon. My brother and I have sent you a painting, but we just wondered if we could do any more to help. We just wanted to offer our assistance.'

I have to admit that I was quite shocked when I realised it was in fact Reggie Kray who was on the phone.

I had always imagined him to be a powerful, menacing man who would speak with a deep intimidating tone. How wrong I was; he sounded just like Corporal Jones off the TV series *Dad's Army*.

I told Reggie that I was organising a charity auction in Wolverhampton and that was going to be it, as far as I was concerned, so I didn't really need any help.

'Well, we just wanted you to know that we're thinking about the boy and if we can help you, we will,' said Reg.

We exchanged pleasantries and Reg said that he would keep in touch by letter to see how James was getting on. I put the phone down and thought no more about it.

The Krays had earned their infamous reputation from the way they had controlled the East End of London during the 1960s. They had beaten, stabbed, shot and even murdered rival gang members on their way to the top of the criminal heap, but were as well known for their charitable acts as their violent outbursts and many in the East End saw them as Robin Hood-type figures. I couldn't see anything wrong with the Krays being associated with the Fallon cause. In fact I thought it could only have been a positive thing. They knew a lot of people and never failed to generate interest where the media was concerned. To raise money for James, I would have to give his plight as much exposure as possible and the name Kray would certainly help me achieve that. For now, I didn't need anything other than the items they had so kindly donated, as they would be enough to give me the publicity I needed.

I booked the Connaught Hotel in Wolverhampton, which is one of the better hotels in the city. I also secured the services of a local band called The Sect, who agreed to play free of charge. A local DJ also agreed that he would provide his services for free. I was reasonably confident that the event was going to be a success.

Ticket sales, however, were non-existent. I could only put the lack of local support down to two factors.

Firstly, at that time, the mid- to late '80s, there was a lot of anti-South African feeling in reaction to the apartheid laws. Trade sanctions had been imposed against the country by Britain and many other Western nations. It wasn't politically correct for people to have anything to do with the country and, particularly, with white South Africans.

The main reason, I guessed, was that as young men growing up in the Wolverhampton area, my elder brothers and I had been nothing but trouble. We had all been imprisoned and convicted of numerous violent offences and people felt intimidated by us. I just don't think that anybody wanted to be involved with anything we were doing, regardless of what or who we were doing it for.

My attitude was 'Fuck them' – I wasn't going to let their petty mindset interfere with my efforts to help a child. As the event drew nearer, my elder brother Paul, who lived in Brixton, south London, my younger brother Michael, who still lived in Wolverhampton, and I decided to visit the pubs and clubs in the city in order to generate interest and sell tickets.

We were going from pub to pub, leaving tickets with landlords and asking customers to buy them, but they were all claiming to be short of money or 'busy that night'. I hate fucking ponces and tight people.

Rightly or wrongly, their attitude didn't put me in the best of moods. I was annoyed that so-called 'decent people' could hold petty prejudices and in a sad attempt to spite me, withhold a meagre £5 note from a 10-year-old paralysed boy who was fighting for his life.

As we continued touting the tickets, we came across what I can only describe as a group of drunken louts who were hanging about in the street. They were behaving like drugged-up monkeys, hurling waste-paper bins, screeching and throwing chips at one other.

As we walked by, somebody threw a chip that hit me on the back and one of them called me a 'wanker'. I turned around and asked who had thrown the chip. Nobody said anything, so I asked who had called me a wanker. Again, nobody answered so I started to walk away with my brothers. I really wasn't in the mood to be dealing with these people. Once more, the abuse started and one or two of them were mimicking me and laughing. They'd had their chance, so I walked up to who I thought was the culprit and punched him in the face.

He immediately lost his swaggering bravado and started whimpering, 'Please don't hit me, please don't hit me. I haven't done anything.' One of his friends began to run to a nearby telephone box – so as to ring the police, I assumed. I didn't relish the thought of being arrested for the likes of these people, so I ran over to try and stop him. Meanwhile the man I had hit, Stuart Darley, was getting brave again and shouting further obscenities, so I left his friend and walked back over to where he was standing. I hit him again to shut his drunken mouth. I know what some people might say – it's violent, it's wicked – but vulnerable people like my elderly mother have to walk those same streets and endure that sort of intimidating, loutish behaviour. The gang quickly dispersed. My brothers and I carried on with what we had set out to do.

The following day, my brother Paul and I returned to our homes in the south and Michael remained in Wolverhampton. Around midday I got a phone call from Michael, who said that the police had arrested him that morning and charged him with assault. They told Michael that they were also going to arrest Paul and me, so we should contact them at the earliest opportunity. It was typical: somebody starts something, comes unstuck and calls the police. No doubt it would have been a different story if the gang had kicked some old man around the streets after he had objected to being called names and having food thrown at him.

I wasn't too concerned. In my mind, I had done no wrong and the police could wait. I wasn't going to jump into my car and go to hand myself in; I would make myself available to them when it suited me.

The event for James was scheduled to take place later that week and everything seemed to be in place. The local newspaper advertised the event and I had even managed to get it a plug on the local radio station. The venue and the entertainment were booked and all the items I had to auction were in Wolverhampton, so my presence was not essential. If I did attend and the police arrested me, then it would have been embarrassing for James's grandparents and everyone concerned, so I thought, for everyone's sake, it would be best if I stayed away. I rang James's grandmother and explained that I wouldn't be able to attend the event because of 'personal problems'. I didn't tell her about the police because I didn't want to concern her; I just said that everything was sorted and that all she needed to do was turn up. The night after the charity auction, Michael rang me and said that there was an article in *The Express and Star* about the event.

He warned me that it didn't make pleasant reading:

CHARITY NIGHT FOR CRASH BOY A SHAMBLES
A charity evening in aid of a former Codsall boy who was horribly injured in a car crash raised barely £40 after only 20 people turned up.

The disco and auction at Wolverhampton's Connaught Hotel last night was described as a shambles by the boy's grandmother, Mrs Rita Nicholson.

Mrs Nicholson of Wilkes Road, Codsall, hoped to raise hundreds of pounds for equipment desperately needed for her 11-year-old grandson, James Fallon. He had a seven-hour operation after a road smash in South Africa last September. James, formerly of Wilkes Road, Codsall, is now back at home with his parents in Johannesburg, but they have been told he will never recover from his paralysis.

His grandparents aimed to buy him a computer he can work with his eyes so he can start to communicate with those around him again. Mrs Nicholson said: 'I don't know why people didn't turn up last night but it was disappointing. The hotel has offered to let us have the room again some time in the autumn and we will be trying to organise another and more successful event.'

I was absolutely appalled by, and ashamed of, what had happened. I couldn't understand how people could snub such a young boy who was suffering so much. I didn't care what they thought about me, but it bothered me that people could turn their back on a boy like James.

A few days later, Reggie Kray wrote to me and asked me how the event had gone. I sent him the newspaper article and explained to him why I had not been able to attend. I told him that I wasn't going to let it end there; I was determined to do something to help James. It felt personal now. I told Reg that if the offer he and his brother Ron had made earlier still stood, I wanted to take them up on it. When Reggie received the letter, he telephoned me and said that I shouldn't worry about other people because he and his brother Ronnie would now assist me with my efforts to help James. One of the many aids James needed cost about £40,000 – a specialised computer that would be attached to James so that he could communicate with people by moving his eyes.

Reg said that he and Ron were going to try and raise the money to buy this computer. To show he was sincere, Reg sent me a letter pledging all proceeds from his book *Slang* to James. I had no idea how much this gesture was worth. I guessed it would be several thousand pounds so I was extremely happy when I rang to tell the Fallons the news. Good news for them had, after all, been rare of late. Reggie's kind offer was reported in several national newspapers and it seemed his generosity knew no limits. *The Sun* reported that the book would make £80,000, and James's mother was quoted as saying, 'I don't care what the Krays have done in the past, to us they are saints.'

Reggie, flattered by the positive publicity that he had received, started ringing me four or five times a day. He said that he knew a lot of people in London, including celebrities, who would help, so, by hook or by crook and using his contacts we could pull this off.

'You will have to link up with a few of my people,' Reg said. 'I will give them your number and they will call you within the next few days.'

What should have been a straightforward fundraising event was turning into a bit of a roller-coaster ride. The police were looking for me, I had been snubbed by the people I grew up with and the event had been a shambles. I had surely endured all of the lows, but now, with the Krays on board, I felt I could achieve what I had set out to do.

My efforts to raise funds for James were now taking up most of my time. I didn't think about it or realise until later, but my own family were beginning to suffer because I was working fewer hours and this had resulted in a dramatic fall in my income. My weakness is that I never do things by half – it's all or nothing with me – and to be honest this has never caused me anything other than grief. The blinkers were on and I was determined to show the locals that their childish snub had not deterred me.

The first of 'Reggie's people' to telephone me was a Scotsman named James Campbell, who lived in Chigwell, Essex. He introduced himself, as is common with people who knew the Krays, not with 'My name's James Campbell', but with 'My name's James. I'm a friend of the Krays.' Reggie, he said, had asked him to get in touch with me and I was to expect another call from a man named Peter Gillett. Campbell told me that Gillett had recently formed a PR company called Progress Management, which had been set up to sell Kray merchandise and campaign for the release of the twins. 'Fine,' I said, 'that will be great. I need as much help as I can get at the moment'.

'Give us a couple of weeks while I look at a few possible events,' Campbell said, 'and then I will be back in touch with you.'

I felt better about the situation, to be honest. With other people now taking on some of the work I could dedicate more time to putting my own affairs in order and earn some much-needed money for my family.

About a week later I got a call from Peter Gillett, who introduced himself as Reggie Kray's 'adopted son'. Gillett had got to know Reggie whilst serving time for armed robbery in Parkhurst Prison. They soon became romantically linked after they had both been interviewed by the press.

Reg was quoted as saying: 'Peter is the best friend I have ever had. He makes me feel young again.'

Gillett, however, was a little more forthcoming when he was asked about his feelings for Reg: 'It's an intimate relationship, but we aren't bent. It's like a homosexual affair without sex and I'm closer to Reg than I have ever been to anyone, even my wife.'

Gillett's ambition was 'to be a pop star' so Reg used his contacts to promote him, but his singing career never did take off. Instead of stardom, he settled for forming Progress Management, which was nowhere near as lucrative or glamorous.

I asked Gillett what I could do for him and to my surprise he accused me of trying to con Reggie Kray out of several thousand pounds. I asked him what the fuck he was on about and who the fuck did he think he was talking to. Gillett claimed that he had done checks on the Fallon family. He said he had found out that Elaine Fallon lived in a huge house with servants and had a bottomless pit of money at her disposal. To cap it all, he claimed that the fundraising for James was a con made up by me to get money out of Reggie Kray.

I politely told him to fuck off and put the phone down. I was totally shocked by what I had heard as I knew the Fallon family were far from rich. I had lived on the same council estate as them and I knew they wouldn't dream of using their son's tragic accident to con money out of people. I was still shaking with fury when I sat down to write Reggie a letter. I asked him who the hell this Gillett was, phoning me up and accusing me and the Fallons of conning people.

'If you and yours are going to give us all this shit,' I told him, 'then I can do without your money and your help.'

It caused quite a lot of bad feeling to say the least. I didn't want to trouble the Fallons with Gillett's allegations, but I felt I had to put them in the picture just in case he contacted them directly. I rang James's grandmother and explained to her about the various allegations being made. She said that she was 'really annoyed about this Peter Gillett. Elaine has a modest, three-bedroom, one-storey house. She has no servants whatsoever. They are in debt up to their eyes. They have had to borrow money for the equipment James needs.' I told her not to worry about it – I had contacted Reggie and I would let her know what he had to say.

When Reggie received my letter, he rang me and explained that I should ignore Gillett as people intent on causing trouble had given him the wrong information. 'He's only looking out for me,' Reg said. 'Somebody told him all that knowing he would react and I might fall out with him over it.'

I wished I had stuck with my original decision to say 'thanks, but no thanks' to the Krays, but I thought that perhaps it was 'all just a misunderstanding', as Reg said.

Shortly after my introduction to Campbell and Gillett, I received a phone call from a lady who introduced herself as Kate Howard. Kate said she was Ronnie Kray's fiancée and he had asked her to contact me. She said that Ronnie had heard about the shambles in Wolverhampton and wanted James's mother's address so he could send her a cheque for £500 to make amends. If I needed any more help with James, I was to speak to Kate and she would get things done if possible. I thanked Kate and told her I would keep her up to date with James and the efforts to raise funds for him.

Kate, a tubby bleached blonde, had only recently got to know the twins. She had written to Reggie in Gartree Prison after she had read a book about their lives. This was how most of their associates had got to know the Krays; few appeared to be true friends and most were more like members of some macabre fan club. Reg said that there was something in Kate's letter that made him think that he could do business with her. What 'business' was beyond me. Kate, I learned, ran a chauffeur-driven car-hire company and, as a side line, a tacky 'strip-o-gram' service.

Reggie had put Gillett in touch with Kate in July 1988 and despite the fact Kate was married, she and Gillett quickly became lovers. Kate began talking to friends about how she was going to live with Gillett and Reggie in a country mansion once Reggie was released. Her plans were dashed, however, when one afternoon, whilst in bed with Gillett, she let it slip that her husband was dying of multiple sclerosis. Disgusted that Kate was sharing his bed whilst her husband was so ill, Gillett ordered her out of the house. A few days later he took her to Gartree Prison in an attempt to convince Reg that he shouldn't have anything more to do with her. Gillett reckoned she was lacking in sensitivity and principles.

No doubt Gillett, himself married, would have considered it acceptable to sleep with another man's wife if the husband was healthy.

Reg did not want to kick Kate into touch completely, as he was afraid she might go to the media with embarrassing letters that he had written to her. To keep all parties happy, but, more importantly, to keep Kate away from the press, Reggie palmed Kate over to Ronnie, his mentally ill, homosexual twin. Kate and Ronnie were hardly compatible, but within a year Kate was announcing her forthcoming marriage to him. I must admit I was surprised that a man like Ronnie, who was said to demand strong moral principles, would marry Kate, a woman who whipped businessmen for money whilst topless. Then again, the image the public and I had of the Kray firm was totally at odds with the people I was encountering. On Monday, 6 November 1989, Kate and Ronnie Kray married in Broadmoor Hospital. Ronnie was said to be extremely happy with his new wife; I guessed Kate was even happier with her new name.

Up until this point, I had only spoken to the Kray brothers on the telephone but the morning after his wedding, Ronnie telephoned and suggested that I should visit him. He said that if I brought a reporter along with me from James's home town, he would give him an interview and appeal to people to send the Fallons donations. I accept Ron Kray was not the Archbishop of Canterbury and his heartfelt pleas wouldn't tug many heart strings, but it would give James's plight more exposure and hopefully get more people involved in helping him.

On 16 November 1989, I travelled to Broadmoor Hospital with a journalist from *The Express and Star* named Jon Griffin. I had known Jon for a few years, as he had been a court reporter in Wolverhampton for some time. Inevitably our paths had crossed as a result of my regular appearances there during my formative years.

Broadmoor Hospital is situated on the outskirts of the village of Crowthorne, near Bracknell in Berkshire. Crowthorne is a picturesque village with a tree-lined winding road leading up to the hospital. You think that you are entering the grounds of a stately home until you reach a clearing at the top of the hill. There you find a long, high, red-brick wall surrounding the hospital like a thick, protective scarf.

We parked the car and walked to a reception area that was bustling with waiting visitors.

'Name please, sir,' asked the hospital official.

'O'Mahoney,' I replied.

'And which ward is that?'

I explained that I was O'Mahoney and that I wished to visit a patient.

'Oh right,' he said, 'and who might that be?'

'Kray,' I replied, 'Ronnie Kray.'

I could feel all of the people in the waiting-room looking at me. Even here in an institution renowned for holding some of Britain's most notorious killers the very mention of the name Kray still prompted a reaction. I must admit it made me feel slightly apprehensive. Who was this man I was going to meet? A monster, it would seem, judging from the way the people in the waiting-room had turned to look when his name had been uttered. After a short wait, a hospital warder appeared with a clipboard and called out: 'All visitors for Henley Ward please.'

Ronnie was on Henley Ward, so Jon and I approached the warder with about five others and gave our names, which were then ticked off a list on his board. We were allowed through a door, which was locked behind us.

Immediately in front of us was another door. We were effectively locked in a very small room. When the door in front of us was unlocked we stepped into another room and then the door behind us was locked. This procedure happened about four times until we emerged into a large courtyard, which we crossed, closely guarded by a hospital warder.

Broadmoor Hospital reminded me of my old secondary school. A big Victorian red-brick building with big arched windows.

There was no 'buzz' about the place, the atmosphere was subdued, controlled, intimidating almost. When we eventually reached the building on the other side of the courtyard, the door was unlocked and we entered a long corridor at the end of which came the sounds one might hear in a school dining-room. There were voices, people moving about, the clink of teacups, chairs being dragged and the odd raised voice giving instructions to others.

At the top of the corridor, I turned to my left and saw a large room where approximately 50 people were seated at tables. To my right was a canteen hatch where a man was serving teas and biscuits. We had, I realised, finally reached the visiting-room.

I scanned the faces of the men sitting at the tables, looking for Ronnie Kray, but he didn't appear to be there. I was looking for a stocky, intimidating figure with brushed-back, raven-black hair. Like most people, when I pictured the Krays I saw the two faces David Bailey had captured in his famous photograph of the twins: Ron at the forefront scowling, his eyes deep, inky, black pools; Reg appearing over Ron's right shoulder, head tilted, brazen-faced, cocky almost.

I was going to ask one of the warders if Ron was coming when at the back of the room, I noticed a man stand up and beckon us with his hand. This was not the Ron Kray Bailey's lens and the police had captured two decades ago.

Ronnie Kray was now short and slightly built, and his intimidating scowl had long gone. He was dressed in an immaculate pale-green-striped suit, white shirt, pink-and-white-spotted tie complete with gold rings, gold watch and diamond cuff links. He was, without doubt, the best-dressed patient in Broadmoor.

As Ronnie stood before me, he put his hands on my shoulders and pulled me towards him. It seems funny now, but I genuinely thought that he was going to kiss me in the way that the Hollywood mafia kiss fellow gangsters. I was aware Ronnie was homosexual and so I instinctively pulled away from him.

Ronnie could see from my expression that I was confused, but he just laughed and said: 'Don't worry, I'm deaf in one ear and I just wanted to say something discreet to you. I was pulling you to my good ear so I could hear your reply.'

We both laughed and sat down at the table. He asked Jon if he would go and fetch him a few cans of alcohol-free lager from the canteen. As Jon walked away, Ronnie said that he wanted to know if I trusted Jon. I told him I wouldn't have brought him if I didn't. Ronnie said that was good enough for him, but he had previously had some bad experiences with the press and didn't want anything going wrong; he was doing this interview to help James.

I found his mood surprisingly philosophical for a man who had spent more than two decades incarcerated for crimes which had shaken the nation in the far-off days of the swinging '60s. Ronnie Kray, friend of the famous, East End gangster and now Broadmoor prisoner, said he had no regrets. 'What happened to me was fate, just fate,' he reflected. 'That's life. You take the good with the bad.'

Flashing Jon what probably would have passed as a menacing leer 20 years ago, he added: 'We had a good life. We were arrested and jailed for political reasons. They wanted to make examples of us but I'm not bitter and I do not resent what happened to me; I accept it.'

I almost burst out laughing when Ron said he had been imprisoned for political reasons. Being convicted of the murder of two men may also have been a factor. At 56, Ron was a grim shadow of the man who had ruled London's underworld. Thin and gaunt, he chain-smoked nervously, his conversation was muffled and occasionally incoherent, but behind the mask was something uniquely sinister about the man once dubbed 'The Colonel' by underworld associates.

Ronnie became quite emotional when he spoke about James. He told Jon: 'James is a very deserving case for help. I am lucky compared to him. If you have got your health and strength then you are a lucky man. I can smoke and drink. I am not complaining about my lot. James's is one of the most terrible cases I have heard of in my life. We have got to raise as much money for him as we can to try to give him some sort of life. I get letters every day from people asking for charity. I like to help where I can, but we're not millionaires, you know, although some papers seem to think we are. I wish I could do more to help James and his family, I really do.'

Ronnie said that if each of the paper's readers gave five shillings each, it would go a long way to helping James's family. When Ron said that I realised just how long he had been locked up and understood how far from reality he had been removed. Shillings went out of circulation around the same time as The Beatles split up. In his fine suit and jewellery poor old Ronnie was living in the past, incarcerated in Broadmoor and locked in a time warp.

Ronnie's mood suddenly changed. 'Well, I think that's enough for now,' he said, rising to his feet. He shook hands with Jon and wandered off to another table to stand on his own.

It didn't occur to me at the time but Ron was acting strangely because of his paranoia. He had been wary of talking in front of Jon before we had sat down and eventually he had just got up and walked away. Ron called me over and said, 'I am sorry, I have really got to go but will you come and see me on your own soon?'

'Of course I will, Ron,' I answered, 'no problem. Thanks for helping James out. See you soon.' We shook hands, Ron smiled and then he was gone, escorted from the room by two warders.

Although I never heard from Gillett again, James Campbell kept in regular contact with me and we discussed various fundraising ideas. The event was going to be a variety show at the Hackney Empire Theatre, but Campbell could not attract enough celebrities for it to be put on. Eventually it was agreed that it would be a charity boxing show. Boxing clubs from West Ham and Newham in the East End agreed to provide the fighters. The donated items that I had received for the failed event in Wolverhampton could now be auctioned off between bouts at the show, which was to be held at the Prince Regent Hotel in Essex.

Campbell was really enthusiastic. He went on about all the people that he was going to invite. 'Everything will go well,' he assured me. 'We will raise a lot of money for James.' Looking back, I regret not asking him exactly which James he had in mind.

2

LOOKING AFTER YOUR OWN

After my first visit to Ronnie, he would ring my house two or three times a day and I would visit him at least once a week. To be honest, I felt sorry for Ron. He seemed like a man who 'knew' everybody, yet in reality had nobody. His life revolved around his infamous name, which after two decades in custody was all he had left. He genuinely believed that people on the outside were worried or interested in what he was up to. Ron was still living in the 1960s when he was a somebody in the East End, a force to be reckoned with. I got on really well with him but thought of him as the sort of old-age pensioner who sits down next to you in the pub and starts reminiscing about his 'war days' rather than some mythical manic gangster. Conversation in the main revolved around the 1960s in preference to the present or the future. Then again, there was very little else he could talk about, having spent the last 20-odd years of his life in a cell. As for the future, I doubted if he had one beyond the walls of Broadmoor.

It was true that Ron was not a well-balanced man. He wasn't foaming at the mouth or barking at the moon, but he was a very paranoid person. Ron the good guy wanted to be liked and do good things for people so he could read what a nice man he really was. He thrived on publicity and it was as if he was screaming out for affection. Ron the bad guy would also court publicity, revelling in the fact he was portrayed as Britain's most infamous gangster, and had no regrets whatsoever about his murderous past. This two-fingered gesture at the authorities cemented his reputation as gangster number one and undoubtedly made him feel as if he had 'achieved' something. Ron the good guy was easy to deal with, while Ron the bad guy was a fucking nightmare.

On one visit to Ronnie Kray, I was surprised to see Roger Daltrey, lead singer with The Who, sitting at the table. In my youth I had been a big Who fan, so I was quite impressed, not to mention pleased, to meet him. Ron introduced me to Daltrey, who listened painfully to me reminiscing about Who concerts I had attended over the years and Who songs I considered to be masterpieces. It soon became apparent to me that Daltrey had endured this conversation a thousand times before so I reluctantly shut up. Given an opportunity to speak, he explained why he had taken the time to visit Ronnie. Daltrey was apparently obsessed with the idea of making a film about the Krays.

He said it was the only British gangster film worth making and, handled the right way, would make as good a film as *The Godfather*, if not better. I learned that very early on in the negotiations Daltrey had been going to Parkhurst Prison to talk things through with Reggie. Apparently, Reggie also thought it was a good idea and had set the wheels in motion for Daltrey to make the film. Daltrey had already paid for three scripts to be written and had even lined up actors to play the lead roles. Hywel Bennett was to play Ronnie and a lesser-known actor, Gerry Sundquist, was to play Reg. Bill Murray, who played Detective Don Beech in the television series *The Bill*, was to play Charlie. Daltrey's idea was that violence wouldn't be a major force in the film. He was more fascinated by the twin element and the fatal power of one brother over the other. The film he had in mind concerned the bond between the twins rather than the fear that they instilled in people. It all sounded a bit too deep and arty for me.

The singer had a binding agreement with the Krays, but he seemed unable to make the film happen. Two other film producers, Dominic Anciano and Ray Burdis, came on the scene and said they were going to make a film about the Krays without the Krays' permission. Daltrey decided that this would be a good time to bail out so he sold all his rights to a company called Parkfield, who were backing Anciano and

Burdis, and who proceeded to make the film. Ronnie Kray was not at all happy about this and a couple of weeks after the visit with Daltrey he asked me and James Campbell to go to the singer's trout farm in Sussex and 'give him a slap'. I had absolutely no intention of slapping Roger Daltrey and Campbell was incapable of slapping anybody. Eventually, Campbell just telephoned Daltrey to warn him of Ronnie's threats. People in the Kray camp thought it was marvellous that Ron was issuing threats to one of the world's most famous rock stars. I knew one of the hangers-on would eventually 'let it slip' to a tabloid reporter. It was, after all, good material to bolster the Kray legend and keep their name in the newspapers.

The 'incident', if it can be called that, was later reported in the *News of the World*.

KRAY'S FURY AT STAR ROGER DALTREY
Ronnie Kray ordered his henchman to sort out rock star Roger Daltrey after he had felt that he had lost out on a film deal. The gangster signed over the rights to use the Kray name to a Daltrey company. He was furious when he learned Daltrey had sold on the contract to a film company. They later made the film *The Krays*. It had profits of around £7 million, but because of the contract, Ronnie and brothers Reggie and Charlie received just £85,000 each.

A pal of the gangland villain said: 'Months later, a film producer met Ronnie and said he would have paid two million for the rights.' Ronnie summoned his lieutenants and said that he wanted Daltrey sorted. The pal said Ronnie was deadly serious, but his men just phoned Daltrey to register his displeasure.

Whether people were genuine friends or imaginary enemies, few escaped Ronnie's wrath. One day he could be talking to you without any hint of a problem, the next his paranoia would kick in and he would be discussing damaging you with somebody.

Ronnie had told me he didn't like Peter Gillett because of his closeness to Reggie and the fact he had slept with Kate. To add insult to injury, it had been reported in the press that Gillett and Kate had sex 'in the back of a Ford Escort'. It wasn't the sort of tacky publicity Ron liked to see his 'good name' associated with. Both denied the allegations, but Ronnie had made up his mind that they were true. In an effort to calm things down, Reg spoke to Ronnie in defence of Gillett but Ron refused to listen and, for a time, the once inseparable twins fell out. What made it worse was the fact both Ron and Reg were putting their side of the story to reporters and the rather distasteful matter was being played out via the press. Eventually Ronnie resorted to what he knew best and asked me to find somebody to sort out Gillett. 'Get somebody to hurt that rat,' he hissed. Ron was really going into one, saying Gillett had caused him and his brother to fall out. Throughout the visit I was barely able to get a word in, but by the time I had left Broadmoor, Ron had changed his mind. The very next morning I received a letter scribbled in his childlike scrawl: 'Bernie, tell that fella I asked you to speak to about Gillett to leave it out. Talk soon, your pal, Ron.'

Daltrey and Gillett were not the only ones to incur Ron's wrath. As Charlie was the only Kray brother outside of a prison cell he had been charged with the task of sorting out a deal with Parkfield, who were making the Kray film. Inevitably, Charlie messed it up. His brothers blamed him for not checking the script (which they did not like), the depiction of their parents (which they did not like) and the financial deal that he had struck. When they learned Charlie had pocketed an additional sum for himself as a consultancy fee, they hit the roof. They claimed he had conspired with the film company behind their backs. To be honest, I felt sorry for Charlie. The man had a family to support and little or no chance of gaining employment. He was just doing the best he could. Charlie was a decent enough sort, who would run around for the twins, doing their errands and taking their flack, yet he never had a bad word to say about either of them. But Ronnie was always against him, saying he was no good, that I should not trust him or speak to him.

As well as his unusually violent streak, Ronnie also had an odd sense of humour. On one occasion, I took my partner Debra to see him. After giving me a lift to Broadmoor, I told her: 'Seeing as you're here, you may as well come in and say hello.' After sitting down, I noticed that Peter Sutcliffe, the Yorkshire Ripper, was sitting at an adjacent table. Sutcliffe was not as I had pictured him. A quite small man with very small hands, he had a dark beard and wiry black hair, although from behind it was obvious he was going bald. Ronnie joked to Debra that if she didn't behave herself, he would get the Ripper to take her out on a date. Ron thought it was really funny and laughed out loud. Debra looked at me and laughed nervously. I quickly changed the subject.

But Ron couldn't control his laughter, so we both sat there in silence, watching him. Occasionally, I would arrive at the visiting-room before the patients were brought in. Looking across the courtyard towards Henley Ward it was quite a sight to see two of Britain's most infamous killers, the Yorkshire Ripper and Ronnie Kray, being escorted side by side to the visiting-room.

Ronnie said that he despised Sutcliffe. Ron had been sentenced to life imprisonment with a recommendation that he serve 30 years for the murders of George Cornell and Jack McVitie, whereas the Ripper had been given a life sentence with a 20-year recommendation for murdering 13 women and attempting to murder a further 7. In Ronnie's mind, the authorities judged his crimes against other villains as being far worse than the Ripper's crimes against innocent women. This troubled Ronnie and made his loathing of the Ripper even greater. What Ronnie failed to realise was that neither he nor the Ripper were likely to be released, regardless of recommendations made by the judges at their trials.

Sutcliffe and Ronnie had an 'altercation' in Broadmoor in the mid-1980s and in the struggle that ensued, Sutcliffe got the better of him. I wasn't surprised; Sutcliffe was younger, fitter and certainly more agile. Ronnie, a man for whom reputation meant everything, was beside himself with rage, but he had to be careful he didn't involve himself in violence inside Broadmoor because the penalties could be harsh. Ronnie told me that he had assaulted a hospital warder during his early days at the hospital. They had put him in the punishment block, which is in a wing of the hospital called Norfolk House.

'It's the most feared place in here,' he said, 'the intimidation and mental pressure in there cannot be explained. If you went in there sane, you would come out mad. Some people never come out of there again.'

I have no idea what went on in Norfolk House. Ronnie felt uncomfortable just mentioning the place and he certainly didn't want to return. This was one of the reasons he never sought to resolve his differences with Sutcliffe.

Preparations for the boxing show continued in earnest. Reggie sent me a list of 150 people he said I should invite to the event. Amongst the broken-nosed and criminally recorded were celebrities such as Roger

Daltrey, Jon Bon Jovi, Sam Fox, Glen Murphy, Ray Winstone, Bob Hoskins and Barbara Windsor.

James Campbell, always eager to assist where money and celebrities were involved, said that as I had enough to do he would contact the people on the list on my behalf. When I eventually saw the printed tickets, I was surprised to see that Campbell and another man, named David Brazier, whom I'd never heard of, had appointed themselves 'promoters' for the event. Alongside their names and self-appointed titles was a photograph of the Kray twins. I assumed they were putting their names on the tickets alongside a grand title and a picture of their heroes as an act of vanity.

'Whatever turns you on,' I thought. So long as the event went well and raised money for James Fallon, I couldn't have cared less.

I telephoned Campbell and asked him who this 'promoter' named Brazier was. Campbell told me that he was his business partner – 'a man with lots of contacts', he assured me. I later learned neither James Campbell nor David Brazier were the entrepreneurs they professed to be. Brazier did have a lot of contacts, but you could only describe them loosely as business contacts. Campbell was, in fact, a mini-cab driver (who was later to lose his licence for drinking and driving) and David Brazier his boss at a mini-cab office in Chigwell. I assume the numerous business contacts Campbell boasted about were the people they ferried around all day in their taxis.

I was concerned about the way the 'promoters' were managing the event. The tickets, priced at £40 each, were being handed out without any money being collected or any record whatsoever being kept of who was getting them. Campbell assured me that everything was in order and nobody would ever think of pulling a fast one where the twins were concerned. Reluctantly, I agreed to let him deal with the guest list Reg had sent me and continue with the sale of the tickets. Having effectively lost control of the event, I was unaware what expenses were being incurred or what revenue ticket sales were generating. The only feedback I got was from Reg Kray and it was hardly encouraging. Reg was writing to me saying that if he and his brother were on the street, they would 'fill the place three times over'.

'You must sell more tickets,' Reg ranted, 'you must try harder.'

I did try to explain the situation to Reg, but a man who had spent his life surrounded by 'yes men' wasn't used to listening.

I asked Campbell why Reg appeared to be so concerned and he assured me it would be 'all right on the night'. In the weeks leading up to the event several newspapers published stories covering it. The *Daily Star* ran the following article:

> KRAYS KO COSTA CROOK IN CHARITY BOXING BASH
>
> The Kray twins have told Costa del Crime fugitive Ronnie Knight to stay away from a boxing match they're organising . . . OR ELSE!
>
> Ronnie, ex-husband of actress Barbara Windsor, thought his old sparring partners would welcome him copying ITV's *El CID* series by cheekily jetting back to Britain for the charity tournament. But the terrible twins have sent word to his Spanish hide-out, saying, 'No can do, Ron Ron, no can do!'
>
> The Krays fear Knight – wanted by British police in connection with a security robbery – could cause a punch-up OUTSIDE the ring. The gangland killers have set up the star-studded bash a week on Friday from their cells. It's Ronnie and Reggie's way of raising cash for James Fallon, 10, a hit-and-run accident victim and son of a friend. Ronnie Biggs – holed up in Brazil – has sent a signed banknote from the Great Train Robbery to be auctioned. Tina Turner, Dire Straits, U2, The Rolling Stones and The Who have all donated autographed gifts. Knight and his wife Sue were eager to join in the £50-a-ticket night in Chigwell, Essex, but now he's said to be fuming at his villa on the Costa del Sol. A spokesman for Ronnie Kray, in Broadmoor, and Reggie, in Lewes Prison, denied the twins were hitting their pal below the belt.
>
> It was just too risky to let Knight turn up, he explained. 'He could attract trouble and we don't want the police getting wind of him being there and bursting in on such a good cause. It would be too embarrassing. Sorry, Ron.'

I knew the story was rubbish. Ronnie Kray had laughed out loud when he saw it and said he couldn't believe how gullible the media were. The story had obviously been the result of a dubious tip-off from somebody connected to the Krays in order to generate publicity for the boxing show, but more importantly, to register Ron's 'good deeds' in the media. Personally, I couldn't have cared less what the Kray hangers-on had printed so long as it publicised the event and ensured it was a sell-out.

One of the people on the guest list Reg had sent me was a man named Keith Bonsor. Reg had told me that his friend was the manager of a nightclub in Basildon called Raquels. Reggie had suggested that as I lived near the club I should go and see Bonsor as he may have been able to sell some of the tickets to his customers.

Reg told me that Gillett had appeared at Raquels when he was launching his pop career. 'Bonsor owes me a favour,' Reg said, 'for getting Pete to perform there.'

I rather hoped Bonsor had forgotten Gillett's performance. From what I had heard of Gillett's singing, it was Reg who owed Bonsor the favour and not vice versa.

Reg was aware that my attempts to raise funds for James had been taking up so much of my income and time that my own family was beginning to feel the pinch. I hardly ever saw my son Vinney. My daughter Karis had recently been born and this added to the financial strain that I was under. Reg suggested that whilst I was at Raquels, I should ask Bonsor if he had any door work for me to do at weekends. Additional income would greatly ease my problems at home and so I considered this a good idea. When I went to see Bonsor, he said he was unable to attend the boxing event himself, but said he would pass on my number to people he thought might be interested. I asked him if he had any door work available and he told me that he contracted it out to a local security company. He gave me their number and told me to speak to a guy named Dave Venables. Bonsor was quite certain, given the fact Reg Kray had recommended me, that Dave Venables would be able to sort something out.

The same evening, I had arranged to meet David Brazier and James Campbell at a pub in Epping where we were to double check everything was in order for the event. However hard I tried, I couldn't get a proper answer out of them about how many people were going to attend. Questions concerning ticket sales and revenue were met with vague answers and assurances that 'so-and-so would be paying on the night'. I hadn't had any dealings with the Krays before so I assumed these men who banged on about loyalty, honour and respect did things on trust.

I had no choice other than to accept what I was being told.

When our meeting was over, I rang Debra to tell her that I was on my way home. My instinct told me something was wrong.

'It's James Fallon,' she said, 'he has lost his fight for life. He died earlier today.'

James had begun to shake violently after a blood clot had formed on his spine. He was rushed to hospital but doctors said he had suffered acute brain damage. For two-and-a-half long hours the Fallons watched their son die; eventually, when all hope was lost, they agreed to allow the machine keeping him alive to be switched off.

I was surprised at just how much James's death affected me. I felt something of a hypocrite for feeling upset because I had never met the boy. I suppose it was because I could not help but admire such a brave child. Despair turned to anger. It didn't seem right for such a young boy to die in such a horrific way. Why did money have to be such a major factor in his recovery? Why should any parents have to go cap in hand to save their child's life?

Hundreds of Kray supporters had recently marched on the streets of London in protest at the length of time the twins had been imprisoned. They demanded their release in letters to their MPs and the Prime Minister. Everybody knew the Kray brothers were two convicted murderers who refused to show any remorse. That fact didn't seem to concern their adoring 'fans' who would send in money for the 'Free the Krays' campaign.

I had been trying to get people to donate £5 to James Fallon, a boy who through no fault of his own had been imprisoned in a broken body. Few had responded until the Krays put their name to the cause. I didn't blame the brothers and I appreciated their help, but it did make me wonder about people's priorities. James had put up a tremendous fight and I felt deeply sorry for him and his family.

I couldn't believe after all the suffering he had endured that his life had been so cruelly snatched away. I went back into the pub and told Brazier and Campbell the sad news about James. Their reaction sickened me; there was no talk of remorse or respect, all they wanted to know was what we were going to do with the proceeds from the boxing show now. I told them in no uncertain terms that James's family had incurred huge debts in their fight for James as there was no

National Health Service in South Africa. All money from the event, regardless of whether James was alive or not, would still go to the family who needed it.

On the night of the event, a telephone was connected to the public-address system. There were 200 diners there who had each paid £40 a ticket. They all fell silent as Reggie Kray, having been granted special permission to telephone the hotel from Lewes Prison, paid a moving tribute to James. It was a sight to see so many criminal heavyweights standing sombrely and paying tribute to a ten-year-old boy. Charlie Kray attended, as did Ronnie Kray's new wife, Kate. Ex-Kray gang member Tony Lambrianou and his younger brother Nicky arrived with TV stars Glen Murphy and Ray Winstone. There wasn't an empty seat in the entire hall.

Several of the people in attendance did not want to publicise their presence as they had risked entering the country from exile in Spain. They were there simply because Reg had asked them to attend. It was at this event that I met Geoff Allen, the man described in many books and newspaper articles as the 'Godfather' of the Krays. Geoff was 70, but he had the mind and attitude of a man half his age. He came across as a country gent but in reality he was a well-connected villain.

Geoff was jailed at Norwich Crown Court for 7 years in 1976 for masterminding a £300,000 insurance swindle after a historic building, Briggate Mill, was burned down. It was also believed in police circles that Geoff was the brains behind the Great Train Robbery. It was Geoff's house in Suffolk where Ronnie and Reggie had gone to lay low after murdering Jack 'the Hat' McVitie. I liked Geoff a lot. With him, you got what you saw. There was no gangster chit chat about how well respected he was or the usual shit the vast majority of Kray hangers-on came out with. Geoff warned me that many of the people present were not what they made themselves out to be and I should be cautious about getting involved with them. 'Steer clear of the Frayne brothers,' he warned, 'and that Tony Lambrianou.'

I had never heard of the Frayne brothers but I had heard of Tony Lambrianou. Tony had lured Jack McVitie to a house in East London where the Kray twins had lain in wait. Once McVitie entered the house, Ron had glassed him and Reg had stabbed him to death. Lambrianou had not given evidence in his defence at the trial and was sentenced to life imprisonment. I was surprised Geoff was telling me to give him a wide berth. Perhaps Lambrianou was an East End psycho and Geoff was telling me to avoid him for my own safety, I reasoned.

Geoff and I spent most of the evening laughing at the guests who had arrived dressed as Kray clones. It reminded me of some of the sad individuals I had seen on Elvis Presley lookalike TV competitions. Nobody but themselves could see the slightest resemblance. They looked absolutely ridiculous, dressed in starched white shirts, black ties, Brylcreemed hair, Crombie coats and a fixed scowl to match, they believed they looked the part. Two Kray clones that were particularly prominent appeared to be very friendly with 'promoter' James Campbell. I thought they looked more like the comedian duo Hale and Pace than the Krays.

When I asked Geoff who they were, he told me they were Lindsay and Leighton Frayne, the brothers he had advised me to avoid. Later in the evening, Campbell brought the Fraynes over to introduce them to me. They seemed polite enough, but I couldn't help but notice the sense of theatre about them. Every phrase, every bit of body language was well thought out, mimicking their heroes Ron and Reg. I also spoke to Lambrianou, who thanked me for a great evening. Why he should be thanking me did puzzle me a little, as he had paid £40 to get in – or so I thought. Lambrianou didn't strike me as a violent man or appear in any way intimidating; he seemed OK, was extremely polite and went out of his way to be pleasant to anybody who spoke to him.

What I did find rather bizarre was the amount of people who asked Charlie Kray, Kate Kray and Lambrianou for their autographs. Another man I met there was a Scot named Alan Smith. Alan had written to me before the boxing show and had organised a sponsored run in Edinburgh to raise money for the Fallons. Alan was in his early 30s, fit and approximately 6 foot tall. He told me he worked as a doorman and often visited London doing security at some of the large outdoor pop concerts. We agreed that when he was next in London we would meet up for a drink.

The evening went really well. A couple of local fools tried to gatecrash, but when Charlie Kray, Lambrianou and a few other infamous faces appeared at the door to see what the fuss was all about, their mouths dropped open and they fled into the night. Flannagan, the self-styled first page-three girl, and 'close friend' of the Kray family, took the bids during the auction.

Out of the various items for sale, including the signed Rolling Stones albums and boxer Charlie Magri's shorts, pride of place went to two official passes for visits to Broadmoor Hospital and Lewes Prison to see Ronnie and Reggie in person. Flannagan, treading the boards of the boxing ring, shouted out: 'If you really fancy an interesting chat and want to do some good at the same time, then let's hear from you.' Both passes were quickly snapped up for £500 each. The event raised a reported £15,000. I was overjoyed that so much money had been made. It also eased the embarrassment I had endured following the non-event in Wolverhampton. With the proceeds from Reggie's book, I thought I had generated about £100,000 for the Fallons. The fact that the police were still seeking Paul and me for the assault on Stuart Darley did not trouble me. All that mattered to me that night was the fact that I had finally achieved my aim and raised a considerable amount of money for James's family.

At the end of the evening, I went to collect the money but I could not find Campbell or Brazier. The hotel and other expenses had been paid, but there was no sign of the promoters. It had been a long day and an even longer night, so I assumed they had gone home and would contact me the following day.

That weekend I contacted Dave Venables at Raquels nightclub and asked him if he had any door work for me. I was told that I could start work immediately. The wages, Dave said, were £40 per night, cash in hand. I stayed at the club for a short while, talking about things in general.

Dave Venables told me that things were not going too well for the local bouncers and I was entering the Basildon nightclub security scene at a time of change following a spate of retirements, deaths and public disorder. A bouncer named McCabe, who was once all-powerful, had recently died in a road accident and the infamous West Ham United football hooligans, known as the Inter City Firm, had taken on the hardcore of Basildon's doormen at a rave held in the town.

Madness had reigned that night. The ICF had come prepared with coshes, hammers, 'squirt', tear gas and knives. The unwitting doormen had nothing to defend themselves with other than their muscle-bound bravado and reputations. They soon lost them both. The ICF rampaged through the hall, hacking, stabbing, slashing and stamping on the retreating bouncers whose crime it was to have had one of the ICF members ejected over a trivial remark. Being a good doorman isn't about going to the gym and throwing your steroid-bloated frame about, it is about diplomacy and understanding the psyche of the psychos you encounter.

The Basildon bouncers were now learning this valuable lesson. Those who escaped tutorial in the main hall were captured in the car park and given the most brutal of lessons. They were beaten and their flesh torn open with Stanley knives. One blood-soaked bouncer was thrown into a lake. It was a miracle nobody died. Many of those who avoided hospital immediately 'retired' from the security industry, declaring almost comically, 'Fings ain't what they used to be.' They were, of course, quite right: things had changed. Lager louts with bad attitudes had been replaced by smartly dressed, drug-fuelled, knife-wielding villains. Commuting to Essex from the East End of London, these villains wanted to flood the county with the 'love drug' Ecstasy. Disco versus rave; bouncer versus firm member; pints versus pills; they were all on a collision course and I was stepping into the epicentre without realising it.

I thanked Dave for helping me out and told him that I would start work the following weekend. After securing additional income and the event for James going so well, I thought things were certainly looking up for me. I still had the incident with the police in Wolverhampton to sort out, but it was hardly a hanging offence.

Over the next few days, calls from Ronnie and Reggie were fast and furious. They shouted at me and demanded that the funds be handed over to the Fallon family. I was in total agreement, but told them that I could not find the two men who actually had the money. Promise after promise followed, meeting after meeting took place, but the money never did materialise. Ronnie accepted what I had to say, but Reggie would not. He was constantly on the telephone. 'You've got to do this, you've got to do that and you've got to hand that money over.'

I kept telling him that I hadn't got the fucking money, that Campbell and Brazier had the money. It just got sillier and sillier.

I could offer no explanation other than the fact that I could not contact the two men or locate the money. Kate Kray joined in the barrage of phone calls, ringing me to tell me what Ronnie had told me five minutes earlier and what Reggie had told me ten minutes before that. Reggie Kray eventually informed me that Tony Lambrianou had been appointed to sort out the problem. He was to find out where the missing money had gone and arrange for it to be given to the Fallons. A meeting was arranged at a pub in Gants Hill, Essex. Campbell, myself, Lambrianou and one or two other people I had never met before attended. When asked about the proceeds from the boxing event, Campbell said most of it had gone on expenses. 'Bollocks. Count the people on Tony's table alone,' I said, '12 at £40 a head, that's £480 – plus whatever they bid for auction items.'

'But Tony and people like that didn't pay, Bernie,' Campbell replied. 'You can't expect them to, they are on the Kray firm.'

It dawned on me: Charlie Kray's table was on the Kray firm, as was Kate Kray's table and no doubt Campbell's and Brazier's. They had used the money genuine people, including myself, had paid to supplement themselves. I went fucking mad and walked out.

When Reg telephoned me to find out how the meeting had gone, I told him exactly what had happened. 'Those bastards have stolen money from a dead child and I want it. If I don't get it, I am going to bash them.'

Reg said that money would be given to the Fallons. 'A couple of grand,' he said, 'but we want you to forget this, Bernie, as Ron and I don't want any bad publicity surrounding ourselves and a kid's charity.' Reg also wanted to forget he had pledged all the proceeds from *Slang* to James. No doubt he thought that now that James had died, his parents' problems were over. It did make me wonder if the Fallons would still consider Reg 'a saint' now.

When Ronnie heard what had happened, he insisted that Lambrianou should pay for his table. 'He isn't one of us,' he said, 'make sure he pays, but as for the rest of it, we are never going to get the money now so do as Reg asks, accept the money he's offered and let it end there.'

Why Ron had singled Lambrianou out, I didn't know. I did know that I was never going to be able to recoup the Fallons' money. A week later, I was told Campbell had given 'some money' to Kate Kray, which I was told had been passed on to the Fallon family. The subject was never again discussed with the Krays in my presence.

It came as no surprise when I read in the *Sunday People* some time later that one of the 'promoters' involved in the charity boxing event for James Fallon had been involved in another charity scam. In a weekly feature entitled 'Rat of the Week' the following story appeared:

STARS GET CONNED BY CHARITY CHEAT

Heartless taxi boss Dave Brazier took the dying for a ride when he pocketed the proceeds of a charity football match. He organised the game between a celebrity 11 and his own firm to raise funds for a local hospice, but his cheque for the celebrities' expenses bounced and he never passed on a penny of the money raised.

He still owes hundreds of pounds to the people who helped publicise the event in aid of the Saint Frances Hospice at Romford, Essex. Hugh Elton, manager of the celebrity side which included boxer Terry Marsh and actors Glen Murphy and Ray Winstone said: 'This leaves a really bad taste. I have been involved in charity matches for 30 years and this is only the second time it has happened. We agreed to play the match because it was a very worthy cause. We didn't charge a fee, only expenses for the players who came from all over the country.

'Normally these are paid after the game but Mr Brazier gave me a cheque for the £450 bill, which bounced, and despite numerous promises, including a new cheque in the post, he has not paid a thing. I understand he has failed to pass on anything to the hospice. It's a rotten situation.' One of those who attended the match last August added: 'there were at least 200 people who each paid a couple of quid entrance money.

'After the match, there was a disco and a raffle in the club house, which raised even more cash, and before the game, collection boxes for the hospice were taken around the town. Even the Kray twins sent an autographed copy of their book and they won't be very pleased to learn that a charity has been ripped off.'

Hospice boss Harry Packham said: 'We are most concerned for the good name of the hospice which relies on public donations to raise the annual £2 million needed to run our 22 beds. We did receive a disappointing £49 from a total of 30 collection boxes, but we received nothing from the match itself.

I am also very sorry that the celebrity 11 have not been reimbursed for their expenses.'

At his home nearby, Dave Brazier claimed that he himself had lost thousands over the match, but when asked to give detailed accounts of the losses his sums didn't add up and he couldn't explain why the hospice did not receive a penny from the hundreds of pounds in cash taken at the event.

It sounded painfully familiar to me. The same promoter was at the helm and the same infamous villains had backed him by donating items to raise money. If they were not in on the scam, they wouldn't have had anything else to do with Brazier after the Fallon fiasco. Ron and Reg were eager for the press and public to know that they were not happy about dying children being ripped off, but despite their position as 'kings of the underworld' and champions of a code of conduct men had allegedly died for breaking, I was more than certain that the Essex cabbie who had committed this despicable act had little or nothing to worry about.

3

GANGSTARS' PARADISE

I had often wondered how my life would end, but I had never imagined anything quite so violent as this. I was staring death in the face and there was nothing I could do. The snarling man in front of me had a hammer and a previous conviction for a gruesome murder.

I was in the front room of Tony Lambrianou's flat with Alan Smith, the Scotsman I had met at the boxing show. Alan had travelled down to London from Edinburgh that day to visit Ronnie Kray and to meet me for a drink.

Half an hour earlier, Alan and I had received a telephone call from Tony Lambrianou, who had invited us to his home. In the '60s, Tony and his brother Chris had lured Jack McVitie to a flat where the Krays had then murdered him. Looking back, I realise I had been foolish to accept Tony's invitation to visit his home.

It was Tony Lambrianou who stood before me now, threatening to 'smash a hammer through your head' and shouting, 'I'll kill you.' Alan and I had called around to see Tony earlier that day, but he wasn't in. According to Tony, his wife had told Alan and me he was out, but we had refused to accept the fact. We were then said to have insisted that Tony was home and we had become abusive. Alan and I were now going to pay for our stupidity.

WANNABE IN MY GANG?

As Tony raised the hammer, which would surely extinguish my life, I instinctively threw my hands up to protect my face. Bang! Bang! I screamed out in pain as my fists struck the headboard behind my bed.

Sitting up and nursing my grazed knuckles, I realised with relief I had been having a rather silly dream. Lambrianou must have had a similar silly dream because in his book *Getting It Straight* (2001) he describes to Freddie Foreman, his co-author, threatening Alan and me in much the same manner. The only significant difference between my version of events and Tony's is that he seems to believe that the attack actually happened. Like so many stories and people associated with the Kray myth, the incidents and non-events they describe have been fleshed out and exaggerated to inflate the egos and reputations of those involved or those who say they were involved.

The truth of the matter is, Ronnie Kray had asked me to visit Tony Lambrianou at his flat, which was on the upper floor of a rundown council block at the Elephant and Castle in south-east London. I had met Tony several times on visits with Ronnie after he had been asked to resolve the mystery of the missing money from the boxing show. He had not seen Ronnie for years and they appeared to get on well, but I sensed something was not quite right because of the way Ronnie talked about Lambrianou to other people. In 1988 Ronnie and his brother Reg published *Our Story* in which they admitted for the first time their involvement in the murders of George Cornell and Jack McVitie.

Lambrianou must have thought that the Krays' public admissions would give him the opportunity to cash in on his own story. Not long after Reg and Ron's book, Lambrianou published his first book, *Inside the Firm* (1991), in which he described himself on the front cover as 'a former Kray gang boss'. When Ronnie Kray saw the book he was livid. Tony had written:

> Up until the time that Reggie Kray admitted his part in the murder of Jack the Hat McVitie, every loyal one of us held our silence over the events of a unique era in British crime. Now perhaps it's time for a member of the firm to have a say. For years we've been hearing what everybody else has had to say about us, in courtrooms, books and newspapers, and the twins have taken their chance to reply in print. I intend, with this book, to set the

record straight for all of us who stood together in the dock and
went to prison for our crimes.

Ronnie told me that Tony was a liar, had not held his silence and was no
Kray gang boss. 'Lambrianou and his brother grassed us up and Tony
was no member of our firm.' Leaning over the visiting-room table in
Broadmoor, Ron whispered, 'I want you to get Lambrianou and jump up
and down on his ribs until every single one of them is broken and he has
no wind left in him.'

I tried explaining to Ronnie that somebody who had served 15 years
for a crime that he and his brother had committed deserved to make a
few quid out of their story. I attempted to reason with Ronnie: 'You and
Reg have admitted the murders yourselves in your own book, so he isn't
doing any harm, is he?'

Ronnie sneered and said that Lambrianou was a snivelling grass
and had not kept quiet, as he was claiming. 'Lambrianou is saying
that he had kept his mouth shut and should therefore be shown some
respect, but that is total shit,' Ronnie said. 'Tony Lambrianou and his
brother Chris made statements against me and my brother in an
effort to save themselves. I will show you the paperwork.' Ronnie was
prone to making false allegations when he fell out with someone or
he thought that people were conspiring against him.

He would often have a go at me, not threatening to kill me or
anything, just asking why I was talking to such-and-such a person and
asking what had been said. Had they mentioned Ron and did I trust
them? He often talked about killing other people who had displeased
him or who he thought had been talking badly of him, but in actual fact
the person concerned had done no wrong. Ron was, more often than
not, suffering from a bout of his paranoid schizophrenia.

I couldn't see how Tony could be guilty as charged by Ron, so I
thought I would go and warn him about what was being said. If I
wasn't prepared to carry out Ron's will, I was 100 per cent sure that
one of the Kray hangers-on would, just to get into Ronnie's good
books.

The Kray gang had stood trial 20 years ago. Tony, since then, had
been mentioned in numerous newspaper articles and books and had
always been portrayed as a man who was loyal to the twins. If he had
informed on them, as Ronnie claimed, I was certain that after 20 years

the facts would have come out before. Whichever way I looked at it, I just couldn't believe what Ronnie was saying.

When we arrived at Lambrianou's flat, I admit Alan and I had taken a drink but we certainly were not drunk. Tony's wife, Wendy, had answered the door and told us that he was out. I thought that he might be avoiding coming to the door because he had heard about Ronnie's ranting. Most 'jobs' in the Kray camp were given to many instead of one. Ronnie had probably asked numerous people to confront Tony and so I wouldn't have been surprised if he was aware of Ron's displeasure.

If I was right about Ronnie just being paranoid, I wanted Tony to know that despite the rumours, he had nothing to be concerned about because I was sure Ronnie would calm down and see sense at some stage.

I told Wendy that there was no need for Tony to pretend he wasn't in and this seemed to upset her. I can see why it would as I hadn't explained that I was there with good intentions and she could have taken it as some sort of insult or veiled threat.

From there on in, it was all downhill. Wendy asked us to leave, so I gave her my mobile-phone number and asked her to ask Tony to call me. Alan and I then walked away. Later that afternoon Tony did call and asked if we would go to his flat. When we arrived Tony said that he didn't think it was right that Alan and I had turned up at his home earlier after taking a drink.

I agreed, but explained that Alan had come down from Edinburgh that morning. 'We had gone for a drink and after discussing what Ronnie had asked me to do, we decided to warn you before somebody else did Ron's dirty work.' Tony's mood changed at once and the conversation turned to Ronnie's paranoia and how it would all blow over. I told Tony I would keep him informed about what was going on.

He thanked me and that was the end of the matter. No threats were made and no hammer was brandished, in spite of what Tony claimed in his book. In fact, Tony had posed for a photo with Alan. At the next visit, Ronnie asked me what had happened regarding Lambrianou. I told Ronnie that I had gone around to his flat but he wasn't in. Ronnie seemed disappointed, but said that he had found out Lambrianou was holding a book launch in Epping and he was going to get him 'pulled' there. I mentioned this to Lambrianou and he immediately cancelled that particular event.

I saw Ronnie a couple of weeks later and I thought that he would have calmed down, but I was wrong. Tony had appeared in the *News of the World* claiming McVitie, whose body has never been found, was buried in a grave 50 miles from London.

> Jack and his hat were dumped into the grave. Then his body was covered by a layer of soil. The next day an unsuspecting funeral procession pulled up at the graveside and a service was held. As the coffin was lowered into the grave, no one noticed that the hole was not quite as deep as it had been the day before.

Tony had not mentioned any of this in his book and Ron said Lambrianou was now making up stories to make money, stories that, he said, could damage Reggie's chances of parole. I had never seen Ronnie so annoyed. He kept saying that Lambrianou was a 'lackey' and a 'grass'. He said he was never in the fucking firm and he was a liar. I found this very hard to believe because Lambrianou's book claimed that he was a 'boss' in the Krays' firm and he and his brother had served 15 years because they had refused to tell police the truth about the McVitie murder.

If Tony had, as Ronnie claimed, grassed them up, then it was inconceivable that he would have been sentenced to life imprisonment and served 15 years. The judge would surely have shown Tony leniency for assisting the prosecution's case against the Kray brothers. What Ronnie was claiming just did not add up, but when Tony and his brother's statements were shown to me, I could not believe what I was reading.

In his book, Tony said that Reggie Kray had told him to invite McVitie to a party. 'It was on Saturday night at a basement flat belonging to a girl called Blonde Carol in Stoke Newington, North London,' says Lambrianou. 'I knew there was a chance of him copping a right hander but I didn't know someone had taken a gun.'

Lambrianou and his brother Chris, plus two brothers called Mills accompanied McVitie to the party. Waiting for McVitie were Reggie and Ronnie Kray, gangsters Ronnie Hart and Ronald Bender and two of Ronnie Kray's young homosexual boyfriends called Terry and Trevor. Lambrianou says:

Ronnie pushed past me and did Jack right underneath the eye with a glass, 'I've had enough of you,' he said, 'keep your mouth shut.' Next thing Reggie was on him. This was the first time I had seen the gun. He tried to shoot him in the back of the head and I jumped, expecting an explosion but the gun wouldn't work. As soon as Reggie pulled the gun I realised it had gone too far. My brother Chris and I had unwittingly set up Jack by taking him to Blonde Carol's so now it was our row too. Jack would come back to us. When the gun failed to go off I said to Chris 'Go and get one of ours.' I knew we might have to do him ourselves. Chris went to our house to fetch a Smith and Wesson .38 police special.

By now Reggie had let go of Jack who was sitting on the sofa asking 'What have I done?' Reggie told him 'You know what you've done.' The gun came out again. Again it just clicked. 'They gave me a duff 'un,' said Reggie.

The next thing I saw was Reggie with a carving knife; it was happening so fast. Jack was in a bear hug and someone was shouting, 'Do him, Reg, go on, Reg, do him.' I saw the first stab go in and turned away. I walked out of the room. I couldn't believe it was really happening. He got it three times with the knife but he must have been dead with the first one. The scene went quiet. I walked back into the room and I didn't want to look but I had to. Then I saw the blood. I saw Reggie pointing the knife into Jack's neck as if he was trying to find his jugular vein. The knife blade was arched and then it went straight through.

I've seen some bad things in my time, men stabbed, near death, but this was worse. And I will never forget the smell.

Death smells like something singeing, like hair and blood burning, a smell that never leaves you. When it was over, Reggie stood there for a second just looking. The knife was twisted to bits. Jack was on the floor in the middle of the room. His hat was a foot from him, crumpled up. Chris wandered back in with the gun we no longer needed. Suddenly everybody seemed to snap out of it. The two boys and the Mills brothers were running out of the room. Reggie Kray turned to me and said: 'Get rid of that, Tony.' And with that, he and his brother and Ronnie Hart had gone.

Jack had been warned by myself and other members of the firm about his behaviour but had paid no attention. How far could the twins let it go when he was persistently challenging their power, constantly trying to undermine their authority?

They could not allow it to happen. Men of their standing could not be seen to have someone like McVitie carrying on like that, particularly in the East End. Had I been in Reggie's shoes I would certainly have done the same thing and the tragedy of it all is that so many suffered for something which the victim himself had decided to cause.

Tony, clearly a leading member of the Kray firm, had decided he and his brother were going to murder McVitie if the Krays failed to do so. McVitie had done the Lambrianous no wrong, but as Tony said, McVitie knew they had lured him to a particularly unpleasant 'meeting' with the Krays and not a party as promised, and for that McVitie would not forgive them. Dramatic stuff, if true, but it isn't – it's fantasy, invented to bolster Lambrianou's ego.

In 1969 Tony Lambrianou had appealed against his murder conviction. In a full and frank statement he told the truth about what happened that night and afterwards in order to try and secure his freedom. Tony said:

> On 28 October, 1967 I met my brother Chris at about 7.30 p.m. and we went to various public houses to have a drink. We went to the Regency Club and upstairs Jack McVitie joined us. My younger brother Nicky was also at the club and he told me sometime after we had arrived that Reggie Kray was in the club. Sometime after midnight when we had gone downstairs to the lower bar, I decided to get some cigarettes from the machine near the office. I went upstairs and while there, Tony Barry came out of his office and walked back in again. He then re-emerged and asked me into his office. Ronnie Kray, Reggie Kray, Bender and Hart were there.
>
> The conversation was to this effect:
> RK: Is McVitie downstairs?
> TL: Yes, he's drinking with us.
> Then something was said about getting him up to the office

and then either Hart or Reggie said, 'We're going to do 'im.'

I said, 'What's it all about?', but I didn't really get a reply.

I was asked if I had a car and I said that I had. Hart told me to bring McVitie round to Carol's and I said that there were others with me and he said that they could come also. But then there was a discussion as to whether the others could come. I also asked, 'What had he done?' Reggie just said that he was 'a fucking cunt' and then they just argued amongst themselves and I was standing in the doorway.

Finally they said that there was a party going on round at Carol's and Hart, I think said, 'Bring him around. We'll have a talk with him.'

I went downstairs and invited the Mills brothers and McVitie to the party. This was not unusual, as normally when they had a party they would invite everyone around.

We went to Carol Skinner's in McVitie's car and when we arrived I was the first one to go down the stairs. There was music playing. McVitie followed me. It was about 12.30 or so. I saw Whitehead and Bender coming out of the back. I was first into the room and Ronnie Kray was standing in front of the fireplace with his thumbs in the waistband of his trousers. Two youths were dancing. Ronnie shook hands with me and almost immediately Reggie jumped on McVitie's back and put a gun at his head. It would not work. Ronnie hit him with a glass and cut his lip. McVitie protested. I cannot remember the words.

The Mills brothers were by this time in the room, and Hart and Bender. I was terrified and I left the room. On the stairs my brother Chris was sitting weeping. We had an argument about it because we realised then what was happening. Chris started to go. Hart came out and I quietened Chris because of him then Ronnie Kray said, 'What's the matter with him?', meaning Chris, and I said he was upset. The Mills brothers wanted to go but no one was allowed to leave.

McVitie had come to the door of the room. He had his jacket off. Reggie hit him and pulled him back into the room. I was just outside; the door was ajar. Reggie had a knife at McVitie's throat. Hart was holding McVitie, the knife would not penetrate. I was terrified. I ran again up the stairs, as I did so I met two children on the stairs and I pushed them into the bedroom.

I stayed there what seemed like a long while but was probably only a moment or so. I came out of the room and started going down again. They were all going out. Bender was talking to Reggie who said 'get rid of him'.

I remember both Ronnie and Reggie's arms were covered in blood. The Krays and Hart left. Bender persuaded me to go into the room. McVitie was lying under the window with his legs underneath him and with half his stomach hanging out. His head was almost severed and his eyes were open.

Bender said: 'It's all over, it's done.' I could not believe it.

Later, my brother Chris returned. He has described how he cleaned up and disposed of the body and it's true. I never knew that this was going to happen to McVitie. I know we should have come to his assistance but I was terrified that without a weapon the same would be meted out to us too.

I have never belonged to the Kray firm. I met them at the same time as my brother Christopher and only really started to see much of them about eight weeks prior to the murder of McVitie. This was primarily because I was also a member of the Regency Club and also drank in the same public house. I personally was never asked to do anything by them but I knew only too well their reputation.

As regards the solicitors the same occurred to me as to my brother. We knew that false statements had been made to Sampsons [the Krays' lawyers], by witnesses and it was more than our lives were worth to try and change solicitors. I told Ralph Hyams [the Krays' solicitor] what had happened and he told me that the Krays would have to be told if I persisted. And so eventually I signed a statement for Sampsons that was quite untrue.

I was in Brixton on remand with the Krays and when they found out that my brother had made a statement to Sampson's that involved them, they constantly threatened me and my family. I was present at the joint conference in Brixton with my brother, the Krays, Bender and Ralph Hyams. Ronald Kray was almost apoplectic with rage over what my brother had said and we both realised that we had to support the Krays to stay alive. I never wanted to go into the witness box but such pressure was put upon me in the trial that I had to do that in the event.

So much for the East End code of silence and Tony's 'decision' to talk about the murder and his time as a 'Kray boss' for 'the first time' in his book.

Chris Lambrianou had made a statement about the murder before the trial, but as he says in the statement he made for his appeal, the Krays terrified him into retracting it.

I made a statement in my own handwriting on three foolscap lined pages. This did not set out the account as I have put it down truthfully above but involved the Krays and told the essence of what happened. I gave it to Ralph Hyams and he read it and said that he would have to show it to the Krays. I told Hyams not to show it to the Krays but he said he would have to. Two days later Hyams came back and said that the twins had said that it was not to be used. I went on about it to Hyams and he kept reminding me that Tony was in Brixton with the Krays. He said that you have got to do it their way. The twins say that they weren't there and you have got to help. He then told me that I had nothing to worry about because the twins had a lot of power. He altered the statement and I was told what to say.

Just before the trial we all went to Brixton for a joint meeting with Hyams, the Krays, Bender and my brother Tony. Hyams told me again that the twins were very upset about my statement and inferred that this meant 'angry' with me. When I saw Ronnie he was livid with me and said 'Are you fucking well putting us in it?'

He was swearing and shouting and I quite honestly thought I was going to get done.

Hyams was present during the whole outburst. Whatever I said always went back to the Krays. I knew that I could not change solicitors because the Krays had told me that I had got to think about my family. I knew that their power extended way beyond prison walls and I thought it was more than my life was worth to go against them.

So much for 'looking after your own', as they preach in the East End. Here were two young men who had been duped into luring their friend to an unimaginable death and now they were being told they would have to protect the murderers and face life imprisonment themselves for something they had clearly not done. What sort of 'man' would allow himself and his own brother to serve life imprisonment because he was too scared to stand up to two bullies and tell the truth? Hard man? Man of honour? Weakling? Tony considers himself to be a hard man and a man of honour. He is 'proud' of the public image he has forged for himself. In his book he says of himself and his 'bosses':

> The twins went away with a lot of honour and a lot of dignity. They could have brought many other people down with them, but they chose not to. I took my punishment, whether I deserved it or not. I was there at the end and hopefully took it like a man. It wasn't a question of my killing anybody. It was a question of 'I was there', and I knew there was going to be trouble of some sort.
>
> I saw what happened. Perhaps I didn't like what I saw, but I kept my mouth shut and that's why I got the sentence that I did.

This from the 'gang boss' who ran upstairs and locked himself in a room with children. His brother hadn't gone to fetch a gun to 'finish McVitie off', as he claims – he had sat on the stairs and wept whilst a man he had enjoyed a drink with that night was butchered in the next room.

The Lambrianou brothers served 30 years in prison between the two of them. During that time their mother and father died. Tony says in his book, 'I blamed myself, if I hadn't have had this sentence, I would have spent more time with him. I felt that we let him down, because we should have been there towards the end of his life.' He states that the death of his parents whilst he was inside is the biggest regret of his life.

I doubt it. In his heart, the biggest regret in Lambrianou's life must be not being man enough to stand up to the Krays and their threats and not making the statement to police he was only prepared to make behind the Krays' backs. But if Tony had had the guts to do that, his 'reputation', his 'name', would have been in tatters. Instead, to promote his sham, he attacks better men than himself, other gang members who refused to be bullied by the Krays into serving time for crimes the Krays had committed themselves. Men like 'Scotch Jack' Dickson who later wrote a book called *Murder Without Conviction*, published in 1986. Tony says:

> A lot of it was untrue [presumably unlike his book]. This was a person who had came to London to put himself on the twins firm. Why didn't he say in his book what he did to us – that he became a grass? If I saw him today, I'd spit on him. I wouldn't hit him – he wouldn't be worth it.
>
> I wouldn't like anyone to harm him: it would be a sin. Let him live to a ripe old age, living with what he did, looking in the mirror and seeing what he is, every day. He's a disgusting piece of work.

This is Tony's opinion of a man who made a statement and gave evidence against the Krays, written, of course, without the knowledge that his own statement would one day surface. Describing the trial and others who gave evidence, Tony is equally scathing.

> The worst damage of all was done by members and associates of the firm who gave evidence against us. It didn't take the brains of Einstein to see that they were out to save their own skins and blame those in the dock for the violence that they had willingly participated in throughout their careers. That was the saddest, most sickening thing, to see people you'd had a cup of tea with, shared a fag with, standing up and showing that when the crunch came their so-called loyalty didn't mean a thing. I think the twins were shocked and disappointed. Let's get it right. We'd all done wrong but some of us didn't try to worm our way out of it by blaming other people. If the grasses had got up there and told the truth we may not have liked it but we could have lived with it. If they had admitted their part and told it as it happened it may not have changed the course of the trial, but at least we would have gone down knowing the truth had been told, but when we heard them telling lie after lie there was no way we could accept that. God Almighty! It was unforgivable.

The Krays destroyed the Lambrianou family and yet Tony still maintains that they were honourable and men of dignity in order to sustain his pathetic image as a gangster.

Many would think him more of a man if he told the truth about the misery and heartache his brief encounter with the Krays had caused him and those he clearly loved. I wish I had heeded Geoff Allen's advice at the boxing show and steered well clear of Lambrianou, because I now know why Geoff thought so little of the individual who calls himself a 'Kray gang boss'.

4

'I READ THE NEWS TODAY ... OH BOY'

The telephone call from my brother Michael was frantic and to the point. 'Mom's collapsed,' he said. 'You had better come home quickly.' It's the news everybody dreads; your mind swarms with every conceivable possibility. I picked up my brother Paul in south London and tore up the motorway, torturing myself with dark thoughts. In my haste to leave, I realised that I hadn't even bothered to ask Michael what had happened.

My mother had, over the years, suffered some horrific injuries after falls. Once she fell down the stairs of her house, fracturing her skull. Mom was rushed to a neurosurgery unit where she underwent major brain surgery. None of us thought she would survive, but in less than two months my mother was up and about and had been discharged from hospital. My heart kept telling me Mom was strong and would be OK, whatever had happened, but my head was telling me she wasn't getting any younger and a similar fall could prove fatal. However depressing my thoughts, nothing could have prepared me for the shocking news that greeted us upon our arrival. My elderly mother wasn't being cared for in a hospital ward, nor was she lying on a trolley in a hospital corridor. My mother, a woman who had never broken the law in her life, had been locked up in a police cell.

WANNABE IN MY GANG?

At 10 a.m. Mom had been in a public telephone box making a call when she had suffered an epileptic fit. In her inside coat pocket was a medical card advising people what to do should they find her suffering from epilepsy. A police car arrived on the scene.

She was picked up off the floor, put into the back of the car and taken to the police station. When they arrived, my mother, who was incoherent, was put in front of the custody officer and the arresting officer told him that she had been found drunk and incapable.

The custody officer ordered her detention and she was put into a cell. When regular checks were made on her, it became apparent that she was ill, not drunk, and so a doctor was summoned. The doctor soon diagnosed my mother as having suffered from a fit and she was treated and released. When Michael told Paul and me what had happened, we went fucking berserk. Together we made our way to the police station and after identifying ourselves, were immediately arrested for the assault on Stuart Darley. A cynic may wonder if we had fallen for some sort of sinister ruse, but nobody could be that sick, could they?

Paul and I were charged with assault and bailed to appear with Michael at Seisdon Magistrates Court the following week. We complained about the arrest of our mother, but red tape, excuses and bullshit encouraged her to ask my brother and me not to pursue the matter. Reluctantly we let it drop.

The legal process is, at best, a fiasco and at times I wonder if it would be cost-effective to plead guilty at the earliest opportunity regardless of your innocence or guilt.

Every other week we had to attend the Magistrates' Court to answer our bail, apply to alter our bail conditions, enter a plea and finally attend to be told the matter was being sent to Crown Court for trial. During that long process, we had to take days off work, travel in the early hours of the morning to arrive on time from London and sit in the court waiting-room for the best part of a day whilst waiting for a meaningless five-minute hearing. Paul said he wasn't going to be fucked about and pleaded guilty. Michael and I rowed with him outside the court, saying his guilty plea would ruin our chances of getting a not-guilty verdict. In his usual devil-may-care manner, he laughed and said, 'Don't worry about your plea, because I won't be turning up for their silly fucking trial unless I'm in handcuffs.'

Paul has never had any respect or concern for the law and those that administer it. As a teenager he was sentenced to six months to two years borstal training. In those days they used to offer the inmates incentives in order to curb their unruly behaviour. If you kept out of trouble you were allowed to wear a blue tie and blue tie wearers were given privileges, such as additional visits. The inmate would then progress through various coloured ties, earning more privileges and eventually freedom. Paul told them from day one they could keep their ties, keep their visits and keep their privileges. Nothing would ever make him change his mind. Eventually, two years and three weeks after being sentenced, he was booted out of the borstal.

After months of being messed about, my brother Michael and I were informed that our trial would take place at Stafford Crown Court. A trial that is scheduled to last two weeks or perhaps even a month may only last a day if the defendant changes his or her plea at the last minute. Because of this, the courts are unable to give the defence a precise date for a trial to begin and so a preliminary date is given and the defendant is put on notice. This means that a couple of weeks before the preliminary date you are told to contact your solicitor every evening to learn if you are in court the following day.

During the time that Michael and I were on notice, we found ourselves working in Newcastle. With at least a day's warning, we could not foresee a problem in returning to the Midlands to arrive at court on time. We rang our solicitor at 5 p.m. and asked if there was any news. He told us that we had been summoned to appear at court the very next morning. I was driving a heavy-goods vehicle and explained to my solicitor that it was doubtful I would be able to make it to Stafford in time as I was only permitted to drive a certain amount of hours, by law, without having a substantial break. His advice was that I should not break the law, but present myself at the court at the earliest opportunity. The next morning, Michael and I set off for Stafford having taken the statutory driving break. We rang the court at regular intervals to inform them we were on our way and that we would arrive around 10 a.m., the time we had been ordered to be there.

We finally arrived around 10.45 a.m. but were told that the case had been adjourned and a warrant for our arrest had been issued. The official said that we hadn't turned up as ordered and therefore we had no defence to the breach of bail. We were once more bailed and told to reappear at the court in 14 days. It was an absolute waste of everybody's time, but much of what happens during the legal process is.

Two weeks later, Michael and I stood trial for the assault on Stuart Darley. We told the court an embroidered version of the truth: Darley was drunk, behaving like a lout, had thrown things and when I approached him had raised his hand; I was in fear for my safety so I had struck him in self-defence. It was feasible, simple and straightforward. We felt the jury wouldn't have to spend too much time deliberating over it.

When Darley went into the witness box to give evidence he was brash and brazen. He answered back to our barrister and the jury could see what sort of man he was. Although I was technically guilty in law, I think he deserved what he got and the jury agreed with me. We were found 'not guilty'. Michael and I were ecstatic as we had been expecting to receive custodial sentences. Looking over at the police, we could see that they were not enjoying the moment as much as we were. Soon, it was their time to smile. The judge released the jury and ordered Michael and me to remain in the dock. He told us that as we had committed an offence concerning our bail, he was going to fine us £50 each. I estimated that my travel costs and loss of earnings in relation to the numerous court appearances I had been forced to make were no less than £500. The court owed me £500, I owed them £50, and so if they sent me £450 we would all be happy. It was the easiest solution I could think of, but I knew nothing concerning the law could be resolved logically. I was told that if I had not paid within the 28 days they had given me to pay, then another warrant would be issued for my arrest. To be honest, as long as they owed me money, I couldn't give a fuck what they issued.

After the Darley trial, Ronnie Kray asked me to visit him to see how things had gone there and were going in general. I travelled to Broadmoor and after discussing events at the trial, Ron told me he was rather concerned about new rules that had been brought in at Broadmoor. Ronnie used to chain-smoke and was being told that if he wished to smoke he would have to do so in a designated smoking room. Ronnie said, 'I spend most of my time now sitting in there surrounded by fucking nutters!'

I laughed and reminded him that he himself was a nutter according to the authorities. Ronnie thought this was funny, in fact he roared his head off over it. 'Bernie,' he said, 'would you do me a favour and write to the Environmental Health Department at Bracknell Council and tell them that the conditions here are very bad for the patients?

'Tell them I am forced to sit in a room full of "fucking nutters" and that it's such a small room, filled with so much smoke, I can barely see my hand in front of my face. Tell them you think it is detrimental to my health. If they ask you how you know this, tell them you were talking to a hospital warder in the pub in the village and the officer was concerned about the effect these changes were having on the patients.'

Ronnie thought that if an outside agency became involved then the Broadmoor authorities might do something about it, especially if they thought that their own staff were not happy about the situation. I wrote the letter for Ron using a pseudonym and posted it, as agreed, to the Environmental Health Department. Within two weeks I received a reply, informing me that the Council were unable to take the matter further as they had no powers of enforcement in hospitals as they come under the Health and Safety Executive. They did promise, however, to pass my letter on to the relevant department at Broadmoor. It was the last thing Ron and I wanted; we both knew it could cause problems for him if either of us were linked to the letter by the bosses at Broadmoor. I rang Bracknell Council and asked them to forget about the complaint, but they informed me the letter had already been passed on. Less than a week later, a letter from Broadmoor dropped through my letterbox.

> I am writing to acknowledge receipt of your letter, the contents of which concern me not so much from the point of view of whether or not restricted practices occur, but that members of staff appear to be discussing matters affecting hospital policy in a public house with yourself and possibly others.
>
> You will appreciate that this is in breach of contract and I therefore must ask you to let me have the names of those members of staff, together with details of alleged restricted practices that you are suggesting occur on the Henley ward.
>
> With regard to the specific point on the smoking policy, this ban is an internal policy matter, which will be dealt with internally.
>
> I look forward to hearing from you with the information requested in this letter.

I was gutted. I knew that Ron had opened a can of worms because of the story he had made up. Hospital warders allegedly discussing internal matters with members of the public in a pub was bound to cause a stink. I knew that on the next visit to Ron, we would have to discuss how we were going to respond to any problems it may cause.

About four days later, I visited Ron and explained to him about the letter, but he told me to just forget it. I emphasised the fact that it could cause problems for him, but he just said, 'Fuck them, what are they going to do, lock me up?' When the visit ended, I said my usual farewells to Ron, but had no idea it was to be our last meeting. I shook his hand, walked out of the visiting-room, across the exercise yard and into the main reception area.

As I went to leave, a man approached me and asked me if I was Bernard O'Mahoney. 'Yes, I am,' I replied.

'Would you mind coming into the office?' he asked.

'No problem,' I said. I thought that they were going to search me for smuggling letters or money out for Ron. I hadn't anything on me and so I wasn't concerned.

The man introduced himself as the general manager of Broadmoor. He told me that I had written a letter to Bracknell Council claiming that I had been discussing internal policy with members of staff in a public house and he wanted to know their names as they were in breach of contract.

I told him that I didn't know what he was talking about. He produced a copy of a letter I had sent to Ronnie and then showed me the letter I had sent to the council. The handwriting in the letters was identical.

'You are Bernard O'Mahoney, aren't you?'

'Yes,' I said.

'Well, you have sent this letter and you are alleging that members of staff have been discussing internal matters concerning this hospital in a public house. I want to know who they are.'

'I'm not prepared to tell you,' I said. I was then asked to leave.

The following week I returned to Broadmoor and told the receptionist that I was there to visit Ronnie Kray. When I said that my name was O'Mahoney, there was a brief delay while the man looked through a file; he then said that my visits with Ronald Kray had been terminated forthwith. The hospital, he said, would not permit me to visit him any more. I was banned from Broadmoor Hospital, home of some of Britain's most infamous murderers, rapists and arsonists. I don't know if anybody has ever been banned from Broadmoor before, I'm sure they have, but I thought it was quite amusing.

I must admit, I missed my visits with Ron, who was unintentionally funny and so appealed to my sense of humour. I certainly met a lot of interesting characters through him. One I had become particularly friendly with was a Scot named John Masterson.

John, a former miner from Hamilton in the west of Scotland, had spent much of his adult life in prison, mainly for robberies and burglaries. In prison he had become a friend of the Krays and they had presented him with a pocket watch inscribed: 'To John from the Kray brothers'.

John was really proud of the watch and was always showing it to people. He had organised lots of petitions for the Krays' release and had fought many issues arising in prison on their behalf. On his business card, John described himself as a 'penal reformer and human-rights campaigner'.

John came to public prominence when he became one of the first prisoners to be held at the now-discontinued control units for subversive prisoners in the 1970s. He took the Home Office to court over the use of the units and pursued the case to the European Court of Human Rights. John wore thick spectacles and was always smartly turned out in a suit, shirt and tie and was well regarded within the criminal fraternity. By the time I met John, he was no longer an active criminal and was always short of money. Despite this, he had recently rejected a £5,000 offer from a tabloid newspaper to set up his good friend Lord Longford. The idea was that he would fool Lord Longford into taking a prostitute into the House of Lords for tea. John was outraged that anybody would even think he would betray a friend's trust.

Whilst John was exercising good old-fashioned values, his 1960s counterparts were busy waging a bloody war over drugs. These gangland icons always banged on about never hurting women and children, but they didn't mind that their drug dealing was the very thing that tears families apart. The first shots fired in this latest drug war were fired into the infamous Great Train Robber, Charlie Wilson. His execution at his villa in Marbella set in motion a catalogue of gangland murders.

It was reported in the press that Charlie had been murdered on the orders of hard man, robber and drug smuggler Michael Blackmore. A year later, 45-year-old Blackmore was himself gunned down in Amsterdam.

A Scotland Yard intelligence officer was quoted at the time as saying: 'Blackmore had a drugs bust up with Wilson and had him rubbed out. They lived by the gun and they died by the gun.' John Masterson was a friend of Blackmore and attended his funeral at Benchley Gardens Crematorium in south-east London. John had known Blackmore well and told me there was going to be a lot of shit over his death. 'Reprisals,' he said, 'are a certainty.'

Alan Smith, the man who had 'survived' Lambrianou's 'hammer attack' with me, was also a friend of John, having met him on visits to Ronnie. When Alan came down to London, more often than not he would stay at John's house in Peckham and we would all meet up for a drink. On one such visit, John was telling Alan and me about the tabloid newspaper that had wanted to set up his friend Lord Longford.

There was a general discussion about the way certain sections of the media behave and somebody said jokingly, 'Well, why don't we try to get one over on them?' Because we had all taken a drink, we were laughing at the very thought of it, but soon we began to kick ideas around.

John was a good friend of the infamous gangster 'Mad' Frankie Fraser, who had recently been shot in the head outside Turnmills nightclub in Clerkenwell, central London. We talked about how Fraser had survived, although his relative David Brindle had not been so lucky. In a separate incident, two gunman opened fire on Brindle, killing him and an innocent bystander, Stanley Silk, in The Bell public house, Walworth, south London. The media seized upon the recent upsurge in shootings, declaring a gangland war had broken out. Overnight, all gun-related crime across London was being linked by the most dubious of threads.

Any tourists on a visit to London who read the newspapers would have thought they were in Beirut. According to the media, a similar war had broken out in Glasgow and soon the shootings north of the border and those in London were linked in the press.

Both Alan and John were Scottish and so the conversation turned to the recent murder of fellow Scot, Arthur Thompson junior. During the 1960s, his father, Arthur Thompson senior, controlled Glasgow in much the same way the Krays controlled London. Arthur senior had ruled Glasgow with an iron fist and was a trusted friend of both Ronnie and

Reggie Kray. Arthur junior, or 'Fat Boy' as he was known, had been serving a prison sentence for supplying drugs before being gunned down outside his house in Glasgow whilst on weekend home leave. Detectives believed that a London hit-man had carried out the shooting. Hours before Fat Boy's funeral, Joe 'Bananas' Hanlon and Bobbie Glover, two men suspected of his murder, were shot dead and their bodies left slumped in a car on the Thompson funeral route.

A senior London detective was quoted in the press at the time as saying:

> Things in the underworld are out of control. These are drug wars, plain and simple. The Glasgow mobs are doing business with the London gangs.
>
> We are trying to find the killers but these are all professional hard men who have learned how to make sure we can't get the evidence we need. Three things are common to the professional murders in London and Glasgow: all the killers and their victims are connected by big-time crime, they are all involved in the drug business and there have been no arrests.

After discussing the press reports and consuming vast amounts of alcohol, we came up with the idea that John, who was known in Glasgow and London for his underworld contacts, would go missing.

The press would be told that Scottish villains who wanted to know who had carried out murders in the recent turf wars had abducted him. John would then suddenly 'be released' by his 'captors' and sell his dramatic story to the press for several thousand pounds. We were all laughing about it but nobody was really taking it seriously. The following day, we discussed it again and agreed that with the media currently desperate for gangland stories, John could probably get £10,000 if he managed to make his abduction story dramatic enough. It was less risky than committing a crime – the scam wouldn't harm anybody and the £10,000 would come in handy, so we decided to give it a go.

Two weeks later, Alan returned to London and parked out of the way whilst John and I went drinking around Peckham. We visited various pubs and ended up in The Heaton Arms. At closing time we left and met Alan at a pre-arranged spot. John got in the car with Alan and drove off. I knocked on the door of a nearby house and told the people who lived there that I had been sprayed in the eyes with CS gas and my friend had been abducted. I kept rubbing my eyes as I wanted to make out I hadn't been able to see anything in case I was asked for descriptions.

The man had already telephoned the police, but he became so concerned about my eyes that he also called an ambulance. When it arrived they washed my eyes out and took me to King's College Hospital. I was trying to stifle my laughter so much that one of the ambulance crew actually thought I was crying. When we arrived at the hospital, they checked me out, the police arrived, recorded my details and left. I was then told that I could go.

I was rather disappointed that nobody was taking much notice of the fact that John had allegedly been kidnapped. I decided that I would contact the newspapers the following day to set the ball in motion. I spoke to two or three journalists and the following morning John's 'abduction' was reported in several national newspapers.

The Guardian published the following article:

KRAY FRIEND MISSING AFTER STREET ATTACK
Disappearance Follows Series of Underworld Killings
Police are investigating the disappearance of a south London man who is an associate of both the Kray twins and Lord Longford. It is the latest of a series of incidents, some fatal, involving members of London's criminal fraternity.

Two men wielding ammonia sprays allegedly attacked John Masterson, aged 47, from Peckham in south London, in the street on Monday night. There were reports of a shot being fired and he has not been seen since.

Mr Masterson had been drinking in two local pubs, The Heaton Arms and The Montpelier Arms in the evening with Bernard O'Mahoney from Essex, who is also a friend and visitor of Ronnie Kray in Broadmoor Hospital.

Mr O'Mahoney said that the two men were walking along Nutbrook Street at about 10.30 p.m. 'The two chaps were aged about 30 to 35 and they sprayed ammonia into our faces. I fell to the floor and there was a loud bang.' Mr O'Mahoney went into a nearby house and the police and ambulance service were called.

He was unable to see for several hours and was treated in King's College Hospital.

Mr O'Mahoney said it was possible that Mr Masterson was bundled into a car. He was aware of no motive for the attack but inevitably there is speculation following the recent killings involving members of south London's criminal fraternity. 'He is always fighting everybody's case for them,' said Mr O'Mahoney, 'maybe he had been asking too many questions.'

Lord Longford said yesterday: 'He liked poking his nose into things like I do. There is always a danger with that. One hopes and prays that he is all right.'

Peckham CID is investigating the disappearance.

The only harm that John may have suffered was the damage to his liver as he drank himself into a stupor with Alan up in Edinburgh.

I spoke to Alan and John two or three times a day, keeping them up to date with the press interest in the story. As the *Telegraph*, *Guardian* and *Daily Star* had already reported the 'incident', we were confident that when John was 'released by his captors' he would be able to sell his story for a substantial amount of money.

By the end of the first week, John had run out of beer money, so he decided that it was time to cash in on his 'ordeal'. I thought John would telephone a journalist and say he had been released and then hope the journalist would ask him for his story. I couldn't have been more wrong.

When I heard what John had done, I must admit I could not stop laughing – he was certainly intent on making as much money as possible out of his ordeal. His 'release' was reported in several newspapers, but the most dramatic account appeared in *The Guardian*:

> John Masterson, a friend of the Kray twins and Lord Longford who had disappeared a week ago after an alleged attack in south London turned up doused in petrol at a Glasgow hospital over the weekend.
>
> Last night, Mr Masterson, who has convictions for robbery, said that he had been abducted because of a dispute over recent murders and attempted murders among criminals in south London.
>
> 'I wasn't the man they were after,' said Masterson. He said

that he had been abducted by two men who had approached him in Peckham, south London and sprayed ammonia in the eyes of his companion, Bernard O'Mahoney, with whom he had been drinking. 'They fired a shotgun and put it to my head to make me get in the car,' said Mr Masterson.

Strathclyde Police confirmed that Mr Masterson had appeared in the casualty department at Glasgow Royal Infirmary late on Saturday night, saying that he had been abducted.

Police interviewed Mr Masterson, but it is understood that apart from saying he had been seized by two Scotsmen in London he gave no details or names. Police in London began an investigation into his disappearance on 14 October after the reported attack.

A Scotland Yard spokesman confirmed that Mr Masterson, who is originally from the west of Scotland, had been traced and interviewed.

Mr Masterson said yesterday that he was already aware of everybody's scepticism about his story. Mr Masterson is negotiating the sale of his story to a national newspaper.

John telephoned me and asked if any newspapers had shown any interest in buying the story of his 'ordeal'. I told him that he had fucked up any chance of making money because newspapers were only willing to pay large sums for exclusive stories and as he had been quoted in the *Guardian* article, he could hardly say he had an exclusive story to tell. John seemed disappointed and said he would get back to London as soon as possible.

I arranged to meet him outside the House of Lords where we had agreed to meet his friend Lord Longford, known to John as Frank, for a drink. As we waited outside for the good Lord, a *Daily Star* photographer took our picture. This seemed to perk John up as it convinced him that there was still press interest in the story, which meant that he would still be able to make money out of it. We spent the evening drinking with Lord Longford in the House of Lords bar. I was pretty certain he knew the 'incident' was not genuine. He kept joking about how well John looked and asked if he had enjoyed his holiday.

Lord Longford knew that a tabloid newspaper had tried to get John to set him up by bringing a prostitute into the House of Lords and so may have guessed this was how John had intended to turn the tables on them. To my knowledge, John never did get paid for his story, but the 'incident' has taken on a life of its own. I have since met journalists who claim they know who abducted John and why.

The story has also been repeated in true crime books, *Gangland* by James Morton being one. The publicity the incident generated created more problems for me than it did John. A couple of days after going to the House of Lords and my photo appearing in the *Daily Star*, I was arrested for the non-payment of the fine that had been imposed when I was late for the Darley trial and bailed to appear at Basildon Magistrates Court.

When I appeared in court, I was asked why I had not paid my fine and when I intended to pay it. I told the magistrates that I was unable to pay until I received the expenses I was owed by the courts. 'You give me my money and I'll give you yours,' I told them. The magistrates were having none of it. I was told my costs and my fine were two separate issues and despite the fact I was owed approximately £500 by the court, they decided to imprison me for one day for failing to pay them £50.

Sometimes I get the feeling that there are laws for some and not for others – it was certainly one of the most bizarre cases I have ever had the misfortune to endure and I've endured a few. The local evening newspaper agreed, reporting the story under the headline:

CRAZY COURT SAGA

A former Codsall man is saying that he is still waiting for £500 court costs that he is owed nearly a year after being cleared of an assault charge, but this week Bernard O'Mahoney was sent to prison for a day in lieu of a £50 fine for breaching bail conditions in the case. Mr O'Mahoney today said that the 'judicial system was completely crazy and it was unfair that the other matter had been pursued'.

Mr O'Mahoney claims that he is still awaiting costs after he was cleared of the charge at Stafford Crown Court in October last year. Before his acquittal, he found himself on a further charge of breaching his bail conditions after he failed to attend court on time for the original assault hearing.

The bail offence was transferred to Basildon Magistrates' Court near his home. A spokesman for Cannock Magistrates' court, with whom Mr O'Mahoney has been in touch, said he should submit a claim in writing via a solicitor.

A month after being imprisoned and more than a year after being found not guilty of assaulting Stuart Darley, my £500 costs arrived. I was tempted to pursue the court for the interest, but I'd had enough of their mind-numbing rules, regulations and procedures for the time being. I also had other, more pressing matters on my mind. My new occupation as nightclub bouncer was taking up more and more of my time. I was involving myself in situations I should have avoided. I was doing what I always do, taking things personally, rising to a challenge and refusing to accept the way things are.

Little did I know, I was walking blindly and unintentionally, deeper and deeper into a fucking nightmare.

5

CONSPIRACY TO MURDER

There was no unity amongst the door staff at Raquels. Most were like me, turning up to earn a bit of extra money. They were certainly not a gang or firm as many nightclub security teams are. In the days before door staff were registered, it was all about being able to counter the efforts of the most violent and disruptive elements in your particular venue. The only way to do this was to bring in an even more violent team of men who were feared (or 'respected', as villains prefer to say) by the locals. Inevitably, this 'team' would all know each other and mix socially when not at work, so they were a 'gang' or 'firm', whichever way you tried to dress up their status.

These days, the council and the police issue door staff with licences, which cannot be obtained without meeting certain criteria. Most men capable of doing the job fall at the first hurdle because they cannot have a licence if they have a conviction for violence or any other crime remotely related to violence. If they have spent their formative years fighting and have been fortunate enough never to have been convicted of an offence, they still have to attend a 'door registration training course'. On this course they learn about fire drills, licensing laws, how to suck up to people who are threatening them, self defence, and of course, first aid. The latter, presumably, for keeping themselves alive whilst awaiting an ambulance after having learned they cannot be taught how to deal with drugged-up psychos in six hours over three evenings in a classroom. My fellow doormen were decent enough people but none of the morons that drank themselves into a stupor in Raquels had an ounce of 'respect' for them. A customer who had glassed somebody or caused mayhem in the club would walk back through the doors the following night without a word being said.

I didn't think it was the right way to run a door, but being the 'new kid in town' I thought it best to keep my opinions to myself. One Saturday night, I was working on the door at Raquels with a man named Larry Johnston – one of the few doormen I felt safe working with. If a fight broke out I knew instinctively that Larry would be alongside me in the thick of it. The problem with Larry was he always had to go the extra mile. When the fight was over, he couldn't resist one last spiteful kick or a stamp on one of the bruised and bloodied bodies that lay motionless on the floor. I was convinced that one day Larry's over-enthusiasm for the job would result in somebody's death.

One evening, a group of men who had left the club minutes earlier approached the door and asked to be let back in. The club was due to close and so I told them that wouldn't be possible. The men were very drunk and became abusive. I wasn't particularly bothered because if you work on the door you endure that kind of nonsense all the time. You have to accept that it goes with the territory. I stood watching them in silence. People were standing around listening to the men giving us abuse and it wasn't doing much for the door team's image, so I thought the best thing to do would be to go inside and close the door for a while. I was hoping they would grow tired of their game and walk away, but they seemed to get more and more hyped up. As soon as we went inside, the men, obviously getting braver because of our lack of response, started kicking and banging on the door. Larry smiled, pushed the door open and we both ran outside. The men began to run. Neither Larry nor myself were built for jogging around Basildon town centre so we stopped and stood in the road. The fleeing men, desperate for a fight moments earlier, also stopped running and stood facing us several yards away.

They started shouting, calling us 'wankers' and chanting, 'Kill the fucking bouncers! Kill the fucking bouncers!' Rather surprisingly (or unsurprisingly in Basildon), they were joined by several other men from a nearby burger bar queue. This group, who had no grievance with us whatsoever, began to hurl pallets and the iron bars that were used to make up the market stalls adjacent to the club. Bottles, stones and anything else the men could lay their hands on rained down on us. It was pretty pointless standing there waiting for their aim to improve so Larry and I went back into the club and closed the doors. Whenever a fight broke out in the club, either bar staff, the DJ or those in the reception area activated an alarm. A light on the DJ's console would tell him which alarm button had been struck so he could then announce over the PA system: 'Door to reception, please' or 'Door to wherever'. Nine times out of ten it was 'Door to the dance floor' because a jealous boyfriend was attacking somebody who had dared to look at his girlfriend. When we walked into the foyer the siren was blaring, the blue light on the ceiling was flashing and all of the other doormen had arrived from upstairs. There were eight of us in total. Everyone armed themselves, some with pickaxe handles and washing-up bottles filled with industrial ammonia – family-size, of course. Others chose smaller weapons such as knuckle-dusters or coshes, which were easier to conceal should the police turn up. I had a sheath knife I always carried and an Irish hurling stick – a bit like a hockey stick but with a broader striking area. When everybody was ready, we opened the door and ran back into the street. One of the men ran towards us with an iron bar, screaming hysterically. I swung the hurling stick, bringing it crashing down across the top of his head; he fell to the floor where he lay bleeding but motionless. Larry ran over and kicked the man in the head and body several times.

Larry's spiteful act incited the crowd and they ran at us. Within minutes, the street had turned into a battleground and was strewn with debris and bodies. Unbeknown to me at the time, there were actually three separate groups fighting. The men that had wanted to re-enter the club had wanted to do so in order to fight another group of men who had earlier assaulted one of their friends. When the alleged assailants had walked out of the club at closing time and into the disturbance that was going on in the street, the group we had originally refused entry to had attacked them. We didn't know who was who and so resorted to hitting everybody who appeared to be involved in the fighting.

Within a few minutes the police arrived on the scene, but rather than restore order, their presence seemed to make matters worse. The crowd backed off at first but then regrouped and started throwing missiles again. The baying mob was now about 100-strong, their number having been swelled by passers-by, revellers turning out of a nearby club and people queuing for taxis. Nobody could see much point in standing in the street and being used as target practice, so the police and ourselves retreated into the club foyer to await reinforcements. As we did so, two officers stumbled on a wooden pallet that had been thrown into the middle of the road and the crowd charged. Soon they were surrounded and were being kicked and struck with weapons. Their colleagues inside the foyer asked us to help them so we all went outside and managed to retrieve the two police officers from the crowd. It wasn't long before police reinforcements arrived, their blue flashing lights and wailing sirens creating panic amongst the crowd, who began to run in all directions. I still had the blood-stained hurling stick in my hand. 'You'd better lose that,' one of the officers said.

I wasn't surprised he had chosen to advise me rather than arrest me, as it had been an extremely dangerous situation we had faced together; the officers who had fallen could easily have died. On Monday the local newspaper published a story about the incident.

POLICEMAN INJURED AS YOUTHS FIGHT

A policeman was taken to hospital after a disturbance outside a nightclub in Basildon. Acting Inspector Ian Frazer was injured when youths turned on police as they tried to break up a string of fights in the town square near Raquels disco.

Scuffles broke out among 100 people at 2.15 a.m. yesterday and back-up police crews were called from Basildon, Billericay, Wickford, Southend and Grays.

Mr Frazer was treated in Basildon Hospital for cuts and bruises but not held overnight. A man charged with assault is due before magistrates today.

It was not an exceptionally violent incident for Raquels. The lunatics who got drunk out of their tiny minds in there thought nothing of stabbing, cutting, glassing or even shooting those who displeased them. I can recall one unfortunate man who was out on his stag night being pushed into a fire exit where he was repeatedly slashed with a Stanley knife. His crime? He had unwittingly shown a local idiot 'disrespect' by bumping into him and then having the audacity to deny that he had a problem. The would-be groom needed 160 stitches – a lesson in 'respect' he will undoubtedly never forget.

Dave Venables had been working Wednesday nights at an Essex venue called Epping Forest Country Club, frequented by footballers, soap stars, page-three girls, the rich and famous and the rich and infamous. Dave asked me if I would cover his shift at the Country Club as he had other commitments and I agreed.

It was whilst working at Epping that I first met David Done, a fanatical bodybuilder from Romford. We got on really well and it was not long before he agreed to come and work with me at Raquels.

He did his job well at first but after a few weeks started arriving late or leaving early, relying on our friendship to ensure no questions were asked – or if they were that I would make excuses for him. Larry Johnston took exception to the favours being showered on David and began making comments about him being a 'part-time doorman on a full-time doorman's pay'. The atmosphere between the two became quite hostile.

One evening, as David prepared to leave early, Larry asked if he would give him a lift home. David said he couldn't as he was going the opposite way, so Larry kicked the door panel of his car. David jumped out and started shouting. Larry responded by pulling out a knife. I couldn't believe how quickly it was escalating. I told Larry to put the knife away but he told me to fuck off and keep out of it. I see very little or no point in holding talks with a deranged man wielding a knife so I took out my bottle of industrial ammonia and squirted him in the face. Larry was temporarily blinded and then sacked. David Done remained. I was annoyed we had fallen out because I liked Larry, but what choice did I have? I couldn't stand by and watch one of my friends kill another friend.

Epping Country Club started playing rave and house music on Sunday nights and it was soon 'the place' to be seen in Essex. Crowds queued for hours to get in and extra staff were taken on to meet the demand. David Done and I were asked to work there on Sundays and we both accepted the offer. Doormen, drug dealers and all 'club people' who had worked Friday and Saturday used to go there, as it was the only night they had off.

It was not long before I got to know many people on the London club circuit. I became friendly with two men in particular: Darren Pearman and Tony Tucker. Darren was a member of a firm from the Canning Town area of east London – a fearless and powerful team, despite the fact the majority of the members were in their 20s.

Darren radiated innocence, was always dressed smartly, always generous and polite, but when there was trouble he would be in the thick of it. He feared nobody, but had respect for everybody.

Tony Tucker was in his mid-30s and a mountain of a man. He ran a very big and well-respected door firm which supplied security at clubs in Essex, Suffolk and London. Tucker was strange in many ways; he spoke to few people and could be quite abrupt. He had a very dry sense of humour and could be quite aggressive towards those who tried to mix in his circle of friends without having been invited.

David Done's obsession with bodybuilding resulted in him having a serious problem with steroids. David's addiction to these performance-enhancing drugs in turn led to problems with money. He even resorted to being a pizza-delivery boy to help finance his drug craving. He refused to listen to reason and his addiction began to affect his judgment. One Monday morning, David rang me up and told me that he had been sacked from Epping Country Club for allegedly selling drugs. I knew this was false. David had nothing to do with drug dealing. I told him that if he was being sacked, then all of the door staff should walk out in support of him. I told him I would pick him up and we would go and see Joe, the head doorman, together to see if we could get to the bottom of it. When we arrived I asked Joe who had said that David was dealing. He said that the club had received an anonymous telephone call.

I got quite irritated and reasoned that if the person who alleged David was a dealer didn't do it openly and with some form of corroboration, then he or she shouldn't be believed. Eventually Joe relented and said that David could have his job back and we both went home. That evening, I received a phone call from Dave Venables who told me that the management at Epping had said I was to be sacked instead of David Done. No reason was given.

What particularly annoyed me was that now I had been sacked, David Done refused to stand by me. He said that he needed the money and the fact that I'd lost my job was unfortunate, but there was nothing he could do. I was fucking livid and my friendship with David became, at best, strained.

David Done worked at the Ministry of Sound occasionally, and in an effort to patch up our friendship he got me a job there to replace the nights I had lost at Epping. The Ministry door team were a powerful firm – nearly every man on the team could have 'a row'. One man I got on particularly well with was Ronnie Fuller. I had first met Ronnie through his girlfriend Larissa, who lived in Grays, Essex. Larissa and I got to know each other when I worked at Epping. Ronnie had been a professional wrestler, but he had given it up as he said the sport was corrupt. 'It's full of villains,' he told me, 'they want you to throw nearly every match so they can gamble on the fight and win.' Larissa constantly nagged Ronnie to give up working the door because she feared for his safety, but he wouldn't have any of it. 'I'm OK,' he would say, 'I've got to know most of the villains who come in here and they get on all right with me.' The trouble with door work is, the longer you do it, the more involved you become in the shit it creates and incidents you consider trivial fester in people's minds.

David Done was a good friend of Carlton Leach's, who had been the head doorman at the Ministry of Sound but had recently been sacked and had his door team removed from the club. Two brothers from south London – Tony and Peter Simms – took over the door and there was immediate conflict between Leach and the Simms brothers.

I asked David if Leach minded us working for the Simms brothers. I felt our loyalty lay with Leach, who was after all David's friend. David told me that he had discussed it with Leach and he had said that it was fine for us to continue working there. A few days later, I learned that David Done had lied to me. When he had approached Leach about working at the Ministry of Sound, he had been told that it would be appreciated if he didn't work for Tony and Peter Simms. When David had explained that he needed the money, Leach told him that he would pay him his wages not to work there. David decided that he would take money from both the Simms brothers and Leach. I said I wanted nothing more to do with it and so David and I ended up falling out again.

I was still seeing a fair bit of Tony Tucker, the man I had met at Epping Country Club. He asked me what was going on between David Done and me and I told him. Tucker, who was also a good friend of Leach, told him that David Done had been taking money from him and the Simms brothers. When confronted, David denied it and slagged me off, telling Leach I was a liar and had been trying to cause trouble. I rang up David and taped the conversation to prove that not only had he taken the money from Leach and the Simms brothers, but the things he had said about me to cause trouble were untrue. Around the same time, an article appeared in the *News of the World* about two of the Ministry of Sound doormen – Mark Rothermel and a South African named Chris Raal.

Rothermel had left before I had started work at the club but Chris Raal was still there, working alongside David Done and me. Chris was in this country on the run from the South African police after it was alleged that he had shot dead a nightclub manager in Johannesburg. I had never met Rothermel and until I had read the *News of the World* article, I had never heard of him.

The Ministry of Sound had recently won one of its many awards and the article was making a big issue about men with violent pasts being employed there. In November 1989, Mark Rothermel had been sentenced to six years' imprisonment for assisting in the disposal of a body. Mark had been working at Hollywood's in Romford – one of Tony Tucker's doors – with another man, Pierre St Ange. Pierre and Mark had got into a dispute with a DJ there named Bernie Burns. They had lured him to a flat in Ilford, where he had been strangled. His body was wrapped in a blanket, put in the boot of a car and taken to a quiet wood near Chelmsford. The head and both hands were hacked off so it would be difficult to identify the body. Mark was reported to have told a friend: 'The hands came off easily but the head was more of a problem because of the veins in his neck.' The DJ was buried in a shallow woodland grave; his head and his hands have never been recovered. Police found the mutilated corpse after a tip-off and arrested Rothermel at the same time – he was hiding in a pond near the grave, up to his neck in water. Mark was found not guilty of murder and not guilty of manslaughter, but he received six years' imprisonment for the disposal of the body. Pierre was found not guilty of murder but was sentenced to ten years for manslaughter.

At first, people blamed Carlton Leach for tipping off the newspaper about Rothermel and Raal's association with the Ministry of Sound. The Simms brothers thought that Leach might have been trying to discredit their door team. David Done told people that it 'must have' been me; it would have been easy to believe as I made no secret of the fact that I had many newspaper contacts which I had made during my time spent working on the James Fallon fundraising event. It was the Kray brothers who had taught me the usefulness and importance of a relationship with the media.

It was a childish and dangerous thing for David Done to assume and then voice; Mark Rothermel and Chris Raal were no fools and obviously extremely dangerous men. I was initially unaware of what David Done had been saying, but the next time I worked at the Ministry of Sound it was apparent something was not quite right and it concerned Raal, who was unusually abrupt with me. You could have cut the atmosphere with a knife but it soon became clear that it wasn't the atmosphere that certain people wanted to cut. I guessed I was under suspicion concerning the *News of the World* article and I was pretty sure who had planted the seeds of uncertainty in people's minds. I went out to the front door and said to David Done, 'What the fuck's going on?' He looked at me rather sheepishly, but said nothing. I could tell by his manner that whatever was going on, he was behind it. Despite the atmosphere nobody accused me of anything, so I decided to sit it out and see what developed. I remained working until the end of the night and then left as normal.

Since starting work at the Ministry of Sound I had met a man named Dave Courtney. To be honest, he looked the part, seemed all right and I quite liked him and those he hung about with. These days Courtney tells people he was a 'gangland boss' or a major player but nobody thought of him as such back then.

I was introduced to him through a mutual friend called Eric Lloyd. Eric lived in the Basildon area and had worked alongside me at Raquels as a doorman. All of the villains in the area, and beyond, knew Eric because he and his family had always been involved in nightclub security. When the Ministry of Sound would close on Sunday morning, the die-hard ravers would go to the nearby Elephant and Castle pub, and then onto The Park nightclub in Kensington. They were good times; everyone was in high spirits and there was rarely a hint of trouble. When The Park closed early on Sunday evening, those still standing would go to The Gas nightclub in the West End or Epping Forest Country Club. Looking back, I don't know how people did it. Most of them were fuelled by drugs so didn't really feel the effects of fatigue until they 'came down' from their drug-induced high.

Courtney and his friends would stand by the huge speakers on the left-hand side of the bar in the Ministry of Sound. They all used to dance about and generally have a good time. The majority of my friends would meet up in the back 'Dark Room' so other than saying hello when we passed, we didn't have that much to do with Courtney or his friends.

Every Sunday evening there was a house and garage night held on a boat which was permanently moored on the Thames at the Embankment. I went there one night and bumped into Dave Courtney, who said hello, then stood drinking with me at the bar. I noticed again that my presence was creating an atmosphere, so much so that everyone around me began to move away – a sure sign that trouble was brewing. I asked Courtney what was going on and he said that he wasn't aware of anything going on; he laughed and said I was just being paranoid.

As I was leaving the boat, I saw Courtney arguing with a man with a ponytail who had a knife in his hand. Courtney was saying to him: 'Not here, not here!'

I am not stupid. It was obvious to me that the man wielding the knife, whom I had never even seen before, was planning to attack me. I went over to Courtney and said, 'What the fuck's he doing with a knife?' Courtney looked embarrassed and denied the man had a knife. I said, 'I'm not fucking stupid, Dave, I saw it.' Once more Courtney said I was mistaken, so I walked off.

As we left the boat, Courtney asked me if I could give a friend of his a lift to a party. I thought that if something was going to happen, it would have happened on the boat, so I agreed to give his friend a lift. The person who got into my car was in his 20s; he told me he was from Coventry. He looked a bit of a mug; I certainly wasn't concerned about him. He told me the party was being held in a house in north London.

It may sound odd, but you can actually sense fear or the coming of violence. The atmosphere in that car was very, very tense. He asked me about David Done and if I got on with Chris Raal. He also asked me if I knew Carlton Leach, in fact, he asked me too many questions. I kept a First World War bayonet down the side of my seat in the car and I decided that the first wrong move this man made, he was going to get it stuffed into his head. The party, he told me, was in a house on a main road heading towards the A1. Every few hundred yards my passenger kept saying: 'This looks like it, this looks like it.' By 'coincidence', every place that 'looked like it' happened to be an unlit, uninhabited area. He told me the number of the house the party was meant to be at, and unsurprisingly, we were unable to find it. He kept saying: 'Pull over here and I'll knock a door.' Each time I ignored him and pulled onto a brightly lit garage forecourt or similar spot. As we were driving up a dual carriageway, I noticed two cars following us.

As we slowed to negotiate a roundabout, I saw that Dave Courtney was driving one of them, and the tall man with the ponytail was in the other. It was apparent to me that this was an amateurish attempt to corner me. My confidence grew when I realised the type of mugs I was dealing with. These 'gangsters' had been watching too many Jimmy Cagney movies. If someone really wanted to harm me, they could have done so on the boat. I couldn't understand why they were bothering with all this theatrical manoeuvring. I stopped the car, grabbed my passenger, shoved him onto the street and slammed the door shut. As I drove away, I noticed he had left a lock-knife on the seat.

The following day, I rang Tony Tucker, who knew all of the characters involved as both Rothermel and Raal had worked for him. I told him what had gone on. I said there was only one way to sort this out – ring Leach, Rothermel, Raal and David Done and arrange a meeting. A 'meeting' is not a democratic discussion; each person says his piece and whoever is not believed does not get to leave the room under his own steam. Later that day, Tucker rang me and said the meeting was on for the following morning in a Portakabin at a car front in Essex. As I was getting ready to leave for the meeting, Tucker rang and said it had been called off, as they had been unable to get hold of David Done. Another meeting was arranged; this time they were able to reach him but he said he didn't want to go. The matter, I was told, was therefore closed. I found it hard to contain my anger.

This had all started because I had suggested Done should show some loyalty to his friend Leach. As a result of that, people had been plotting to stab me for no reason and now I was being told to forget it. I decided I would forget it and carry on working for the Simms brothers and if people didn't like it, that was their problem. I have not seen or spoken to David Done since.

The next time I saw Dave Courtney was in the Café de Paris. He was with the same people he had been with on the boat, and the same bad atmosphere soon descended around me. I wasn't going to play their silly gangster games so I walked over to Courtney and asked him what was going on. Courtney, puffing on his cigar, said he had heard things about me and he didn't like them. I was hardly flattered. 'What have you heard and who fucking from? That wanker David Done?' I asked him. I told him to get his facts right or keep his nose out of matters that didn't involve him. In fairness to Courtney's friend Ian Tucker, he agreed Courtney had only heard talk from people in clubs rather than facts from people who'd know, and so I walked off.

I did attend a party a few weeks later at the house where I was supposed to have been killed and our host was the knifeman with the ponytail – my would-be murderer. He did speak to me a couple of times, asking me who I knew and who I was associated with, but the earlier incident was never raised by either of us. I saw little point. Why ask someone why they were going to do something they clearly had no intention of doing?

One night, whilst working at the Ministry of Sound, I hit a man in the face with a lead cosh. He had been threatening Ronnie Fuller and me as we had refused him entry due to his drunkenness. We had politely asked him to go away several times, but our good-natured requests were only repaid with increased hostility and further abuse. Eventually the man was told to 'Fuck off or else'. His response was to step forward with a raised fist. Smack!

The sound of the lead cosh making contact with his jaw and cheekbone echoed all around us. I knew something had broken in his face, I knew I had hurt him. He fell motionless to the ground and I was advised to disappear. The following day Peter Simms rang me and said the man had suffered a broken jaw and a fractured eye socket. 'The management would prefer it if you didn't return,' he said. Peter and his brother Tony are decent men and had been good to me. I didn't want to repay them with grief, so I said I understood. Out of the Ministry meant out of circulation in London, so it was some time before Courtney and I were to meet again.

Paul Trehern, a Basildon doorman who used to work at Raquels, announced he was getting married and telephoned the club to say he would be popping in on his stag night for a drink with approximately 30 other men. It was expected that they would be rowdy – most stag nights are – but Paul had worked with us and had the courtesy to telephone and inform us of his intentions, so I said it shouldn't be a problem. I advised

Venables that he should go and see Paul and explain to him that there would only be four or five of us working that night. It would be inconceivable for us to control 30 men, so we would expect Paul to supervise his own friends. That way there wouldn't be any problems and therefore they would be most welcome to come into the club. However, Dave discussed it with the management and together they decided that Paul Trehern and his friends would not be welcome. I thought it was ridiculous.

When the night came around, Paul and his friends turned up and were quite rightly disgusted to learn they were being refused admission. Paul ended up grappling on the floor with Venables and, despite Venables' best efforts, he and his friends still entered the club.

Apart from the initial scuffle, they were well behaved and didn't cause any problems whatsoever. I thought the situation had been handled badly and was extremely embarrassed as Paul was a friend and ex-work colleague. The following night Dave Venables didn't come into work. He knew I had the serious hump with him. The next morning I received a phone call from the manager. He asked me to come in and see him as Dave Venables had resigned. He told me Venables had said he could no longer work with me. I was in total agreement: I could no longer work with him. The manager shook my hand and said security at the club was now mine to run. I decided there and then things would change dramatically. I would run the door my way and if the local villains wanted trouble, they could have it.

Prior to my arrival at the club people had taken liberties all the time. By using excessive violence to combat violence, I had reduced the amount of trouble and people were thinking twice about starting anything in the club. It's easy to say with hindsight now, but I should have realised that excess would eventually be met with excess.

I told Tony Tucker about the problems I was having with poor door staff at Raquels and said I needed the back-up of a strong firm to get rid of the local trouble makers who had been dictating policy for too long. I told him I would run the door and he could reap whatever benefits there were from providing invoices and any other 'commodities' such as drugs, protection, debts and so on. I would not bother him with the day-to-day running of the club. The only time I would call on him was if I had a severe problem and I needed back-up. We shook hands and on 4 September 1993, Tony Tucker and I began our partnership at Raquels.

6

DEBT AND DESTRUCTION

The agreement with Tucker brought new faces onto the Basildon scene. Men who had worked for him in London began to replace the local doormen Venables had employed. The door team were extremely firm, but fair. Mark Rothermel, who had worked for Tucker before being imprisoned in the case of the DJ who had his head and hands hacked off, was introduced to me and he agreed to come and work at Raquels. Chris Lombard, a giant of a man who had worked for Tucker at Hollywood's in Romford, also joined us. Within a short period of time none of Venables' old door staff were left. The new team had never heard of the local faces and so cared little about the reputations they had. 'Somebodies' and 'nobodies' were all treated in the same way and if they didn't like it, they didn't get in. Local hard men concerned about losing face began to go to other clubs and the violence in Raquels was dying a death. I became increasingly involved with Tucker, both socially and in his murky door-and-drug business. Everywhere we went, doors and opportunities were flung wide open for our benefit. Tucker told me he was having his birthday party at The Prince of Wales public house, near Grays. He asked all of the door staff who were working at Raquels if they would attend. The party was a real success. Doormen from across London and the south-east turned up in force. Most were out of their face on cocaine, a veterinary drug called 'Special K', Ecstasy or a cocktail of all three and more. Surrounded by such a large and powerful firm, Tucker was in his element.

In the early hours of the morning I was sitting on the floor of an upstairs room in the pub talking to some people I knew from Bristol. A man in his mid-20s pushed open the door, striking me with some force.

I was expecting an apology, but when none was forthcoming, I said, 'You've just knocked the fucking door into me.'

The man looked at me and said, 'Well, you're a doorman, aren't you?'

It was a stupid thing to say because he must have known it would cause trouble. I got up and walked after the man, who had turned his back and left the room. Friends of Tucker followed us. I grabbed the man, but before a fight could start we were separated. One of the doormen told me that the man was Tucker's closest friend, Craig Rolfe, and that Rolfe was extremely possessive of his friendship with Tucker. I was warned to 'watch my back'. I wasn't really concerned. I told Rolfe that out of respect for Tucker, he shouldn't cause trouble at his birthday party. Rolfe seemed OK afterwards, but he still had an attitude.

It was Tucker who told me about Rolfe's past a few days later, when I was explaining what had gone on. On Christmas Eve 1968 Rolfe's father had been found murdered in a van near Basildon. On Boxing Day, a 19-year-old man named John Kennedy had been charged with the murder, together with 23-year-old Lorraine Rolfe, the wife of the murdered man. Lorraine was at that time the mother of three children and expecting a fourth. At their trial Kennedy was found guilty of murder and jailed for life. Lorraine Rolfe was found not guilty of murder, but was sent to prison for 18 months for making false statements to impede Kennedy's arrest. While serving her sentence Lorraine gave birth to Craig in Holloway Prison. Little wonder he had a chip on his shoulder and he'd chosen a life of crime. Craig and I never really did see eye-to-eye after that first meeting. Our views clashed on most things. Fortunately, we rarely mixed socially, but we did have to meet most Friday afternoons on various pub car parks where he would deliver the door staff's wages to me.

Before too long, the heavy-handed door policy I was implementing at Raquels made the club trouble-free. Any violence that did occur was behind the scenes or away from the premises. The rave scene, which had just taken off at that time, had no place for violence: all the kids were into the peace-and-happiness thing that went with their recreational drug taking. It wasn't long before the management at Raquels were approached by a rave promotions company. They said they were currently hiring out a club in the Southend area, which didn't hold enough people to fulfil their demand. They were looking for larger premises and had heard about the change 'in clientele' at Raquels. The management agreed to let them hire the club for their rave nights and a date was set for their opening night.

One evening, a drug dealer named Mark Murray came into Raquels and asked to speak to me. He told me that he sold most of the drugs in the clubs around the Basildon and Southend area and he had heard that the promotions team from Southend were due to start putting on raves at Raquels. Murray said the nights would be very lucrative and asked me if we could strike up a deal where he would be allowed to sell his drugs exclusively at the rave nights. I called Tucker, as I had agreed to let him profit from any illicit business at the club, and he told me to let Murray start. The fee Tucker wanted in return would depend upon the amount of drugs sold per night. It was going to be my job to ensure there was no trouble from other dealers and to ensure an early warning was given to Murray if any police entered the club. When the rave nights started at Raquels, the demand for drugs such as Ecstasy was phenomenal. In order to meet the demand, Murray had to employ additional dealers, who would fan out through the club asking people if they were 'sorted'. Money poured into 'the firm', as we had become known locally, and I was earning more in an evening than I had previously made in a week.

Everyone, it seemed, was happy. The management had a club filled to capacity, the police had a trouble-free venue and the revellers were guaranteed a good night out. Unfortunately, where there are drugs there is money and where there is money there is trouble and where there is trouble you will find violence. Villains who got to hear about the success of Raquels soon wanted a part of it. Instead of fighting drunks or jealous boyfriends, we found ourselves confronted by villains from out of town who wanted their dealers in the club or their door team on the door. The violence that surrounded the firm became more extreme and I soon found myself carrying a gun. Associating with Darren Pearman, Tony Tucker and other villains I had met whilst working at various clubs catapulted me into a world of gang warfare, punishment beatings, debt collection and countless incidents of mindless violence which left men blind, scarred for life or horribly disfigured. I knew the path I was taking was not only wrong but life threatening, but I was in so deep there could be no turning back.

Not long after my partnership with Tucker began, a man named Pat Tate was released from prison after serving four years of a six-year sentence. In December 1988 Tate had robbed a local restaurant. Tate was arrested and on 29 December 1988 appeared at Billericay Magistrates' Court where it was decided that he would see the New Year in at Chelmsford Prison. Tate, however, had made other plans. He jumped over the side of the dock and made for the door. Six police officers joined the prison officer who was trying to restrain Tate, but he still managed to break free and run out into the street. One WPC received a black eye and another police officer was kicked in the face as they tried to block Tate's escape. Once outside, Tate jumped onto an awaiting motorcycle and roared off up the road. Several days later, Tate surfaced in Spain.

He remained there for a year, but then made the mistake of crossing over to Gibraltar where he was arrested by the British authorities. Everybody in Basildon had a good word for Tate, but after he had become a drug user in prison there was a marked change in his character.

When Pat Tate left prison all he had was his drug habit and a bad attitude. He wanted the world to know he was out and not happy about the way he had been treated. Tony Tucker warmed to men like Tate, the sort of man he deemed 'useful'. Tate was 6 ft 2 in., extremely broad, 18 stone and fearless. He also had a glamorous bit of history. His escape from the court on the motorbike and his fight with the police in court were talking points in criminal circles. Tucker soon befriended and recruited him for the firm, but a few members met Tate's arrival with resentment. A man named Chris Wheatley had returned from America some time before Tate's release. Tucker had latched on to him, becoming a 'close' friend and giving him control of one of his venues, Club Art, in Southend. However, when Tate came out, he dropped Chris as if he didn't exist. He also began to badmouth Chris to other doormen, casting doubt on Chris's ability and sneering at the way he handled incidents which arose inside the club. I really liked Chris Wheatley and couldn't understand why Tucker turned on him. There was no room for sentiment in the firm though: Chris had fallen from grace and Pat Tate was to take his place.

Tate brought with him ideas of grandeur. He had met lots of useful contacts in prison that he thought we could work with or exploit. Tucker and Tate began to talk about lorries bringing in drugs from the continent and small aircraft dropping shipments in the fields around Essex. However many times I told them it was risky, they wouldn't listen. Being king of your own backyard is one thing, but going on an international crusade with the kind of attitude and regard for other people they had was a recipe for disaster.

Tucker and Tate embarked on a journey of drug-fuelled madness. Instead of just living it up at the weekends, they were taking drugs from early in the morning until late at night, seven days a week. It was apparent to everybody who knew them that their drug habits were out of control. Both were using ridiculous amounts of steroids, which they mixed with a lethal cocktail of cocaine, Ecstasy and Special K. The latter is a drug generally used to sedate horses, but it did little to calm the drug-crazed duo that were stampeding around Essex causing mayhem. Tate also dabbled with heroin, which made him sometimes depressed, occasionally euphoric, but always on the brink of a violent outburst. Tucker, once level-headed, had also become irrational and unpredictable. The drugs were really fucking up their heads but they couldn't see it – or didn't want to admit it. Occasionally Tucker would emerge from his chemical-induced gangster's paradise and say he was going to give up drugs and start training again. I wouldn't see him for a couple of weeks, but soon he would be back in the club and back on the gear. When Tucker and Tate were together they considered everyone to be a fool. They took liberties with people and, more often than not, with the wrong people. The adoration being piled on them from the wannabes who hung about with the firm was driving them on and on.

I could see through the 'gang groupies' gathered in the club, shaking Tucker's hand, hugging Tate and buying them both drinks. I could see how easy it was for Tucker and Tate to believe they were kings of the heap, untouchable and all-powerful. I could also see that they were fooling themselves, pissing off the wrong sort of people and ignoring the subtle warnings offered. Everybody on the firm knew that our reign was not going to last. Tucker and Tate were going to end up getting us all locked up in prison or buried in an early grave.

I had started visiting Reggie Kray after he asked me to take part in a documentary which was being made about his family. I politely declined as I believed taking part in a programme that glorified the crimes he had committed would damage the slim chance he had of securing parole. Reg accepted my reasons and asked me if I would help instead to organise a 'Free the Krays' concert at Docklands Arena in east London. He gave me the address of U2's manager and asked me to invite the band to play, but the response I got was brief and to the point: unsurprisingly, the band were not interested in getting involved. The concert never did happen.

Reg was totally unlike Ron. He certainly wasn't intimidating, nor was he unapproachable. He struck me as the kind of man who would give someone chance after chance before exploding when he finally accepted he was being mugged off. I've no idea why people say he had a good business brain – everything he got involved in failed because of his 'good nature'.

Even the murder Reg committed was a bloody mess, executed in a moment of madness with little planning. He was destined to be caught. McVitie had let Reggie do him favour after favour and repaid him with humiliating remarks, disloyalty and disrespect. It's not uncommon in the underworld, where many men take a favour as a sign of another man's weakness. Ron Kray was cold and ruthless, while Reg, who was forgiving and weak, would never do anything that might have upset his twin, even if it was to cost him his life.

At their trial, the Krays would have received a far more lenient sentence if they had allowed their defence team to use the fact that Ron had been certified insane and was a dangerous paranoid schizophrenic. Ron would have been found guilty of murder but with diminished responsibility. In mitigation, Reg could have used the fact he was drunk, drugged, on the verge of a nervous breakdown following his wife's suicide and dominated by his homicidal twin. Ronnie's counsel, John Platts-Mills, and Reggie's, Paul Wrightson, had wanted to introduce these facts but the twins would not hear of it. Reg said he felt like he would be betraying his brother, despite the fact Ron had urged him to save himself. The truth was the twins didn't want to destroy the legend the trial had created. They couldn't bear the thought of their Mafia-type deeds being reduced to the uncontrollable outbursts of a homosexual madman and his weaker twin.

DEBT AND DESTRUCTION

Weaker is not an insulting term. Reg was simply more understanding than Ron, reasonable even. Reggie used to ring me on a regular basis, and I used to go and visit him a couple of times each month, first at Blundestone Prison in Suffolk, then at Maidstone Prison in Kent.

The lucrative drug market created by the new rave culture had infected every part of the criminal fraternity like a cancer. From dodgy second-hand car dealers laundering drug money to nightclub bouncers taking rent from dealers, everyone appeared to be making something out of the illicit trade. Even Reg, who I believed epitomised the old school, was taking drugs and looking at the money that could be made in deals. Reggie was using Ecstasy, cocaine and cannabis and was always asking what was going on in the clubs regarding drugs. When I expressed my surprise, Reg laughed and said he was a villain not a vicar. 'If there's money in it,' he said, 'then we want to be a part of it.'

Reg said that he and his brothers had always taken money from the drug trade and he couldn't understand why people refused to believe it because in *Our Story* they admitted the fact. When describing the murder of Jack McVitie, Reg had written:

> McVitie did a crazy thing. He cheated Ron out of some money
> he owed on some purple hearts. It was only a hundred quid but
> it upset Ron. He felt that if you let one villain cheat you and get
> away with it, then others would start fancying their chances and
> start taking liberties.

Murdering somebody because that person owed money for drugs was something I was destined to learn a lot about in the near future. Reg asked me if I could arrange a meeting for him with Tucker. He said he had a man in Hull whom he thought we could do business with. I said I would speak to him and try to arrange it. When I did mention it to Tucker he said he had no interest in Reggie Kray's plans. He said Reggie was a has-been. Tate, he said, had met far more useful people during his time inside. The firm was moving into the importation market and Tucker said we wouldn't be needing the likes of Reggie Kray. However, he did say he would meet him, out of interest, but as far as business was concerned, Kray was to be excluded.

On Reggie's birthday, Tucker decided to send him in a parcel of

Ecstasy and cocaine. I'd often taken Reggie bottles of Napoleon brandy on visits. It was quite easy getting things into Maidstone, but they were tightening up. One of the firm's dealers was appointed to come with me to smuggle in the drugs. He was quite nervous about being searched and so before going into the prison he went into the toilets of a pub opposite the main gate to ensure the parcel was securely secreted. He put the bag of Ecstasy and cocaine in his underpants and then joined me at the bar for a drink.

Just before it was time to go into the prison, he said he had to go to the toilet again. He went in, took down his trousers, sat on the toilet and when he had finished he pulled up his trousers and flushed the chain. When he returned to the bar he suddenly turned pale and dashed back into the toilets. I thought he was ill but when he returned he told me he had dropped his trousers as he went to sit down and the package had fallen out of his pants and into the toilet. He was unaware this had happened and when he had completed his ablutions he had flushed Reggie's birthday present away. The parcel was worth approximately £350. That was probably the most expensive visit that man will ever make to a toilet.

Tucker, Tate and Craig Rolfe turned up at Raquels one evening with a man they introduced as 'Nipper'. His real name was Steve Ellis. Nipper, from Southend, was a very likeable man and in time I got to know him well. He was inoffensive and very funny. Everybody seemed to like him and it wasn't long before he became established on the scene. Everywhere the firm went, Nipper was there.

One evening Tate, Tucker, Rolfe and Nipper went into a 7-Eleven store in Southend. Nipper threw a bread roll at Tate and Tate retaliated by throwing a cake at Nipper. They were all high-spirited and were soon engaged in a full-blown food fight. The shop assistant kept telling them to stop, but they just got more and more carried away. Eventually the assistant said he was going to call the police. Tate ripped the phone out of the wall and told the man, 'You shouldn't say things like that.' Tate said he would pay for the damage but as they were talking, the police arrived. Tucker, Tate and Rolfe walked off and Nipper was arrested. It was no big deal. In fact everyone thought it was rather funny.

Shortly afterwards, Tucker's teenage mistress, Donna Garwood, was trying to get in touch with him, but she couldn't ring Tucker at home in case his wife answered the phone. Garwood rang Nipper to ask him if he could locate Tucker and speak to him on her behalf. True to form, Nipper made a joke of things and said rather sarcastically, 'He's probably at home giving his old woman one.' Nipper hadn't said it maliciously. You could never get a straight answer out of him as he was always joking. Garwood, though, later told Tucker what Nipper had said and made it sound as though Nipper had spoken with some venom. The next time I saw Tate and Tucker, they didn't mention the phone call. However, they did say that Nipper had grassed them up to the police about the 7-Eleven incident and they were going to make him pay. Usually friends were allowed in the club for nothing, but Tucker instructed us that when Nipper turned up, we should charge him, but make sure he went in. Once he was inside the club, we were to ring Tucker, who would come down to get hold of Nipper. Fortunately, he never showed up. The following day Tucker and Rolfe turned up at Nipper's house with one or two henchmen in tow.

Tucker, high on crack cocaine, stuck a loaded handgun into Nipper's temple and said he was going to kill him. He was threatened with a machete and Tucker said he was going to hack off one of Nipper's hands and one of his feet. Gangsters always like to think of themselves as having manners so Tucker gave Nipper a choice: 'Which limbs do you want to lose, your left or right?' Before he could start hacking lumps out of Nipper, Rolfe and others grabbed Tucker and managed to get him out of the room. Nipper's house was looted before they plastered their excrement over everything they left behind. Nipper fled, understandably terrified.

The following Friday night, Tate and Rolfe came down to Raquels, saying they were looking for Nipper.

I said he wasn't in the club, but they insisted on looking to check to see if any of his friends were. They had a walk around for about 15 minutes and then left. Tate rang back later that night, obviously out of his head, to ask me if Nipper had turned up; I said no. I could hear him banging as if he was punching a wall. He was shouting, saying that he was going to kill Nipper. He said if he couldn't get hold of Nipper, he would 'do his family'. He said Nipper's sister, who was only 15 at the time, would be abducted, and he would cut her fingers off one by one, until Nipper was man enough to show his face. There wasn't a lot I could say to Tate, so I just replied 'OK' and put the phone down.

On Friday, 18 November 1994, I had arranged to visit Reg with Tucker. When it was time to leave I rang his home number and mobile, but I couldn't get an answer.

Reg had been promised a percentage of takings from a person who wanted to install fruit machines and video games in pubs and clubs. Reg thought Tucker might be able to help him out by putting machines in venues where he worked and that is why he had asked Tucker to visit him. I didn't think Tucker would want to get involved with fruit machines, so taking him on the visit didn't seem that important. I couldn't wait any longer so I decided to visit Reggie alone. I decided to tell him that Tucker had been unable to make the visit because a family matter had arisen which he had to attend to.

On the way home from Maidstone Prison, I heard on the radio that a man had been found dead in a ditch in Basildon. I didn't think anything of it as stranger things were happening in Basildon all the time. When I got home, I continued to try and contact Tucker, but he wasn't answering his phone.

On Monday, 21 November, a detective based at Basildon police station telephoned me, saying he needed to see me urgently. Everything was fucking urgent with the police so I guessed it was something trivial, but I was wrong. When we met, the detective said he wanted to know if I had heard anything about Pat Tate being shot. I said I hadn't. He also asked me if Craig Rolfe had been up to anything in the past few days. I said I didn't know what he was on about. I wasn't being very helpful and so he said I could go, but he would be back in touch, adding, 'You'll know what Rolfe has done before too long.'

I contacted Tucker and he was very keen to hear what the police had to say. He asked me to meet him in the car park at Pitsea Cemetery as soon as possible. Tucker had a thing about meeting out in the open in public places, whatever the weather. We usually met outside the casualty department at Basildon Hospital, but I soon realised why he had decided to change the location.

Tucker told me that he and Rolfe had gone to Nipper's house because Nipper had grassed them up over the 7-Eleven incident. He said they had been trying to get him all week. He had also gone there on separate occasions with Tate. Nipper had confronted Tucker and Rolfe with a pump-action shotgun and they had been forced to flee. Tucker said that on Sunday Tate had been at home, getting ready to go out. He was in the bathroom when somebody threw a brick through the window. Tate peered outside and a rather irate Nipper had opened fire from close range with a revolver. Tate raised his right arm to shield his face. A bullet hit him in the wrist, travelled up his arm and smashed the bone as it exited through his elbow. Nipper fled and Tate was taken to hospital. Tucker said that when Tate got out, Nipper was going to die.

This incident was not our firm's main problem. Kevin Whitaker, from Basildon, had been a friend of Craig Rolfe's for some time. He had introduced Whitaker to Tucker and he had started using Whitaker as a courier for drug deals. Whitaker had been involved in a £60,000 cannabis deal with a firm from Romford which had gone wrong and Tucker had lost out.

As Whitaker had been the go-between, the debt was down to him and Tucker wanted to know how he was going to pay. Whitaker, who knew what was coming, tried to stay out of the way. A wise man would have left Essex because Tucker and Rolfe devoted their days to trying to get hold of Whitaker. Eventually Rolfe contacted him via his pager and assured him there was no problem, he just wanted to congratulate him on the birth of his new-born son. Surprised by Rolfe's friendly manner, Whitaker agreed to meet Rolfe so that they could have a celebratory drink together to 'wet the baby's head'. Whitaker was picked up in Tate's BMW and greeted by a smiling Tucker when he climbed into the back seat.

Once the car had picked up speed, the mood changed. Tucker demanded to know how Whitaker was going to repay him for the drugs lost in his care. Whitaker blamed the loss of the cannabis on the firm from Romford, so Tucker and Rolfe said they would take him to confront the people concerned. Tucker and Rolfe were getting increasingly annoyed. It was dawning on them that they were not going to get their money or drugs back. They pulled over and grabbed hold of Whitaker and kept saying to him, 'If you like drugs that much, have some of ours.' They were forcing him to take cocaine and Special K. Whitaker was becoming more and more terrified. Tucker was laughing. He said Whitaker was pleading with them to let him go. Tucker used a syringe and needle he had been using himself for steroids to inject Whitaker three times with massive amounts of mind-bending drugs. Whitaker, who was shaking with fear, eventually passed out.

They left Basildon and travelled along the A127 towards Romford. Tucker said that as they reached the Laindon/Dunton turn-off

Whitaker was drifting in and out of consciousness. They drove up the slip road as there didn't seem much point in taking him to Romford. They turned left to go towards Laindon and then pulled up before telling Whitaker to get out of the car. There was no response. They grabbed the motionless Whitaker and dragged him from the car, all the time ordering him to 'get up'.

But Whitaker was never going to get up. Like Kray victim Jack McVitie, Kevin Whitaker had been lured out on a pretence by a friend and murdered by two power-crazed thugs because he owed them money for drugs. They got in the car and drove off but Rolfe suddenly pulled up and ran back towards his 'friend'. 'Fucking leave him,' Tucker ordered.

'You can't leave him here,' Rolfe replied, 'everyone's coming out of work and they'll see him.'

Reluctantly, Tucker agreed and so they returned to where Whitaker's body lay and put it in the car. They then drove back over the A127 to Dunton Road. Tucker said they looked at Whitaker and they knew he was dead. They dragged him out of the car and dumped his body in a ditch. I asked Tucker what he was going to do. He just laughed, and said, 'Fuck all,' but I knew he was concerned. He said the police would not treat Whitaker's death as murder. They would just think that he had overdosed on drugs round somebody's house and died. Nobody would want the body of a junkie in their home and so it would be reasonable to assume Whitaker would have been dumped anyway. He kept laughing, saying: 'We certainly won't be having any more trouble with Mr Whitaker.'

I told Tucker what the police had been asking me. He did seem rather concerned that they had been linked to Whitaker's murder so quickly. However, he kept saying, and I think he was trying to convince himself, that they could never prove that he and Rolfe had murdered Whitaker. Tucker was later proved right – detectives could find no evidence to support any murder claims. Whitaker was written off as a junkie who had overdosed.

At the inquest, coroner Dr Malcolm Weir called the death 'most inexplicable'. Friends told how Whitaker had made no secret of the fact that he was heading for a rendezvous with Rolfe on the night he died.

A message asking him to contact Rolfe was also logged on his radio pager. Rolfe was called as a witness at the inquest and asked to explain his rendezvous with Whitaker. He denied meeting him and said he only spoke to him on the phone to enquire about his baby son. Tucker also attended the inquest, but did not give evidence. An open verdict was recorded.

Tate was laid up in Basildon Hospital after the shooting at his home. He had lost a lot of flesh from his upper arm, but he seemed in good spirits. Tucker was making sure of that. Despite being in a hospital bed under medication, Tate was supplied with a steady stream of drugs. A side effect of his heavy drug habit was that Tate suffered from extreme paranoia. He had convinced himself that Nipper was coming back to finish him off, so he asked Tucker to give him a firearm to keep in his bed. He was immediately supplied with a revolver. Within a couple of days a nurse discovered the gun while making up Tate's bed. The shocked nurse immediately contacted the police and Tate was arrested. Because he was still out on licence from his six-year robbery sentence, Tate was automatically returned to prison for being in possession of a firearm, a breach of his parole-licence conditions.

Nipper remained off the scene. I did ring him to say I would stand by him but he has since told me that he didn't trust me because of my association with Tucker. Little did he know that I was growing tired of Tucker's irrational behaviour myself. Fearing a reprisal attack, Nipper bought a Smith & Wesson for £600 and a bullet-proof vest for £400.

When Nipper was finally arrested for the shootings, the case against him was never pursued because the judge ruled that the gun that he had on him at the time of his arrest was not the gun that was used to shoot Tate. Nipper did, however, serve seven-and-a-half months in prison for illegally possessing a firearm.

I could see the writing was on the wall for the firm and myself. The drug-taking and the violence were completely out of control. As soon as somebody put a foot wrong his loyalty was questioned and once that happened his popularity quickly diminished until he was deemed an enemy. Once deemed an enemy, that person became the subject of some sort of violent attack.

On a morbid high because he had literally got away with murder, Tucker started to rant about killing one of the firm's doormen, whom he thought was a grass. J.J. was a good, decent man who lived in Chelmsford and had known Tucker for years. However, Tucker's drug-induced paranoia had turned him against J.J. Unsure he could take on

J.J. alone, Tucker turned Carlton Leach and a number of other friends and associates against J.J. by saying he knew for sure he had been giving information to the police. One drug-crazed night, Tucker, Tate, Rolfe and a fourth man went to Epping Forest Country Club with the intention of carrying out Tucker's murderous plan. They filled two syringes with a cocktail of drugs they called 'champagne'. A third was plunged into Rolfe's vein so blood could be extracted. This was then topped up with pure heroin and shaken so it resembled the contents of the other two syringes. The plan was to get J.J. in the car, let him see Tucker and Tate injecting the 'champagne' and then offer him the syringe containing the heroin. If he refused, they intended to 'jab' him with it and if that failed the fourth man, who was sitting in the back of the car, had agreed he would shoot J.J. through the head.

When they arrived at Epping they found out Carlton Leach, who knew nothing of the murder plot, had arrived there earlier with his firm and J.J. had decided it would be best to leave. Back in Basildon that night, Tate was so drugged out of his mind and hyped-up at the thought of killing somebody, that he had tried to shoot Craig Rolfe. The following day Tucker and Tate were laughing about Rolfe, who had been so terrified he had climbed out of a window to escape. They told him it wasn't personal, Tate was just hallucinating. Everybody knew it wasn't right, whatever Tate's excuse. Deep down, we all knew the way things were going somebody else was sure to get murdered soon.

The next time I met Dave Courtney was in a place I had never expected to see him. He was in Maidstone Prison visiting Reggie Kray. Going to see Reggie was totally unlike visiting his brother in Broadmoor. Reggie, in an effort to see as many people as possible, used to ask fellow inmates who didn't receive many visits if they could send their visiting orders to his friends. The end result would be that you could end up sitting at a table with a person you had never even met. On average, Reg would send out about four or five of other people's visiting orders, so there would be five or six tables full of his visitors on any particular day. Reg would move from table to table, thanking his 'fans' for coming, spending a few moments with each of them and then moving on. On this particular visit, I spotted Courtney at a table and assumed he was there visiting an inmate he knew, so I was surprised when he came over, said hello and told me he was there visiting Reg Kray.

DEBT AND DESTRUCTION

I asked Courtney about the night I had thrown his friend from Coventry out of my car. He laughed and said that it was a genuine party and I was just being paranoid. Because he was denying anything untoward had been planned, there was little point in debating the matter further.

Courtney did not know the Kray brothers – like so many of their fans he had written to them in the hope that his heroes would write back. Reg had fulfilled Courtney's wish and invited him to visit. To be honest, my heart sank when Courtney said who he was there to visit. I took comfort in the fact that visits only lasted about an hour and so I wouldn't have to put up with too much bullshit from my would-be 'killer'.

Thankfully Courtney was sitting at a different table to me and so the visit passed off without me having to converse with him too much. Over the next few weeks, Courtney appeared at Maidstone more and more often. He was very keen to visit Ronnie Kray but Broadmoor had tightened up on who was allowed to visit patients, so Courtney's wish was never granted.

7

AN INDECENT PROPOSAL

On the morning of 17 March 1995, a reporter rang me on my mobile phone and told me that Ronnie Kray had died of a massive heart attack. Ronnie had passed away at 9.07 a.m. at Wexham Park Hospital in Slough. He was 61 years of age. I tried ringing Maidstone to offer my condolences to Reg, but the prison had been inundated with calls and none were being accepted.

That evening I got a call from Reggie. Naturally he was upset about his twin brother, but his grief, he said, was a private matter.

Over the next few days Reg rang me regularly. He told me that Dave Courtney 'and his men' were guarding Ron's body at a funeral parlour in Bethnal Green. He asked me if I would go to the parlour to do a shift as Reg wanted to ensure ghouls or publicity seekers didn't pull a stunt. I said I would get in touch with Courtney and sort it out. I had no intention of doing so. I thought this type of gangster theatre was a step too far. What harm could anybody possibly do to a dead man? Hard men who employ minders have always puzzled me, but a dead man needing protection was beyond comprehension.

On the morning of Ron's funeral I arrived at the funeral directors at around 9 a.m. and made my way inside. Crowds had already begun lining the street and some teenagers had scaled lamp-posts and buildings where they hung precariously, waiting for a glimpse of Reg, Charlie, Ron's coffin and other ex-members of the Kray firm, who were to be united on their turf for the last time. Bouncers in dark glasses stood all around, gloved hands clasped in front of them. There was no air of sombreness or sense of mourning, but more of a carnival atmosphere.

I was surprised to see Kate Howard outside the undertakers; she was talking to a journalist. Kate had been divorced by Ronnie after she had published her tacky book about her brief spell as 'Mrs Kray'. In the book she had described having an extramarital affair in lurid detail.

Ronnie, for whom pride and self-respect meant everything, was understandably upset that not only was somebody having sex with his wife, but she was letting everybody know about it. To add insult to injury, Kate revealed that whilst married to Ronnie she had been charged and convicted of using a stolen credit card in an attempt to try to obtain goods from shops at the Lakeside Shopping Centre in Essex and she had spent time at her friend's sleazy phone-sex call-centre listening in on perverts.

Ronnie was also upset that Kate had graphically described her own appalling manic behaviour in the book. Sounding more like an East End fishwife than a Kentish housewife, Kate described kicking her lover in the face, stabbing him with car keys and attempting to run him over because he had thrown her sunglasses out of the car. Apparently, her lover had not suffered enough for his misdemeanour – Kate said she turned around and drove at him again. 'Then I went really mad,' she wrote.

> There was a wooden stake lying by the side of the road. I picked it up and began to beat him . . . I'm not a violent person, but something in me snapped. By now, the police had arrived and they pulled me off him. Good job too – I think I could have killed him.

Mrs Kray could have kept her sordid secrets to herself, but the whole point of mixing with the Krays, for most of their fans, was to tell people how hard you are or how close to them you were. Given the opportunity of seeing a combination of the two in print was obviously too much of a temptation for Kate. Ronnie divorced her, but Kate chose to hang on to his greatest asset: the Kray name.

I went into the funeral parlour and saw Reg standing in an office with a female prison officer. He was reading a meaningless framed certificate on the wall. Reg looked vulnerable, a broken man, his twin brother's death having devastated him. I asked his prison escort if we could have a few seconds alone. The officer said that she couldn't leave Reg, but she would not intrude. With that, she walked to the window and looked out, leaving us looking at her back. I was in no doubt that she thought we wanted to share a few private words, which we did, but first I whipped out a metal flask of brandy and offered it to Reg. He smiled, gulped down what he could and gave it back to me.

'Thanks, Bernie,' he said, 'you're a good friend. I will need that to get me through today. It's going to be hard saying goodbye to Ron, but I've got to keep my composure because so many people are going to be there.'

I told Reg he would be OK. He embraced me and invited me to go in to see Ronnie. I entered the Chapel of Rest and approached Ron's coffin. He looked extremely peaceful which, to me, seemed odd for such a violent man. Ron looked older and thinner than when we had last met. His hair, brushed back in the familiar style, had turned white. In his coffin, people had placed mementos – a packet of cigarettes, photos and the odd red rose. I brushed Ronnie's face with my hand, said goodbye and walked out. I couldn't feel sorry for Ronnie, a man who had inflicted fear, pain and even death on others. He chose the path he took and revelled in it. I did wonder if behind the face of 'The Colonel' was a man who would have lived his life differently if he had known what was in front of him. Despite what Reg had told the media on a regular basis about having no regrets, I knew he did have them and that, given the choice, he certainly wouldn't have taken the same path.

When I walked out into the reception area, there seemed to be more bit-part bouncers around than genuine friends and family. The kings of the London underworld, who seemed to have everything, at the end didn't have anything or anyone. I looked around at my fellow mourners. When they weren't flexing their muscles and trying to look mean for the cameras they were laughing and joking amongst themselves. It was obscene.

The prison officer told Reg we would all have to leave soon. I looked across at Reg then nodded towards the Gents. Reg asked the officer if he could use the toilet and she said, 'OK'.

Once Reg had disappeared inside, I went in and once more produced the flask of brandy. He held it, raised it, said, 'To Ron', and took three or four mouthfuls. Walking outside the funeral parlour, I was amazed at just how many people had now gathered. Bethnal Green Road was a sea of people; the bouncers stood in a row outside the funeral parlour, now buried in a mass of flowers. As soon as Reg stepped outside, Courtney, who was dressed in a long coat more suitable as a prop on a sci-fi film than for use at a funeral, began to usher him through the well-wishers as if he were incapable of walking the ten or so steps from the undertakers to his car. When Reg reached the car Courtney continued to move through the crowd, organising men who didn't need organising. He was trying to look busy and important, trying to be a somebody. The fact that we were at a man's funeral was totally overlooked. A mass of bouncers pushed people back as if their very presence posed a threat to Reg. Some were shouting at people who looked back at them in total bewilderment.

On a visit a few days earlier, Reg had asked me if I would remain with him and Charlie throughout Ron's funeral, as he was concerned 'some nutter' was going to cause a scene and he didn't want the service disrupted. For that reason, I agreed I would.

Now that the macabre circus was on the move and I had witnessed the legions of fools trying to promote themselves, I decided there and then I wanted no further part of it. I was sure the prison officers, police officers, countless journalists, underworld cronies and hordes of Courtney's merry men would be sufficient to 'protect' hard man Reg Kray.

I saw Annie Allen (Geoff's wife), Alan Smith and John Masterson getting into a limousine and so I joined them. Tony Lambrianou and his wife Wendy didn't have a car and so they also joined us. The journey from Bethnal Green was something that I don't think Londoners have ever witnessed, or will ever witness again. I saw *EastEnders* actress Patsy Palmer, who played Bianca, at various points along the route. As soon as Ron's coffin and the limousines carrying the invited guests had passed, Patsy would jump into her jeep and reappear somewhere further along the route. People ran up to our car, wanting to shake Tony Lambrianou's hand; a few asked for his autograph. There was only one brief incident. Two women, their faces contorted with hate, screamed, 'Fucking murderers,' but their voices were soon drowned out by the clapping and cheering of others. It was a bizarre cavalcade, like one of those Victorian travelling freak shows where the locals would come out to gaze in wonder at weird and dysfunctional people.

My thoughts turned from the crowds to the man sitting opposite me – Tony 'the gang boss' Lambrianou. What must be going through his mind, I wondered. These people are cheering, these people think that he is one of the men who held his silence, when both of us know that's total nonsense. How could he attend Ronnie Kray's funeral and pretend to mourn, when Ronnie had bullied him and his brother into accepting a life sentence? How could Lambrianou show anything for this man who had allowed him to rot in prison while his parents died? How could this man opposite me tell the press that the Krays were men of respect, men of dignity, men who looked after their own? Together we sat watching thousands and thousands of people, cheering and clapping the corpse of a schizophrenic homosexual who had shot a man through the head, butchered another and ordered the murder of at least one other. What was it about these Krays? What was it about these people that so many found glamorous?

I know people will call me a hypocrite because if I felt that way I should not have been there. A failed friendship is no different to a failed marriage. Everything goes well at first, but when you really get to know the other person, their faults and failings begin to annoy you. They eat away at you whilst you do your best to dismiss them. Eventually, reality hits you and you have to accept your life has to take a new direction because you have grown to loathe those you're with. That is just how I felt maintaining my friendship with these people. Knowing the truth about them made it feel so wrong. I would tell myself that nobody is perfect, but their deeds and words would keep gnawing away at me.

I began to look at myself. I thought long and hard about what I had become and what I was involved in. The members of the Essex firm I was part of were no more than latter-day Kray hoodlums. Outwardly, they commanded the same respect but within, the same bitterness, backstabbing and disloyalty were rife. It was survival of the fittest, every man for himself. The rules and criminal codes that both firms preached were fabricated, produced for the benefit of the media and those whom they didn't want to betray them. Both firms were criminals, by definition: they broke rules, laws and had no intention of abiding by anything that didn't suit them. The criminal code was as dead as the corpse of Ronnie Kray.

When I got home from Ronnie's funeral I got washed and changed and went straight into work. To be honest, I didn't really fancy it. There had been a private get-together at Lenny McLean's pub after the funeral and I'd had a fair bit to drink there. I now had the taste for it and fancied going out, but decided against it. I could, after all, continue to drink when I got to Raquels. By the time I got home from work that night I was drunk and Debra, understandably, was annoyed. We began to have a heated row and the next thing I knew there was a knock at the door. It was two police officers from Basildon. I wasn't in the mood for them and became quite abusive. They said they had received a complaint about a disturbance. I told them to go away and leave me alone but they kept saying they wanted to come in and talk to me. I told them that there was no way they were getting into my house, adding that if they fucked off now there wouldn't be any disturbance, as I was going to bed. The officers tried stepping into the hallway, but I pushed them out. Debra got quite upset and stepped outside to talk to them. Again they tried to come into the house and I blocked their way. 'If you want to talk to them, then talk to them, but I'm going to bed,' I told Debra. I slammed the door and went upstairs.

I had weapons in the house, including a gun, and I began to panic. The gun was fairly well hidden in the ceiling in the kitchen but there were bayonets, knives, CS gas and ammonia around the place. I thought I had better get rid of the gun and the gas, as they were the only two things that I could be arrested for possessing illegally. I looked out of the window to see if the police had gone and it appeared they had. I removed the gun from the ceiling in the kitchen and the gas from the cupboard near the front door. I knew I had to get them out of the house because the police would probably return mob-handed before too long.

I felt like Saddam Hussein waiting for the weapons inspectors to arrive. Should I ditch the hardware or should I take a chance and hide it? I looked out but couldn't see where Debra or the police had got to. I guessed Debra had gone to her mother's, so I rang and asked if she was there. Her mother said she hadn't seen her. Ten minutes later her mother rang back and said that Debra had rung her from the police station. She said that Debra was upset and would not return home because she had rowed with me and I had turned on the police. I decided to go and sort things out with her, so I rang a taxi, switched off all the lights and went outside. I hid the revolver and the gas canister under a large plant pot and went back into the house to wait for the taxi, which arrived a few minutes later. When we got to Basildon police station a police van swung in front of the taxi and another pulled up at the side. A third police vehicle pulled up immediately behind us. I got out of the car and officers in blue overalls with Koch machine guns crouched down behind a van, their weapons pointed directly at me.

They shouted, 'Put your hands in the air and kneel on the floor.' When I did so I was handcuffed and led into the police station where I was told that they had received information that I was in possession of a gun. They said I would be held in custody whilst a search was conducted at my home. I didn't get much sleep that night or the next morning. I don't know what it was, I just knew the police would find the weapons I had hidden in the garden. Detectives finally came to interview me at about 3 p.m. the following afternoon. I was told that they had searched my home and in the cupboard immediately behind the front door had found a bayonet which was approximately 18 inches long and in a sheath. They also found a rounders bat with the word 'dentist' engraved on it.

While searching the main bedroom they said they had found an eight-inch sheath knife bound in blue tape. Finally, they said, at the edge of the lawn at the end of the path in the garden they had found a small aerosol can and a small leather holster which contained an automatic handgun. I was told the items would be sent off for forensic tests and I was bailed to reappear at the police station in a few weeks' time. I got back home at about 6 p.m. that evening.

I had been due to visit Reggie that day. However, the police had been kind enough to ring the prison to tell him that I was otherwise detained. I sat in the house considering my position. If I couldn't get out of this mess, I would get convicted, lose my door licence and as a consequence of that, lose the security contract at Raquels. I began to wonder if that was such a bad thing. Perhaps this was the excuse that I had been looking for. Then again, I had to provide for myself and my family. I really didn't know what I was going to do. I sat reading the newspapers, which were full of stories about Ronnie Kray and his funeral. The amount of publicity the event generated had propelled Dave Courtney into the media spotlight. He had paraded up and down the street in his ludicrous long leather coat looking like Wyatt Earp, eager for any photo opportunity, and the photographers had not disappointed him. His face was splashed all over the newspapers and Dave Courtney really thought he had arrived.

Shortly after the funeral, the *News of the World* revealed that some of the people who had elected themselves to guard Ron Kray's corpse at the funeral parlour had been involved in a series of sick and disturbing incidents. The article claimed that they had snorted lines of cocaine off Ronnie's half-open coffin, set up a Ouija board next to his casket and tried to contact his spirit.

They had then put a Sony Walkman on Ronnie and laughed at him. One is said to have remarked, 'Don't he look stupid with the earphones on?'

Reggie was quoted as saying, 'I'm not happy: I've heard some stories and I'm disgusted.' Reg had heard that staff at the funeral parlour in Bethnal Green discovered tell-tale smudges on Ronnie's highly polished oak coffin. They also found pieces of paper with letters scribbled on them used for the Ouija session. What sort of scum would do such a thing to a corpse? It was beyond me. The very same people who had done this had attended the funeral, pretending to pay their respects to a man they aspired to be. The funeral had been more of a circus than I had imagined. When I spoke to Reg he was deeply hurt by what people had done to his twin brother. He said he was determined to find out which individuals had done what and get them tidied up, as he put it. The phone calls to my house came almost on the hour, every hour, for a week, but fortunately I had refused to have any part in guarding the dead man at the funeral parlour and so I was unable to assist. So much for these people having respect and looking after their own. The man Reg should have been asking was Dave Courtney, who had put himself and his cronies in the undertakers to guard Ronnie's corpse. If they were not directly responsible, they were certainly guilty of failing to do their job efficiently. How hard is it to guard a dead man?

The Kray firm and their fans had become as depressing as their Essex firm counterparts. A particular thorn in my side was one of Reggie's more avid fans, a man named Bradley Allardyce. I had met him whilst visiting Reg in Maidstone Prison where he was serving a sentence for robbery. Recently he had been moved to Whitemoor Prison in Cambridgeshire where Pat Tate was also serving his sentence. Reg had asked me if Tate would look after Allardyce, as he was rather vulnerable.

I was reluctant to ask Tate, but I did so as a favour to Reg. Soon Tate and I were both regretting ever hearing the name Allardyce. Tate rang me a few times, saying, 'Who the fuck is this person you've put on to me? He's becoming an embarrassment.'

Allardyce would ring or write to me, asking why I hadn't bothered visiting him. It was as if he thought he was a somebody because he knew Reg Kray. He told anybody who would listen that he was Reggie Kray's 'right-hand man'. Allardyce would reveal years later that Reggie was using him for more than just his right hand. The caged love birds were in fact an item. In one letter Allardyce, believing he was a fully fledged Kray firm gangster, wrote to me about an associate of Reggie's called Gary Piper claiming he had cheated Reg on a deal:

Gary Piper is in a lot of trouble, Bernie. He's used us and I will never let that go unpunished. Never. I'll bide my time, but when I get out, Bernie, he will be finished. Nobody crosses Reg without crossing me. I will make that cunt pay for what he's done. I am not stupid, Bernie, he will be finished. I do not intend to end up back in prison down to him. But he will be sorry he ever crossed us. Reg means the world to me, Bernie. A lot of people think he has a lot of friends, but you and I know different. It's up to us to protect him. He is like a father to me, Bernie. I love him very much. Gary Piper is finished. Take it from me; Reg listens to me, Bernie, and he will always do as I ask. Because he knows I will only do what's best for him. Sometimes people take advantage of him. Well that's all stopped now because I am his right-hand man. You're a good friend, Bernie, and Reg knows that. I've seen Pat Tate, he sends his very best to you.

In another letter he sent me a visiting order pleading with me to visit him. He asked if I could bring some 'birds', slang for doves, a type of Ecstasy, and some 'Mickey Duff', Cockney rhyming slang for puff, or cannabis as normal people call it. He also said he would get phone cards and start up his own 'food boat', prison slang for contraband which is then used as currency. Censors who read his letter would hardly be fooled by somebody saying 'could you bring "birds" and "Mickey Duff"'. I am surprised the police were not kicking my door down.

Reg had another prison friend from the Midlands, whom I shall call 'Ryan' as he has suffered enough as a result of his association with the Krays. Reg had also had a sexual relationship with him despite the fact Ryan was below the age of consent. Everybody had known Ron was homosexual, but few suspected Reg had such tendencies. One day Reg rang me and asked if I would travel up to the Midlands as a matter of urgency as Ryan had been arrested and needed somebody to stand surety for his bail. I had never met the boy in my life, but when you're wrapped up in that gangster shit you tend to give the required answer rather than the sensible one. 'No problem,' I said, 'I will help him out.' I travelled up to the Midlands from Essex only to find out that Ryan was in custody and the police had no intention of giving him bail. I contacted his solicitor and was told Ryan was due in court the following morning and a bail application was going to be made then. The solicitor said, if needed, I would have to offer the court something substantial if I was to stand bail for him. The only substantial thing I had to offer as surety was a house I owned in south London. The solicitor said the courts preferred cash, but added, 'We will see what we can do.'

The following morning I turned up at court and saw Ryan, who I could only describe as a young boy, sitting in the dock.

The proceedings got under way and very soon afterwards he was walking past me out of the door having being granted bail without any surety being required. When I went outside, he and his solicitor had gone. It's hard to describe how I felt – mugged-off, disappointed and fucking angry all spring to mind. I had travelled over a hundred miles to gamble a house on a stranger and he did not even have the decency to say 'Hello', let alone 'Thank you'.

When the case was finally heard Ryan was sentenced to a term of imprisonment. During that sentence it was revealed in the press that Reg Kray had taken an Aids test. Ryan, Reggie and their sexual relationship were soon linked by probing reporters. Reg, who had heard Ryan had been talking about going to the press upon his release, wanted him silenced. Reg told me about the nature of his relationship with Ryan and said because he was under the age of consent he feared he would be branded not only homosexual, but a sex offender. As bold as brass, he sat facing me and said not only would this affect him publicly but it could cause problems for him in prison. Reg said he had received two official warnings to stay away from young offenders in prison and any publicity concerning young men below the age of consent could result in him losing privileges or being segregated. Therefore Ryan needed to be advised to keep his mouth shut or else. It takes a lot to shock me, but here was a man saying to me that if it ever got out that he was sexually abusing a boy it could prove embarrassing, so would I silence his victim? I told Reg I didn't want anything else to do with Ryan or matters that involved under-age sex. Reg started to rant about his name being rubbished in the papers, friendship, loyalty and being let down, but I wouldn't change my mind. He made me feel sick.

I couldn't threaten a young boy who was going to allege he had been sexually abused. Dress it up any way you want, but this was child abuse. Reg turned instead to Dave Courtney and Gary Piper, the man Allardyce claimed was not only finished but eternally unforgiven by the Kray circle.

Together they travelled to Ranby Prison in the Midlands where Ryan was being held. During the visit they produced a pre-written affidavit which stated any information Ryan may give to the press now or in the future regarding sexual abuse by Reg Kray was made up for financial benefit only and was wholly untrue. Gary Piper told Ryan, 'If anything gets in the press, you will get hurt, really hurt.' The trembling youngster was then encouraged to sign the affidavit, which he did. Feeling pleased he had forced a young boy to stay silent about his abuser, Piper wrote to Reg: 'It's all off, the chap is not going to go through with it, neither ever will he. It will not come up again, you will not hear another thing of, or about, the nonce, he's been taken care of.'

No doubt these men of respect were pleased with themselves. No doubt they have never actually thought who the nonce in this matter really was or about what they actually did. I really had to get away from these villains – everything they did contradicted every word they uttered.

8

FOUR FUNERALS
AND A DEATH THREAT

Roger Mellin was a really nice kid. Young and impressionable, he had never been in trouble in his life and lived with his girlfriend Tracy, who had a disabled child. Roger was desperate for money and had often asked about selling Ecstasy for Murray in Raquels. I told Roger not to get involved in that shit, that he was not cut out for it and ought to forget it. Murray, however, told Roger that he would pay him £50 a week just to store drugs at his home. I told Roger not to do it, but he had made his mind up.

One morning Murray asked Roger if he would count out the pills and put them in bags for the various dealers. Roger didn't like the idea of the dealers coming to his house, so he booked a room in a local hotel. He sat on the bed and set about counting the pills into different bags. There was a knock on the door, and when he opened it police officers poured into the room. On the bed there were 1,500 Ecstasy tablets and quantities of cocaine and amphetamines. Roger had been caught red-handed. The police had been watching Murray's dealers and had followed them to the hotel. When they were quite sure that drugs were being distributed, they moved in.

Roger was devastated. He knew he was going to serve a lengthy prison sentence despite the fact it was his first offence. Roger pleaded guilty at his trial and was sentenced to five years' imprisonment. He refused to name Mark Murray or any of the other dealers. In return for his loyalty, Roger's partner and her disabled child received nothing from the firm or Mark Murray whilst he was away.

A few weeks after Roger's arrest, Reg rang me and asked if I would go to visit him as he was due to be interviewed by Mary Riddell from the *Today* newspaper and wanted me to be there. I don't know why he wanted me there, but I decided to go as I had made my mind up that it would be the very last time I would see him.

I also told myself that once I had lost my door licence for possessing the gun and the CS gas, I was going to sever all links with my criminal associates and start living an uncomplicated, stress-free life. Even if I didn't deserve it, my children did. I didn't want them growing up surrounded by people like my friends and me, I wanted them to have a future. If I was to ever awake from the nightmare I was living in, now was the ideal opportunity to begin to stir. Sitting with Reg, surrounded by his half-wit wannabe entourage, confirmed to me that I was doing the right thing. When the visit was over, I shook Reggie's hand and told him I'd see him soon, but I knew I would never see him again. When I walked out of Maidstone Prison after the visit, I felt nothing but relief, I just hoped shedding my associates in the Essex firm would be as easy.

In August 1995, a 19-year-old man from Essex came close to death at Club UK in south London after a mixture of cocaine, speed and Ecstasy brought on a fit. Tucker's dealers had already caused the death of one young reveller in the club: 20-year-old Kevin Jones had died after taking Ecstasy supplied by the firm. This latest victim attracted a lot of publicity and there were demands for the club to be closed, so Tucker decided to withdraw all dealers from the premises for six to eight weeks until the dust had settled. He rang me and asked how Mark Murray and his dealers were performing in Raquels as he would need new faces when he started supplying drugs in Club UK again. I told him they were discreet and no problem. Murray ran exactly the kind of operation Tucker was looking for and so Tucker asked me to bring Murray over to his house for a meeting. Tucker told Murray that he wanted him to take over the sale of drugs in Club UK. Murray would have to buy all his drugs from Tucker and pay £1,200 rent each weekend, but in return, Tucker said, he could earn in excess of £12,000 a week.

Murray did not bother checking Tucker's mathematics. He stuck out his hand without hesitation. The deal was struck. He was to start as soon as the recent bad publicity had subsided. Less than four weeks after Murray and his minions started dealing in Club UK, it was raided by the police.

Murray's dealers threw all their pills and powders on the floor in order to avoid arrest. Murray lost 800 Ecstasy pills in total, pills he had not yet paid Tucker for. He had lost 468 pills a few weeks earlier when three of his dealers had been stopped in a car and searched by the police. He had also lost 1,500 pills when Roger Mellin had been arrested counting his drug stash in a Basildon hotel room. With the 800 pills his dealers had dropped in the Club UK raid, his crumbling drug business had lost a total of 2,768 Ecstasy pills with a street value of £41,520 in less than two months. Murray now owed Tucker about £20,000. Prison would have been a salvation for him; an early grave was more likely.

There are no financial advisers in the drugs world and there are certainly no overdraft facilities. Tucker wanted his money and he wanted it immediately. He came around my house with Rolfe and asked me where he could find Murray. We all got into my car and I took them around to Murray's flat. His girlfriend answered the door. Rolfe barged his way into the front room and demanded to know where Murray was. The terrified girl said that she didn't know. Rolfe asked if he had taken his phone with him. The girl said he hadn't, he had left it in the flat. Rolfe picked it up and began making calls to all the people whose numbers were stored in it. Tucker sat on the settee with me and was laughing.

'Are you watching this programme?' he asked Murray's girlfriend.

When she replied, 'No,' Tucker ripped the plug out of the wall, wrapped it around the television and told Rolfe to go and load it and the stereo into the car, which he did. He then told Murray's girlfriend she was coming with us. She was very frightened and said Mark would be home soon. He said, 'Don't worry about that, get in the car.' We then drove around to my friend Mark Shinnick's house. Shinnick had been a good friend of Murray's, but of late he was having less and less to do with him. This was because his wife Carol was Roger Mellin's sister and she had resented Murray ever since Roger had been locked up.

Everyone thought Murray had pulled a shit trick on Roger when he had asked him to look after his drug supplies for £50 per week. The real kick in the teeth had been when Murray refused to give Roger's partner and her disabled child one penny whilst he was imprisoned. We sat drinking and talking and when Tucker had calmed down he seemed to forget why – if he'd ever had a reason – he had taken Murray's girlfriend around to Shinnick's house. I think he did it to ensure she didn't forewarn Murray about Tucker looking for him. Whatever, tired of waiting, we all went home, leaving Murray's girlfriend stranded at Shinnick's house. That night Tucker and Rolfe returned to Murray's flat and grabbed him when he answered the door. Tucker pulled out a huge bowie knife, held Murray by the neck and pressed the point into his throat. He said, 'I want my money, Murray, and for every week you owe me, you pay £500 on top. If I don't get it, you're dead.'

Murray, terrified in the knowledge Tucker was more than likely to carry out his threat, and equally concerned his debt now carried interest, contacted everybody he knew asking for financial assistance. When people learned that Tucker was Murray's creditor, they didn't want to know.

In desperation, Murray turned to a man he had recently met on the Essex club circuit.

John Rollinson was a small-time drug dealer whom I had met once or twice when he had visited Raquels with Murray. Rollinson was a mature, scruffy, short and overweight individual who worked during the day as a hairdresser. By night he gave himself the rather grand title of 'Gaffer'. He peddled drugs and sat in the quieter pubs telling anybody who would listen that he was a face in the Essex underworld.

It was John, or Gaffer, who came to Murray's aid, although he didn't have the capital to settle his debt in full. Gaffer scraped together £2,000 for Murray, a generous amount by most hairdressers' standards.

Murray, who still feared Tucker was going to damage him, or worse, asked me to arrange a meeting with him at Raquels so he could pay him the cash and ask for the interest agreement to be dropped. At the meeting, held upstairs in the diner, Murray pleaded with Tucker to give him more time and to drop the interest charge as he had only been able to raise two grand. 'I will have what I owe you soon,' he said, 'if you don't let me carry on, I won't be able to get the money to pay you.' Tucker reluctantly agreed and dropped the interest clause, but said Murray would have to purchase all of his drug supply from him and the cost would be inflated so that his debt could be paid off sooner rather than later.

Unfortunately for Murray there was another but. Tucker had recently acquired a batch of Ecstasy pills that were known as 'apples' because they had an apple motif imprinted on them. Tucker said that they were extremely strong and people who had taken them had complained of headaches. 'The dealers can't get rid of them once everyone knows what they're like,' he said. 'Sell them.' He took the £2,000 which Gaffer had given to Murray and handed the pills to him.

Breathing a sigh of relief as Tucker strode off, Murray felt safe for the moment. He was back in business; soon those extra-strong pills would be in the hands of his dealers and being distributed in Raquels. Soon, he thought, his troubles would all be over.

The following Friday night I was standing at the bar in Raquels talking to Tucker and Craig Rolfe. The assistant manager was also with us. One of the barmaids telephoned the assistant manager and asked him to go and see her as she had a problem. Tucker and I were asked to go with him to resolve whatever the problem was. We went to the bar near the main dance-floor area and the barmaid told us she knew that a girl in the club was under age, had refused to serve her and now the girl was getting stroppy.

We called the girl over. She looked distressed. I asked her if she had any ID on her to prove her age.

She said, 'I haven't. My purse has been stolen.'

I said, 'I'm sorry, if you have no ID, then you will have to leave. The barmaid says she knows you and you are under age.'

The girl became very irate. She said, 'I have had my purse stolen. I showed you my ID on the way in, why are you asking for it now?'

I said, 'You may appear to be 18, but the barmaid says you are not. Therefore you must show your ID or leave.'

'I've had my purse stolen,' she repeated. 'There is £300 in it. My dad's a policeman. I'm going to get him and you'll all be in trouble.'

'Look, any story you tell me, I've already heard,' I replied. 'If you haven't any ID, you will have to leave.'

The girl began shouting: 'My dad's a policeman, I've had my purse stolen.'

I said, 'I'm sorry, you'll have to leave. If your dad is a policeman, he will understand that if you haven't got ID we cannot let you remain here.'

Eventually the girl left. To be honest, I couldn't have cared less if the girl was 17 or 18. I have always judged people on the way they behave. Most 17-year-old girls who came in the club were trying to act older than they were and so were well behaved. It was the 30-year-old men who behaved like 12-year-old boys I objected to. If the barmaid hadn't said anything, I certainly wouldn't have asked the girl to leave.

At closing time, I was putting the chains on the fire doors and waiting for the staff to leave before going home myself when I heard shouting. I thought somebody was being attacked and so I went to see what the problem was. At the front door I found the barmaid who had told me the girl was under age.

She said she had just fought with the same girl, who, she claimed, had waited outside the club to have it out with her. I told the barmaid she had better wait inside until the girl had gone. Half an hour later, when I was satisfied the incident was over, I went home and thought no more about it. It wasn't until some time later that I discovered the truth about what had happened. Somebody who had objected to the way the girl had been treated told me that the barmaid had stolen the girl's purse from the toilets. The girl knew that the barmaid had her purse and had demanded that she return it immediately. The barmaid had then telephoned the assistant manager to say that the girl was under age so that we would eject her and the accusations would cease. Leah Betts, the girl who had her purse stolen, was rightfully upset. Leah had waited outside the club after being ejected and after confronting the barmaid, she had been assaulted.

Because of this incident, Leah was barred from coming into Raquels. I didn't know at the time that she had been a victim of this theft. I knew she was 17, and that is why she had to be excluded. If the row about the purse had not happened, she wouldn't have been barred. If she had been allowed in the club, would the tragedy that struck later ever have happened? If this, if that. I have turned it over a million times in my mind.

On 31 October 1995, Pat Tate was released from prison and Tucker organised what he thought would be a huge party to welcome him home. It was to be held at a snooker hall in Dagenham. Tucker rang me and said he wanted me to go to the party with all the doormen; he and Tate had something they wanted to discuss with me.

I rang Tucker back that night and said I would be unable to go because I had to go to my mother's in the Midlands. It was a lie. I was trying to get out of the situation I was in, not get more involved, and I wasn't the only one who felt like this.

Only 15 people attended Tate's coming-out party – a stark indication of his declining popularity. Tate and Tucker called me a few days later and we met in the car park at Basildon Hospital. They said they had a bit of work coming up in the next few weeks and they wanted me to go along with them. A bit of work meant robbing someone, usually drug dealers. I told them I wasn't interested. Tate was agitated, as though unable to understand the words 'no' or 'will not'. 'This is fucking big,' he said. 'All we have to do is turn up, rob a couple of fucking idiots and we will all earn a fortune for a half hour's work.'

I told him I still wasn't interested. Tate and Tucker became hostile, telling me I was a waste of time and I wouldn't be offered anything in the future. I still felt something for these people. Before mashing their brains with drugs, they had been my friends. Now they were blind to any danger, oblivious to reality. I warned Tucker to be careful, but as usual he just laughed and turned my advice into ridicule.

Leah Betts, the 17-year-old girl I had banned from Raquels six weeks earlier, was planning her 18th birthday party. Leah was looking forward to becoming an adult, as she hadn't enjoyed the happiest of childhoods. Her parents had separated after her father Paul began a relationship with his current partner, Janet, who was married to one of his friends. Paul was in the police and his friend was a fellow officer based at the same station. When Leah's mother Dorothy learned of Paul's extra-marital activities she divorced him for adultery and he left the family home when Leah was just three years old. Dorothy met a man named Chris and together they moved into a house in Basildon with Leah.

On 1 September 1992, Leah's mother collapsed and died. She was 45. Leah, who had just turned 14, was naturally devastated. It was only when Dorothy died that Leah's father involved himself more in her upbringing. Leah chose not to live with her father, remaining with her step-father, but she did begin to visit him regularly and formed a relationship with her new family.

Leah attended Basildon College and worked in Alders department store, opposite Raquels in Basildon town centre. For months she had been telling her class and work mates what a great party she was going to have on her 18th. Whilst planning the celebrations, her father and step-mother agreed that she could have a party at their home, but they insisted there would be no alcohol because some of the guests would be under age. They also stipulated that they would remain on the premises throughout the evening.

My 14-year-old daughter and 16-year-old son think I am past it so you can only imagine how Leah must have felt when she contemplated celebrating her 18th birthday with soft drinks whilst being monitored by her parents. Leah realised that she was never going to have the great party she envisaged. Foolishly, Leah decided that she would enjoy herself regardless, by taking Ecstasy. Like thousands of other teenagers at that time, it was not the first time that Leah had experimented with drugs and so she was confident just one would do her no harm. After several failed attempts by girlfriends to get sorted, a male friend named Stephen Smith was asked to go into Raquels and purchase the Ecstasy pills for her party. Smith agreed that he would see what he could do.

On Friday, 10 November, it was business as usual in Raquels. Ecstasy, cocaine and amphetamines were being sold discreetly near the top bar. Because of his financial problems, Murray was selling the drugs himself that night. A nervous teenager sidled up to Murray and asked him if he could score. Murray nodded; the teenager held the folded notes in his hand, Murray held the Ecstasy pills in his. They pretended to shake hands. Murray took the money, the teenager the pills. The fate of Leah Betts was sealed. That deal was going to end her life and change a lot of other people's.

Unfortunately for Leah, the drugs which were purchased from Murray were the Ecstasy pills with the apple motif that had come from Tucker and had been indirectly financed by John 'Gaffer' Rollinson.

That night in her father's home, Leah, against the advice of her closest friend who had been given a warning about the strength of this particular batch, took one Ecstasy pill. As the party wore on, some of the other revellers took Ecstasy and others smoked cannabis. Ex-policeman Paul Betts, who had danced with Leah in the room where all the revellers were, later said he had neither smelt the cannabis nor noticed anything unusual.

On Monday, 13 November 1995, I was filling my car up with petrol at a garage. I was thinking about Christmas of all things. It had been a bad year. Once Christmas was out of the way I could concentrate on the New Year, a fresh start and hopefully a new beginning. I had severed all links with the Krays and their hangers-on and my pending court case for possessing a gun would soon see me out of Raquels and out of the Essex firm's murky circle. Things, I thought, were looking up for me.

As I walked to the garage kiosk, I glanced at the news stand. Every newspaper had a picture of a girl on the front page. Her eyes were closed, her mouth slack, agape and there were tubes everywhere. I picked up a tabloid out of curiosity and paid for the petrol. I looked at the picture and thought to myself, what a waste. I turned the page and a picture of Raquels leapt out at me.

The article said an 18-year-old girl was on a life-support machine after taking an Ecstasy pill bought at the club. My heart sank. I knew this was going to cause serious grief. When I got in I sat on the stairs and put my head in my hands. I wasn't sure what to do. I rang Mark Murray but his phone was unobtainable. Then I tried ringing Tucker, but like Murray, he had gone to ground.

The following day I was out of town. I had a court case in Birmingham I had to attend – various driving offences, nothing serious. I was banned for 12 months and fined £330.

Driving back down from the court case I heard nothing but reports about Leah's condition and the police enquiry on the radio. Four addresses were raided that morning in Basildon. One of them was Tate's flat, where Tucker's mistress Donna Garwood was living. A quantity of amphetamine was found, not a lot, just a bit of personal, but the fact that they'd raided Tate's flat indicated the police knew the firm was involved in the supply chain. I didn't think it would be too long before they rounded us all up for questioning.

A couple of days later at around 11 p.m., I received a telephone call from a man who introduced himself as Steve Packman. He told me that he was on police bail for 'the Leah thing'. 'I've got to go back to the police station for supplying the pill which Leah took,' he said. I told him I had no idea who he was and asked him what he wanted from me. He said he had heard the door staff at Raquels had a problem with him over Leah collapsing. I told him that nobody I knew had a problem with him or anybody else and he should forget anything he had heard. Packman asked if I would meet him, but I told him it was very late and I was very tired – if he really needed to speak to me, he should call me at a reasonable hour.

I didn't have a very good night's sleep that night. The call played on my mind.

In an effort to help me distance myself from my criminal associates, I had decided to move out of Basildon. Debra and I had purchased a house in Mayland, a small village located about 15 miles outside Basildon.

We were due to move the following morning. Debra had left before I got up because she had to go and wait for items that were due to be delivered to our new home. I took the children to school and then drove to Mayland where I found Debra standing at the front door. 'Have you heard what's happened?' she asked. 'Leah Betts has died.'

I knew at once that the firm was now living on borrowed time; if Tucker and Tate's ludicrous robbery plans didn't bring us down, Leah's death surely would. Around lunchtime Tucker rang me. He was going mental. He was saying he wanted this Betts mess sorted out and he wanted it sorted out today. There was too much attention both on him and on the firm in general, he said.

Because Packman and his co-accused were under 18, police had been unable to name them. This lack of information resulted in investigative reporters descending on Basildon en masse and they were being told in confidence by people in pubs that Murray, Tucker and myself were involved in the drugs chain which had supplied Leah. The reporters were then questioning people about our other activities and Tucker convinced himself they would soon open a can of worms he would never be able to re-seal. Now Leah had died, Tucker said, 'the shit is going to hit the fan'. He had been planning his retirement with Tate and didn't want this to interfere with it. I explained to him about the phone call from Steve Packman and he suggested we let people know exactly who was being blamed for supplying Leah so that the media interest in the firm would fade away and he could get on with his business. 'Look, if he's on fucking bail for it, he's the one who's going to be nicked for killing her, not us,' he said. 'If he's already in the frame, there's nothing we can do about it. It's not grassing and I don't need this shit now.'

Tucker was like a demented tyrant. He knew his empire was crumbling but he wanted to cling on to it until the bitter end.

The Thursday night after Leah's death, I sat down at work, trying to decide what to do about Steve Packman. I had to face the fact that the only way to stop reporters trying to unearth evidence against myself and the firm would be if Packman was identified in a newspaper. That way everyone would know that a person had been arrested and he was not a member of our firm or in any way connected to us. I rang Tucker to discuss it, but he didn't want to know. 'Do what you think is best, but get it sorted,' he snapped.

It was all right for him to take a back seat. I was the head doorman at Raquels, the fucking fall guy everyone had firmly in their sights. Uncertain and uneasy, I decided to put my foot in the water. I had to sort this out.

I spoke to a reporter I'd known for several years. I told him about Packman and said I was going to arrange a meeting with him. The reporter said he would be keen to get the first photograph of the man who had allegedly supplied Leah and said he would be there when the meeting took place. I rang the reporter a few days later and told him I had arranged to meet Packman at a garage in Basildon. The reporter said that when I did meet Packman, the conversation would have to be recorded. He said this was to safeguard his newspaper in case Packman tried to sue them for any reason. Reluctantly, I agreed.

'What went on, then?' I asked when Packman and I finally met.

He said that he knew Leah and her friend Sarah Cargill. They had been planning Leah's forthcoming 18th birthday party. Leah and Sarah had said they wanted to get gear for it.

They approached a friend, Louise Yexley, who was unable to get anything, but said she would ask her boyfriend Stephen Smith if he could help. Smith and his friend, Steve Packman, had gone into Raquels after a night out at Romford dog track. Smith had made some amateurish efforts to obtain drugs, but when he had approached people and asked if they had Ecstasy for sale they told him they didn't know what he was on about. Smith said to Packman that if a dealer approached him, he was to come and tell him. While Packman was standing at the top bar, a man asked him if he was sorted. Packman described the man to me as wearing a blue Schott bomber jacket, with long, curly shoulder-length hair. I knew at once that he was describing Mark Murray. He said he returned to Stephen Smith, who gave him the money. He told me he then bought the pills, which were later passed down the chain of friends to Leah. Packman told me he hadn't said this to the police. He'd told the police he was so drunk that night, he couldn't remember anything. I told Packman that he hadn't caused us any problem, it was just one of those things. We shook hands and he walked off into the night. I went over to the reporters who had been photographing Packman from a van. Nothing untoward had been said about me and nobody had implicated the firm. The reporter now had an exclusive photograph of the man who was on bail and who was going to be photographed in any event when he finally appeared at court.

Tucker would be happy because attention would be taken away from him and the firm as soon as Packman's picture appeared in the press. The management at Raquels would be happy because Leah hadn't been in the club on that night and so they couldn't be held in any way responsible for her death. I was happy because it was all over, or so it appeared.

I gave the tape to the reporters, said I didn't want to see them again and walked off. I wasn't offered money for the story or the pictures and I have never received any.

Whatever happened regarding the Leah Betts inquiry, common sense told me that matters were coming to a head.

There was Tucker and Tate's ridiculous plan to rob a shipment of drugs and the fact that when I appeared in court for possessing the gun and the gas I would lose my door licence and, as a consequence, my income. We had reached the end of our reign. I had been told Tucker had consulted a solicitor about the possibility of him being arrested in connection with the Betts case, but he denied it when I asked him. I did not know it at the time but Murray had been arrested, questioned and released by officers the morning after Leah had collapsed. As soon as he had been bailed, he fled without saying a word to me. I did not know anything about what happened to Leah until I picked up that newspaper two days after she had collapsed. The ship was sinking and it was clear to me that it was now every man for himself. If I was put out of work, nobody was going to pay me any money and nobody was going to look after my family. I decided I couldn't wait for the end, I was going to start rebuilding my life immediately. I had been waiting for too many tomorrows to arrive – if I didn't act now I would never get out of the mess I was in.

The night after I met Packman, I went into work and called all of the doormen into a meeting. I told them I was leaving. I'd had enough of Raquels and all that shit that went with it. I was meant to work until 2 a.m. that night, but by 11 p.m. I'd had enough. I went up to the office and told the manager of my decision. I went downstairs to the main dance area, said goodbye to the barmaids and the assistant manager and walked out of the door.

The following day I received a telephone call from one of the doormen who said that Mark Murray's photograph was in the *News of the World*. I had expected Steve Packman's picture to be in the paper, but not Mark Murray's. I went out to buy a copy to see for myself.

On the front page there was a picture of Murray and an article which said that Murray was one of the men being quizzed by police investigating the death of Leah Betts:

> Jobless Mark Murray, 35, of Pitsea, Essex, was among six people held after Leah's death at her 18th birthday party last week. He faces further questioning after the *News Of The World* handed cops a secret tape containing new evidence.

The verbal undertaking I had received about the tape remaining confidential had been ignored. I felt sick knowing the police had the tape, as I knew they would be questioning me about it sooner rather than later. I was also annoyed that Murray had not bothered to contact me as he had been arrested and could have briefed me about police lines of enquiry.

The following day, Monday, 20 November, Tucker rang my home, but I wasn't in. He left a message on the answering machine. He was shouting, being abusive and threatening. He said I couldn't just walk out of Raquels and he wanted an explanation. He also said I was responsible for Murray being in the paper. He said, 'I thought that other kid was going in. You shouldn't have put Murray in. I'm going to fucking do you.'

Debra heard the message first and was quite concerned, but I reassured her Tucker wouldn't do anything. 'Cracked out of his head no doubt,' I said, 'Tate's probably listening to him in the car so he's going over the top for his benefit. I've done nothing I regret, so fuck him.'

I was still owed a week's money as we were paid in arrears at Raquels. I rang the doormen and told them I would be down on Friday to collect my money. One of them said, 'You had better ring me before you come, as I have heard that Tucker has got the hump.' I told him I didn't care.

It was not about the couple of hundred pounds I was owed, it was the fact I wanted Tucker to know his threats didn't concern me. I didn't want to involve the door staff in my problems, so I agreed I would ring before I turned up to ensure there would be no unpleasantness. I armed myself. I put a huge bowie knife in the back of my trousers, a bottle of squirt (industrial ammonia) in my pocket and went down to Basildon town centre to collect my money. Two of the doormen, Maurice and Gavin, met me outside McDonald's and advised me not to go round to the club. Maurice told me, 'Tucker's there now with Tate, Rolfe and a few other people I haven't seen before.'

I said, 'I don't give a fuck, I want my money.'

Gavin said, 'Tucker's told me that he's holding your money and if you want it, you should get it yourself, but I wouldn't advise it as he's firmed up.' I got really annoyed. If Tucker was going to do this and that why didn't he turn up as I had done, alone?

'I'll give you my wages,' said Gavin, 'and get yours off Tucker. You can go round if you really want to. You know I'm with you.'

Gavin needed the work at the time, and Tucker knew he was loyal to me. I didn't want to cause him any unnecessary problems, so I agreed. Gavin gave me his money and went back to the club. Tucker asked Gavin if he had seen me. 'I know he's your mate, but we've got a problem with him,' he said.

'Well, I've given him my money and now I need to get paid,' replied Gavin.

Tucker apologised and gave Gavin my money.

As far as I was concerned, that was the end of the matter. Everyone was happy. I was out of Raquels and out of that way of life, while Tucker now had gained complete control of Raquels. There was no need for anyone to continue with a vendetta.

The brothers grim: Reg, Charlie and Ron Kray

Mark Murray, who supplied
the Ecstacy pill which
killed Leah Betts

David Done, friend
Tracey and O'Mahoney
at Epping Country Club

O'Mahoney with his arm around Darren Pearman and other 'Towners' at Epping Country Club where Darren was later murdered

Kate Kray at work as a strip-o-gram

The old Raquels door. Head doorman Dave Venables is second from left

Tony Lambrianou (right) in his flat with Alan Smith on the day we were 'attacked' with a hammer

Charlie Kray and 'close family friend' Flannagan at James Fallon's boxing show

O'Mahoney and partner Emma Turner

Shielsie (left) and Adam of Mesh 29

O'Mahoney with
Tucker at his birthday
party, the night he met
Rolfe

O'Mahoney, Reg Kray and
Dave Courtney in Maidstone Prison

O'Mahoney, Kate Kray, Charlie Kray and Tony Lambrianou
at James Fallon's boxing show

O'Mahoney outside Raquels on the night he left

FOUR FUNERALS AND A DEATH THREAT

On 29 November I appeared at Chelmsford Crown Court for possessing CS gas and a gun. I was sentenced to six months' imprisonment, which was suspended for twelve months. I was thankful that the threat of prison had been lifted. Within days of the case ending Basildon Council revoked my door licence and I was banned from working on the door for seven years. It was all too little, too late. I now had only to deal with the threat from Tucker and those members of the firm loyal to him.

The following day I received a phone call from Essex police. A detective told me that I ought to watch my back as they had received information that a firm was going to shoot me. He said Tucker was the man behind it and I should take the threat seriously. I take all threats seriously, but life has to go on. You can't put everything on hold because some loser decides he wants to have a go at you. I asked the detective if the police had any further information. He told me they hadn't; a couple of people claiming to be close to Tucker had called Crimestoppers, the confidential phone service, claiming they had heard it being discussed. They had refused to give their names or any other details. I didn't expect a gold watch when I quit the firm, but I certainly didn't expect to get shot, either. The next day I rang Tucker. 'I hear you want to speak to me,' I said.

'I've been told that you put Murray in the paper,' he replied.

'I don't care what you've been told,' I said. 'You know it isn't true. I told you Packman was going in the paper, and you said you didn't give a fuck so long as the attention was took off the firm.'

'Why didn't you tell me you were leaving Raquels?' he asked.

'I'd had enough of everything,' I explained. 'I admit I was wrong not to discuss it with you, but I just wanted to walk away. You've not lost out. It is still your door. In fact, you have complete control now, instead of going down the middle with me.'

'But people are talking,' he said.

'I don't give a fuck about people, Tony,' I replied. 'I'm out of it.'

Tucker sneered, 'I don't believe you,' and then the line went dead. I assumed he had switched off his mobile phone.

On 6 December I was asked to attend South Woodham police station as DI Storey, the policeman heading the investigation into Leah's death, wished to speak to Debra and me. He said he needed to speak to everybody who had worked at Raquels on the night the pill which had killed Leah had been obtained. Debra was employed to search females as they entered the club, but I guessed this had nothing to do with her – it was just a ploy to get me down at the station.

When we arrived, four detectives met us at the door. Two said they wanted to speak to Debra and I was told that DI Storey wanted to have an informal chat with me. Storey was well aware of the firm's involvement in just about everything. He knew what he could prove and he knew, despite knowing the facts, what he could not. Murray had been pulled and questioned, but nobody was going to give evidence against him. I could see Storey's task was painful, but he knew at that time the only people who could realistically be prosecuted were Packman and Smith. He asked me about the tape which had been given to him against my wishes by the journalist. What could I say? I could hardly deny I was the person on the tape. He asked me if I would make a statement. I didn't have to implicate anyone. All I had to say was, yes, that is my voice on the tape.

He said that there was always the possibility that if I refused I could be subpoenaed to court. He made it clear he wasn't offering me an ultimatum, he was just being honest with me.

I told him I understood my position, but I wouldn't put my family at risk for things I had done. I told him I would have to go away and give it some serious thought, discuss it with my family and speak to him again in a couple of weeks. I wanted the problem with Tucker sorted out first. Despite what the police had warned, I didn't believe Tucker was a threat to me. It was the wannabes, the fucking gang groupies around him, who were trying to stir it up. The conversation with Storey ended around 4 p.m. When I came out, Debra was waiting. She said they had only kept her for half an hour. She had been asked about who was working on the night and other trivial matters – facts they already knew. I guess they had to speak to everyone who was in the building on the night the pill was bought. Procedure these days demands it.

As we drove away from South Woodham police station snow was falling. It had settled and was perhaps three or four inches deep. We had arranged for Debra's mother to look after the children whilst we spoke to the police so we drove over to her home, where we arrived at about 5 p.m. We stayed for a cup of tea and then drove to Wickford, where we had something to eat. Heading for home we drove from Wickford up to the Rettendon turnpike on the A130, which is the main roundabout between South Woodham Ferrers and Chelmsford. We reached there at about 6.30 p.m. It was a miserable night. The sky was pitch black and the surrounding fields were bleached white with the snow, which was still falling. Unknown to me, around the very same time, Tucker, Tate and Rolfe were driving along the very same road.

That night I went to bed early. I had an appointment the following morning with a solicitor in London. I was involved in a civil case at the time and I had to discuss a few points with my counsel.

I had travelled on the train, as I didn't fancy battling through the traffic. At about 11 a.m., I rang home to see if any messages had been left on the answering machine. There was one. It was from a detective who asked me to contact him as soon as I got his message. I rang him from one of the public call boxes inside King's Cross station.

He said to me, 'We've found a Range Rover with three bodies inside. They've all been shot through the head. We think it's your mates.'

'What do you mean?' I asked.

'Do you recognise this registration number: F424 NPE? I am sure it is them. We were watching them on Tuesday and they were in it then.'

I was confused. I said, 'I don't know what you're talking about, explain to me what's happened.'

He repeated that they had found a Range Rover. Tucker, Tate and Rolfe were inside, but they had not been formally identified at that stage.

I said, 'Are they dead?'

'They're very dead,' he replied.

I knew instinctively why they had died: it was their stupid plan to rob a shipment of cocaine they believed would net them enough money to retire. They were certainly in retirement now and few people would be shedding tears over their premature departure.

The day after the blood-spattered bodies were discovered in the Range Rover, the police charged Stephen Smith and Steve Packman with being concerned in supplying the Ecstasy tablet that had claimed Leah Betts' life. It made sense: the investigation that sought to expose those at the most lucrative end of the supply chain was going nowhere and the police's most-wanted now lay dead. In an ironic twist, the detectives who had been trying to gather evidence against Tucker now switched their efforts to gather evidence against his killer.

On 25 January 1996, I met DI Storey, who wanted me to make a statement in relation to the conversation I'd had with Packman. I told him I couldn't bring myself to do it. I had been trying to give up my life of gangs and crime since March 1995 and every step I took towards sanity I was knocked back three by one incident or another.

With Tucker, Tate and Rolfe dead, surely now my time had come. Did I really have to put myself centre stage in a high-profile trial to get my chance? Storey explained that the Crown Prosecution would never let me just walk away. He said they could subpoena me to attend court and the press would then attack me for being a hostile witness in a case concerning the death of a young girl who was currently on the front page of every national newspaper. I knew he was talking sense and he could see that I was struggling with the very thought of accepting that fact. Storey suggested I take another week before I made my final decision. For two or three days I wrestled with my conscience. I knew in my heart what I had to do, this nightmare had to end some time. I will never, as long as I live, forget the next meeting I had with DI Storey at Maldon police station.

The upstairs office we sat in overlooked a quaint row of shops and below people were going about their everyday business. As I sat there watching the normal world go by, I was talking about the unnecessary deaths of young people caught up in a very different and murky world. I was astride two very different worlds at that moment and my decision would leave me in one or the other. I knew which one I wanted to inhabit. I agreed to make the statement validating the tape. As I uttered the words 'I will do it', the door to my previous life slammed firmly behind me.

9

MURDER AND MAYHEM

On Thursday, 23 May 1996, my old friend and Raquels colleague Larry
Johnston fulfilled my grisly prophecy and murdered a man. Larry always
had to go over the top and it was inevitable that it was going to happen
one day. Larry had gone to a theme pub in Rush Green, Romford, called
Big Hand Mo's. He had got into a dispute with a 31-year-old doorman
named Steven Poultney. After refusing Larry entry, Poultney had been
stabbed in the side. An ambulance was rushed to the scene but the
doorman was pronounced dead on arrival at Old Church Hospital.
Larry was arrested the following day and charged with murder. He was
subsequently convicted and given a life sentence.

Two lives wasted and for what? Stupid fucking bravado. But that is
what these gangsters think it's all about: being a face, being a somebody.
Preferring to murder a man rather than face the 'humiliation' of not
being allowed in a pub.

My decision to assist the police had been met by them with relief and
caution. Their investigation now had few loose ends and would appear
neat and tidy, but my life, they warned, was now in danger of being
ended prematurely. My home became a virtual fortress care of Essex
Police. Debra and I were told to carry small pager-sized panic alarms
and electronic boxes tuned into the local police headquarters were in

every room of our home. If the telephone wires were interfered with, an alarm would be activated and an armed-response unit would come running. It was an awful way to live, not so much for myself but for my family.

On Thursday, 20 June 1996, two detectives, whose job it was to escort me to court for the committal proceedings concerning Packman and Smith, picked me up from my home. The night before I could not sleep.

I had sat at the end of my bed in the dark, wrestling with my thoughts. I'd made the agreed statement about my meeting with Packman, but I knew that today was the day that mattered. If I didn't turn up the case would collapse and I could face three months' imprisonment for ignoring a witness order. It almost seemed worth it. It would solve many of my problems and I would be back on-side with my associates. I looked in at my sleeping children and realised I could betray my associates but I could not betray them. Any chance I had of making my life worthwhile lay with my children. I had to do what was right despite the fact that doing right felt so wrong.

I walked out to meet my escort. I wasn't stupid – it wasn't there solely for my protection, it was also there to make sure that I turned up at court. On the journey to Southend Magistrates' Court, the detectives made casual conversation, most of it about Tucker, Tate and Rolfe. One of the detectives had been present at Broomfield hospital in Chelmsford when the three had been laid out in the morgue. He told me that Tucker and Rolfe had been badly disfigured. 'Big fucking geezers, weren't they, Bernie? Their heads were a right mess,' he said. I wanted him to shut up, to not make any conversation with me. I didn't even want to hear him speak. The thought of getting friendly with the police made my stomach churn. It wasn't the men – I had known decent police officers – it was their authority, their uniform and the past experiences I had endured that filled me with loathing.

When we arrived at Southend, I was driven straight into the police station via a back entrance. I was told they didn't want the press or cameramen getting anywhere near me. 'Let's keep it low-key, Bernie,' one of them said.

Once inside I was led through a maze of corridors, the detectives flashing their warrant cards to get numerous locked doors opened. We passed through the custody area and eventually into the court building. We climbed a dozen narrow, wooden steps and emerged into the dock of the court. The proceedings had not yet started so the court was empty. I looked across from my more familiar position in the dock to the witness stand. I was going to have to stand on that platform and publicly assist those I had spent my life resenting. I was once more in turmoil. If I walked out now, I would be condemned as the man who had brought about the collapse of the Leah Betts trial, a girl who in death had become a national icon in the war against the evil drug trade.

The papers would have a field day speculating as to why I would rather face prison than awkward questions. The bitter finger of suspicion would once more be levelled at me.

I could face prison, I could endure the press and the gossip, but could my family? They didn't deserve to have to endure anything, as they had done nothing. The detectives must have sensed my anguish as they suddenly decided that we should all leave the court and get some tea sent up to another room. I laughed out loud, but I didn't tell them why I was laughing. I was thinking of my mother. Whatever the crisis, however dire the situation, she always resorted to saying, 'We had better make some tea.'

At 10 a.m. I was called into court. Packman looked sheepishly around the room, wanting to avoid eye contact with me. Only he and I knew the truth about what really happened at our meeting on the garage forecourt. I had nothing to lose and I genuinely hoped that he would be acquitted. Once I had been seen to fulfil my promise, neither the police nor the press could criticise me.

Old-style committals are, in effect, dress rehearsals for a Crown Court trial. The magistrates listen to the evidence and the witnesses under cross-examination and decide whether the matter should proceed to a full trial with a jury. I was in the witness box for an hour and three-quarters and at the end of it, the magistrates decided that the case would go to trial. I felt dirty leaving the court, but the police were jubilant. It was a real kick in the teeth when they actually thanked me. I couldn't wait to get home. I wanted the events of 1995 to have some sort of closure. The police dropped me off, wished me luck and disappeared down the drive. I wondered if they would be slagging me off and laughing. Paranoid? I doubt it.

My conversion from regular defendant to prosecution witness did little or nothing for my relationship with the police – other than those connected with the Betts case that is.

For several years I had rented out a house I owned in London and a flat in Staffordshire for a bit of additional income. To be honest, it was hardly lucrative, but I kept it going so my children could have a bit of capital in the future. A young couple moved into the flat in Staffordshire but despite assurances, they didn't appear to have any money to pay the rent. They told me they were employed; I don't know why they lied. It would have made no difference to me if they had claimed their rent from the benefit agency or paid it to me themselves. When I contacted them about the rent, which was getting seriously in arrears, they told me they had been paid by cheque and were waiting for it to clear. Then when pressed, they said the cheque had been cancelled as they were no longer going to be paid monthly. Eventually, after receiving no money whatsoever, I went to the flat to talk to them, but nobody was there. I let myself in and found amongst the post, various letters from the DHSS regarding their claim for benefit.

It soon became apparent that they had fraudulently signed my name and entered my details to claim housing benefit for the rent. I waited for them to come home and told them they had to leave within seven days. When I went back at the end of that period, they were still there so I started to put their possessions in the street – admittedly via the upstairs window.

As I dragged the larger items outside, they locked the door and called the police. Two police officers arrived and told me I wasn't allowed back into my own flat and if I had damaged any of the couple's property I would be arrested. I couldn't believe what I was hearing.

Amongst the letters in the flat, I had found one from a magistrates' court stating that the man who had rented my flat had a warrant out for his arrest over non-payment of fines. Yet here were the police giving him sanctuary in my fucking flat. I told the police that whatever they said 'these people were going today'. The officers called for back-up on the radio and within minutes five police cars came roaring down the road, blue lights flashing and sirens wailing. It was a total farce. Four officers went into the flat, two stood guard at the door and the others surrounded Debra, who had come to see what the fuss was about. The police told us that we had to prove that the flat was ours, so Debra rang our solicitor and asked him to attend in person. The solicitor arrived an hour later and confirmed to the police that we owned the flat. However, the police said that the couple in the flat still had rights. 'You can't just go in. You have to get a certificate from a magistrate backing your claim that the flat is yours and then show it to the squatters.'

I totally flipped. 'Fucking squatters, fucking ponces! When you're gone I am going to put them out and back in the gutter.'

One of the police officers grabbed my shirt and I pushed him back.

For a moment it looked as if it was all going to end in violence but one of the officers, who knew me well, stepped forward and asked everybody to calm down. 'Bernie, we're leaving a WPC to guard the door. Go and start the legal process. Whatever you think, you are not going to get into that flat today.' I knew that if I remained, I would end up being arrested so I stayed at my mother's home that evening and went to the flat the following morning. What I found was a scene of carnage.

The police had gone and the front door was ajar. All the furniture in the flat, which I owned, had been slashed with a Stanley knife. The bed had been slashed, the three-piece suite had been slashed and used tampons and excrement had been smeared on the walls. The place was totally wrecked. The incident was reported in the *Daily Mirror* after a reporter who had heard about what had happened to us contacted Debra.

SQUATTERS TRASHED MY HOME AS POLICE STOOD GUARD

Squatters destroyed a mum's flat while police guarded the front door to keep her out. The intruders ripped open furniture and daubed excrement on walls, but hairdresser Debra King was left outside in tears after police told her these people have rights. Mother of two Debra, 30, has asked the *Mirror* to investigate and demanded £1,000 compensation from the police. She said the money would only replace what has been destroyed, 'the police couldn't afford to pay for the upset this has caused me'. She said, 'I tried to get in with my boyfriend, but five police cars pulled up and we were threatened with arrest. A policewoman was put on guard in case we harassed the intruders.

'I called my solicitor but he could do nothing and police told me, "These people still have rights, you can't go in."'

Police told Debra that she could not get in without a certificate from magistrates backing the claim that the flat was hers and it would have to be shown to the squatters. But while she started the legal process, the squatters fled, shredding a three-piece suite, two double beds and curtains with a knife, and spreading excrement, urine and used tampons around. 'I returned the next day to find it completely and utterly trashed,' she said.

She has since discovered that there was an arrest warrant out for one of the squatters for non-payment of fines while another made false claims for Social Security benefits using her address. 'I was warned not to intimidate or harass these squatters but no one warned them not to damage my property or do the awful things they did.

'The police officer may have protected the squatters' rights but they certainly didn't protect mine. I am a victim of a system that simply doesn't care. It's pathetic.'

Staffordshire police said last night that they could not comment as a complaint had been received. A spokesman said, 'The matter is being investigated. An act of law covers the squatters' rights which is a very complicated issue.'

If this is how law-abiding people were treated, I knew going straight was going to be hard. If I had still been involved with the firm, these people would have been ejected there and then, and probably through the same window as their possessions.

On Wednesday, 13 November 1996, my friend Mark Shinnick was arrested in possession of drugs with an estimated street value of £2,000,000.

Five kilos of cocaine, 24 kilos of amphetamine and 10 kilos of Ecstasy were discovered hidden in a false floor of his van. Mark Shinnick was married to Carol Mellin, whose brother Roger had been sentenced to five years' imprisonment after he was caught with Mark Murray's drugs in a Basildon hotel room. When Roger had been sent to prison and Murray had fled following Leah's death, the villains at the top of that particular drug supply chain had demanded their money back. Roger had no money and neither did his family. The villains, a family who it is said run north London, were not prepared to listen to excuses. In an effort to repay them, Mark had 'agreed' to drive a van back from Holland to settle the debt.

Customs officers thought Mark had been acting suspiciously and so they followed his van, stopped and searched it and discovered the £2,000,000-worth of drugs hidden within. I had always got on well with Mark. He wasn't a violent man – quite the opposite in fact, he was quiet and held a well-paid job. Mark had told me that he came out of work one day and a young member of this notorious crime family was waiting for him.

'It was all very friendly. The man was at pains to point out that he understood my position and that it was a shame Roger had been nicked and the gear had been seized. But these villains still wanted their money.' Mark was under no illusions as to his position and he 'agreed' to smuggle the drugs into the country from the continent using his works van. I felt desperately sorry for Carol – her brother was serving five years for drug offences and Mark received a twelve-year sentence. It was a story I saw unfold many, many times. Bait the victim with friendship, promises of huge rewards and protection, get him or her into debt, give them a drug habit or both. Then, through fear and intimidation, offer the victim a way out, the end result of which is usually a prison cell or a grave.

I wanted to talk to Carol, to try and help, but she had enough problems without me adding to them by my presence. I drove around to their house early one morning to put a note through the door. They lived on a normal working-class estate, children's bicycles lay discarded in gardens, while Fords, Vauxhalls and vans adorned with adverts for plastering and dry lining filled either side of the road. As I sat there, I recalled all the events that had occurred in their street. Opposite Mark's home was Jason Vella's flat. Vella was a notorious Basildon villain who had stabbed one of his victims with a sword before the man had leaped from an upstairs window. Vella was later sentenced to 17 years' imprisonment. He would have received a lesser sentence if he had killed the man.

I thought about the night Tucker, Rolfe and I had gone to Mark and Carol's house looking for Murray, his terrified girlfriend in tow; about Mark's son's birthday party which my own children had attended; parties when Raquels had closed for the night but we were still in the mood for more; Murray on the settee boasting openly about his big plans; Murray sidling up to me, quietly asking for advice on his crumbling empire and the ever-present threat of violence from Tucker. They were all gone now: hiding, locked up or dead.

I put the note through the door. All I wanted to say was that I was sorry about Mark's imprisonment and that I was thinking of him. I felt bad not knocking and saying it to her face, but I thought it was best that way.

If 1995 had been a bad year, 1996 was proving to be no better, if not worse.

Raquels doorman Chris Lombard had left our firm because he said the club we worked in was too violent and had gone to work instead at the Island nightclub in Ilford.

I hadn't heard anything of Chris after that until Thursday, 5 December 1996, almost one year to the day since Tucker, Tate and Rolfe had been blown away in their Range Rover. I had stopped at a newsagents outside Liverpool Street station in London to pick up a newspaper, as I had to wait half an hour for a train to Essex. I glanced at the front page and then stared in horror. I could not believe what I saw nor what I began to read. The headline read: 'Murdered doing his job' and alongside that headline was a picture of Chris Lombard. The report said Chris had been shot dead and another man seriously injured after a hail of gunfire ripped through the Ilford nightspot where they worked. Chris, aged 30, was fatally wounded when seven shots were fired through the glass of a locked door at the club in High Road, Ilford at 3.35 a.m. A group of young men had turned up a few minutes after the doors had closed to customers.

They demanded to be let in, but Chris had told them he was not allowed to do so because a condition on the club's licence prevented people entering after a certain time. The men became abusive, vowing to return. Shortly afterwards, as the door staff chatted in the foyer, shots rang out and Chris lay dead. The club, which I knew well, was just yards from the local police station, but this fact had not deterred the gang. Chris had been shot once in the head and twice in the chest with what police believed was an automatic pistol.

The head doorman, Albert St Hilaire, 40, had been shot once in the back, the bullet lodging itself near his spinal cord. The third doorman escaped injury when a bullet grazed his neck. Having regained the 'respect' they thought they had lost by not being allowed into the club, the gang fled into the night. Despite my initial shock, I was not entirely surprised when I thought back to how Larry had murdered a man for the same stupid reason.

I was more shocked by the fact that I was not surprised a decent man had died for such a ridiculous reason. Chris, a giant of a man, had a passion for basketball. He had coached a local school team and had taken part in tournaments in America as a semi-professional player. He hated doing door work and always said he was only doing it to tide him over. Now some wannabe gangster had snuffed out his life because he had dared to refuse him entry to a nightclub. It was a terrible waste of life. My former friends appeared to be dropping like flies. I was glad I was out of it.

As the year drew to a close, I looked back and realised I hadn't moved forward at all. I had been wishing away 1995 12 months earlier and now I found myself counting the days to the end of 1996. I kept telling myself that once the Betts trial was over I could get on with my life.

On Monday, 9 December 1996, the Betts trial finally opened at Norwich Crown Court. The first day was taken up with legal arguments, which I didn't have to concern myself with, but I was told to prepare myself to be called the following day or the day after. I spent that night like a caged animal, unable to sit down or think straight. I paced up and down, trying to talk myself in and out of my forthcoming ordeal. The trial at Southend Magistrates' Court had, in effect, been a dress rehearsal for this trial, which would be scrutinised and reported by all sections of the media. Now, if ever, was the time I was going to take some flack. The police telephoned me a couple of times to see if I was OK, but I knew they were just checking that now the pressure was on I hadn't done a bunk. I was also treated to the sight of a patrolling police car, which drove up and down the lane outside my home. I lived at the end of a remote farm track, the sea to our right, a mile of woodland to our left – hardly mean streets and certainly not worthy of a regular police patrol.

On the second day of the proceedings, the first witnesses were called after opening speeches were made to the jury. Leah's best friend, Sarah Cargill, said that they had decided to buy Ecstasy for Leah's party and had eventually managed to obtain four tablets through a network of friends. The girls were warned that the apple Ecstasy pills were stronger than normal and Cargill had advised Leah just to take half. But Leah had told her that she had done it before and taken a whole one. She said that Leah then drank some Malibu before switching to lemonade for the rest of the evening.

When Stephen Smith gave evidence, he agreed that Leah's friend Louise Yexley had asked him to obtain the pills and said that he had agreed to do so. When he and Packman had gone into Raquels, Smith said Packman had told him, 'Give me the money,' and ten minutes later he returned with four Ecstasy tablets with an apple motif on them.

That night and the following morning, the case attracted a lot of media attention. All the participants so far had been innocent teenagers experimenting with drugs. None were hardened criminals, none were drug dealers. All had been treated sympathetically. I had a gut feeling I wouldn't enjoy the same treatment.

My escorts finally came for me at 8 a.m. on the third day of the trial. Two detectives arrived in an unmarked van and told me to get in the back and make myself comfortable, as it was a good two-hour drive to Norwich. They had planned my arrival and departure at the court well. I was driven to the outskirts of Norwich and then told to lie down in the back of the van; a coat was then put over me. The van drove into the court car park, past the awaiting photographers and TV crews, and then past a security barrier to the rear of the building. The police checked every path we had to take before we actually entered the building.

Once inside, one held the cuff of my shirt as I was led through the cell area, various corridors and then finally up a flight of steps into the dock of an empty court. We then walked out into a waiting area where I saw Packman with his mother and father. I looked at Packman and he quickly looked away.

I was then put in a small room on my own and told to wait. I hated having these people around me – they made me feel inadequate and weak. I didn't need or want their fucking protection. I wanted to go out and sit amongst the people outside the room, but was told I could not be seen talking or even making eye contact with anybody. A glance or a glare could be interpreted as a threat.

I sat in the room alone, reading the newspaper. An elderly man entered and announced that he was from the court service. He gave me a questionnaire to fill in and began to describe the court procedure, telling me where to stand, where the judge would sit and advising me that I should speak clearly and directly at the jury. I didn't have the heart to tell him to fuck off.

He obviously got pleasure out of being so important. To pass the time I filled out his questionnaire, giving him a glowing report in the comments column. I kept thinking about his next staff meeting, his fellow volunteers patting him on the back because of the crap I had written. I wrote that it was my first time in court and I had been helped enormously by the court service volunteer. I had probably spent more time in the back of police vehicles than he had spent in court.

The door opened and I was told that I was wanted. As I entered the court, I could see a few familiar faces in the public gallery. They were expectant and visibly excited: 'Will he, won't he?'

The press gallery was packed. Packman sat alone in the dock wearing a grey suit and tie, his long hair in a ponytail. He radiated innocence. I was pleased. Paul and Janet Betts sat in the front row of the public gallery, approximately three feet from the witness stand. As I approached, the stand beckoned like an electric chair.

I stood in position and gripped the handrail. I was given God's good book and asked to swear an oath on it – a pointless exercise in this Godless day and age, but I had no reason to lie. Packman's barrister, John Cooper QC, wasted no time in describing me as a violent man with serious criminal connections.

He told the jury that I was Tucker's right-hand man, had attended Ronnie Kray's funeral with Reggie Kray and that I had convictions for robbery, wounding, assaulting police and possession of firearms. It wasn't a pretty picture that he painted and all I could do was agree. There was one light moment, however. Whilst in full flow, Mr Cooper said to me, 'And you stood next to the coffin with Ronnie Kray, didn't you, Mr O'Mahoney?'

'No,' I replied.

'Are you saying you did not, Mr O'Mahoney?'

'No I did not, Mr Cooper. Ronnie was the one in the box. It was Reggie I stood next to.' Everybody in the room, including the jurors, laughed.

Packman had admitted meeting me and that it was he who had confessed on the tape. However, it was alleged that I had threatened Packman, saying I would burn down his house and break his legs if he implicated the firm. It was suggested that I was putting pressure on him to confess in order to save myself and Tucker. I told the court that wasn't the case. I felt sorry for Packman. I could see the line his defence team were taking and so I tried to follow it.

'He's not an evil drug dealer,' I told the jury, 'he's just a kid caught up in this mess. Mark Murray supplied the pill that killed Leah Betts. I'm sick of that scumbag sitting out in Spain while eight or nine people rot in prison for him. He killed Leah Betts and I am sure he will kill other people.'

A steady stream of visibly excited journalists left the court, trying to reach a phone in order to file their copy. I could almost feel the atmosphere behind me; Paul and Janet Betts and Detective Inspector Storey appeared relieved that the true story was being made public.

I was cross-examined for the whole afternoon and when it was all over, the police escorted me back to the side room. Alone at last, I felt a great sense of relief. I just wanted to get out of there. Nothing happened for ten or fifteen minutes and then suddenly I was off in a rush between two detectives. I was taken outside and told to lie in the back of the van again. A blanket was thrown over me.

When Leah's parents emerged from the court, the press surrounded them and at the same time, the van I was in slipped away into the evening traffic.

I sat at home the following day waiting for news of the trial. Packman gave evidence, saying that he was totally paranoid when he met me. 'I said what I thought he wanted to hear,' he said, 'because I feared for my safety.' His friend Stephen Smith told the court he was 'more frightened of me than he was of Mike Tyson'. I don't know why he said that – we have, to my knowledge, never met.

The final witnesses gave evidence on Friday, 13 December, and the jury were told that they wouldn't be sent out to deliberate until Monday, as it was too late in the evening to begin now. That weekend dragged on like no weekend before or since.

On Monday, 16 December, the jury retired but there was no further news all day. The judge arranged for the jury to spend the night in a hotel and they deliberated throughout the following day. Eventually, they told the judge they were unable to reach a verdict and were discharged. I was absolutely devastated. I knew the prosecution wouldn't throw in the towel. I knew I would have to go through the whole thing again. I realised that 1997 was yet another year I was going to spend wishing away.

10

CROSSING THE THIN BLUE LINE

Because of the never-ending court cases I found myself involved in, I had been unable to take on any work on a permanent basis. In the 1980s I had worked in the haulage industry driving tipper lorries and so I returned to that on a casual basis. The pressure surrounding the court cases and the financial pressures brought about by the lack of a regular income were also putting a huge strain on my relationship with Debra. We did our best to put on a brave face for the children, but I think we both knew our relationship was living on borrowed time. Few, if any, could have faced what we endured and come out unscathed.

On Saturday, 22 February 1997, I took my son Vinney to watch Manchester United play Chelsea at Stamford Bridge. The Betts re-trial was due to start the following Monday and I wanted to take my mind off it, to enjoy myself with my son. We had a great time at the game: United drew 1–1, a good result for any team visiting the Bridge. When the match was over, Vinney said that he would like to get the United players' autographs. I had been telling him how as a boy, I had waited outside Old Trafford to get the autographs of great players like George Best, Denis Law, Bobby Charlton and Brian Kidd. We walked to the players' entrance where steel crash barriers had been erected, and a group of five burly security staff were stood facing a group of young fans. Eric

Cantona, David Beckham and a few other United players came out to get on the coach.

The children were leaning over the barrier trying to get their autographs, but the security staff began shouting to get back and shoved the steel barriers into the children. I grabbed one of them by the arm and told him to take it easy, but he slapped me across the nose with his glove. I then had my shirt grabbed by his colleague. I considered myself to be in danger and so I head-butted the security guard who was holding me and he fell back, blood pouring from his nose. Vinney was naturally upset by all of this and so we walked off to the car. The security guards regrouped and advanced across the car park towards us. There were approximately eight of them. All I did was turn towards them in a threatening manner and they backed off. I got in the car with Vinney and we drove away from the scene. Rather foolishly, I thought that would be the end of the matter.

On Monday, 24 February 1997, the Leah Betts trial resumed at Norwich Crown Court. It was far more low-key on this occasion, as the media had milked the story dry and the whole country was suffering fatigue from tales of Ecstasy. I was called to give evidence on the second day of the trial.

Once inside the court building, I had refused to wait in the solitary waiting-room I had previously been confined to. I was sick of being hidden away, so I sat amongst the others waiting to go in. Friends of Smith and Packman moved away or averted their gaze. Only Steve Packman's mother gave me a look of contempt. I didn't care – I admire people who speak their mind. John Cooper QC awaited me in court. At the last trial, he had done his job well, making me lose my temper so allowing the jury to see just how explosive I could be. Fortunately, on this occasion, the judge, Mr Justice Wright, was having none of it and wouldn't allow Cooper to draw on my association with other criminals.

This left Cooper with very little he could really ask. The whole point of cross-examining me was to portray me as a violent criminal with serious criminal connections so Cooper could convince the jury Packman would have been so frightened of me when we met that he would have said anything I wanted to hear. So, within a short time, I was told that I could leave. The prosecution said they had decided that I would no longer be required. I savoured those words. They had entered my life like a runaway train, fucked up my head with worry and now they were saying, 'We've finished with you, goodbye.' At the outset, the police had talked about assistance with moving, even arranging a new identity for me, but I had declined. I had made my decision and was going to live by it. I wasn't going to pretend it hadn't happened or deny who I was for anybody. We all make mistakes.

My final day in court had ended at 10.20 a.m. I had only been in the witness box for 20 minutes. When I walked out, I went straight to my waiting-room of solitude. I attacked a plastic tree in the corner, kicking its leaves in the air. I then sat down, my head in my hands. I felt so relieved, angry, elated, depressed and, also, disgusted with myself. The man from the court service came in and handed me a form. He began to tell me how to claim my expenses. I took the form from him, tore it into pieces and threw it next to the plastic leaves on the floor. I thought about his next staff meeting: what would he tell his colleagues now? Probably about a vicious thug who would benefit from national service. A detective came to the door and asked me if I would talk to the media. 'They've asked me to ask you, Bernie. It's nothing to do with me.' I declined, I had said enough for one day; I just wanted to go home.

When the police dropped me off, they thanked me and wished me well. I had got to know them quite well on our trips to and from court, about the trouble one of them had with his mortgage and their silent admiration for some of the more colourful, less serious criminals. I could not thank them, though I did wish them well.

On Friday, 28 February 1997, the trial ended and the jury retired to consider its verdict. But once more they could not agree. Mr Justice Wright formally found Packman not guilty after the jury foreman said that there was no realistic chance of reaching a majority verdict in the case after four hours of deliberation. Stephen Smith, who had pleaded guilty, was given a two-year conditional discharge. I was pleased for Packman and Smith. My evidence hadn't harmed anyone but Mark Murray, who was only affected socially, as the authorities couldn't touch him. He didn't give a fuck about me, Tucker or anyone else. After Leah Betts collapsed, he just upped and went without even giving us a warning phone call. I had no allegiance with or loyalty towards him whatsoever.

Shortly after the trial had ended the *News of the World* published an exclusive exposé on Mark Murray, with the headline: 'Leah Drug

Monster Pedalling Death Again'. Murray had washed up on the streets of Puerto Rico, Gran Canaria, where he was once more plying his trade. The paper said that Murray had become a minor celebrity due to all the publicity from the trial. The *News of the World* printed posters adorned with Murray's picture and the caption: 'This man could kill your kids'. They flooded holiday resorts with thousands of them, warning people of his activities. I've not seen Murray since, but somebody did text me claiming to be him in April 2003. The message, which was sent from an unregistered mobile phone, asked how things were between us.

All I can say to Murray and anybody else from those days is, I've moved on and what's done is done. I have neither the will nor the need for petty vendettas.

In March 1997, I read in a local newspaper that ex-firm member Chris Wheatley had been jailed for seven years after admitting his part in a major drugs operation in Southend. Detectives had swooped on Chris after a lengthy undercover operation. They found more than 200 grams of cocaine, 2.63 grams of amphetamine, 357 Ecstasy pills and £950 in cash. The court heard that Chris had become addicted to drugs in 1995, had been unable to work and that his marriage had been ruined. I know Chris took the treatment he had received from Tucker badly following Tate's release. They had been good friends until Tucker had got involved with Tate and kicked Chris into touch. From being Tucker's right-hand man to being the subject of Tucker's jokes and snide remarks hurt Chris deeply.

On New Year's Eve 1995, Chris had worked on the door with me at a private function and he had told me he was glad Tucker and Tate had been murdered. He was rambling on in a drugged-up, confused, barely audible mumble. It was terrible to witness. I never saw Chris alive again. His drugged, vacant features are another of the many final images my friends have left me with which I have been trying to erase from my mind ever since. Shortly after Chris had been released from prison he died after collapsing outside a gymnasium. Another of our number dead, another family devastated.

On Friday, 6 June 1997, two police officers called at my home to arrest me. Debra was walking out of the door with the children to take them to school when they pounced. I wasn't in and they wouldn't tell Debra why they wanted me.

They were very intimidating, saying I had to get in touch as it was urgent and it was in my best interests that I did as I was told. Debra took the children to school and the police car followed them. She rang me on her mobile phone to tell me what was happening. I rang the number she had been given and asked the police what the fuck was going on. I was told I was wanted for assaulting a security guard at Chelsea. I had forgotten all about the incident at the football match – it was, after all, 15 weeks ago. I asked Essex police if they could forget about arresting me until I had spoken to the other force. What normally happens is that your local police force arrests you and then keeps you in custody until the police force that wants you comes to pick you up. I said, 'Don't bother nicking me yet, let me speak to the police in Chelsea. I will arrange to go to them. There's no reason for you to arrest me. I'm not going anywhere.' Essex police agreed and the police in Chelsea arranged for me to hand myself in. When I got to the station, I was formally arrested for assault, charged, fingerprinted, photographed and dumped in a cell while they sorted out my bail.

It was dawning on me that however hard I tried, I could never conform to their way of life. I was eventually granted bail and told to appear at West London Magistrates' Court. When I walked out of that police station, I knew I was going nowhere. As one case ended, another one loomed. As an active criminal I would have sorted out a few bogus witnesses and intimidated the victim. The police may even have warned him that it wasn't worth going through with the case. This had often happened, but now I was trying to do things right, I was being slaughtered.

About three weeks later, a detective telephoned Debra and expressed his dismay at the firearms incident at my home. He said that he hoped that I was OK. Debra didn't know what he was talking about. He said that an officer from the firearms unit had been told that a man had been arrested outside my home with a shotgun. If this were true, then nobody had told us. I rang the police officer who had called Debra and he assured me that he had received the information from the police firearms unit. He said he would get back onto them and then report back to me. In the meantime, he warned me to be cautious. I told Debra to take the children to her mother's and I would go to my mother's until the situation had been cleared up. If somebody was looking for me with a gun, I didn't want my children being in the same county, let alone the same house. In the meantime, I would discover exactly who, if anybody, was behind this and find them before they found me.

On Saturday, 12 July, I left Essex to travel to my mother's. When I arrived, I went over to the village store and on my way back I saw two of my old school friends sitting outside the pub. It was a warm evening so I sat talking with them. There were about 20 or so other people sitting at adjacent tables in the garden of this rather quaint village pub. I had only been there for about two or three minutes when a police sergeant came walking by. The officer and I had known each other for years and there was certainly no love lost between us. As soon as he spotted me, he headed straight towards me. Naturally, everybody who was sat nearby began to look. He stood in front of me with his hands on his hips and said, 'You've made a name for yourself, haven't you, O'Mahoney? Are you staying at your mother's? When are you going back to London?' I sat there in silence.

I had endured years of this crap as a boy. When I used to walk home from school with my friends, one particular PC used to drive along beside me at walking pace. He would park outside my girlfriend's home and wait for me to come out. Needless to say, concerned parents objected to their children being in my company.

I sat looking at the policeman, listening to his shit and thinking, 'I am only here because I've helped these bastards. My family's lives have been torn apart, people are keen to see me dead and now this prick is giving me grief.' I looked straight at the sergeant and politely told him to fuck off.

The sergeant replied, 'And how's your mother, Bernie?'

I took this to be a veiled threat. I had not forgotten, nor will I forget, when my mother was arrested for being drunk and disorderly when in fact she was having an epileptic fit. One of these fine men had put my mother in a cell for no reason.

I personally never saw this incident as an error of judgement on the part of the police, rightly or wrongly. The police sergeant saw that he had struck a nerve and very wisely walked off. I was embarrassed about what had happened as everybody was looking and talking about what had been said. I told my friends that I was going home until later. About 10 p.m., I went back to the pub and had a drink with my friends. When it closed, I walked to a nearby Indian restaurant to see the manager, a friend whom I had not seen for a few years. I stayed there until about 2 a.m. and left alone. The streets were deserted. I had drunk a fair amount of alcohol, but I wasn't bothering anyone.

A police riot van drove past and when the driver spotted me he pulled up next to me. The driver said, 'All right, mate? You been anywhere nice?'

I just wanted to be alone. I had not bothered anybody and I was not doing anything to warrant police attention.

I told him to 'grow up or fuck off'.

He wouldn't leave it, saying, 'There's no need for that,' so I told him to fuck off again.

He tried to get out of the vehicle so I put my hands on the door and told him to stay where he was as I wanted no problems. He kept on at me, threatening to arrest me, and I guess I just flipped. I couldn't take any more of his shit. I let go of the door and he jumped out and went to lay his hands on me. I whacked him across the head and then punched him in the face. As he fell back I gave him a fierce open-handed slap around the ear. It knocked him sideways. There was a struggle as a second officer who had been in the van jumped on me as I was trying to hold the other policeman down on the floor. Within minutes I found myself overwhelmed by several officers who had been called to give assistance. I wasn't surprised the sergeant from the earlier incident was one of them. I was handcuffed and loaded into the van. The handcuffs were so tight they cut the tendons in my wrist. My forehead was bleeding and I had three wounds in the back of my head. I later learned that my finger was broken and I had a bruise on my stomach in the shape of a boot.

At the police station, I remained with my hands cuffed behind my back. I could feel my wrists bleeding, but they wouldn't remove the cuffs. I was presented to the desk sergeant and the arresting officer said that I had been detained for using abusive words and threatening behaviour. No mention was made of assault. I was put in a cell, still handcuffed, and left alone to contemplate my rapidly decreasing good fortune.

Over the six years I had worked with Tucker and the other members of the firm, I had never endured crap like this, but now I was at pains to toe the line I ended up being crucified. I lay on the wooden bench face down. I couldn't lie on my back as my hands were still cuffed behind me. The blood ran down my face from my forehead and onto the bench. My wrists were starting to swell, making the pain more intense. I took some satisfaction out of the fact that I had managed to hit the officer – at least I wasn't going to be charged with that, or so I thought. Not only did the handcuffs prevent me from lying on my back, I was also unable to undo my trousers so I couldn't use the toilet. Unable to control myself any longer, I had to lie face down in my own blood and suffer the indignity of urinating myself. As a 14-year-old boy, I had been locked in the very same police cell I now found myself in. Over 20 years had passed but nothing had changed. The same anger, the same sense of injustice and the same feeling of utter hopelessness ran through me. My lifelong struggle with authority had certainly buckled and warped me, but the pressures of the last two years had broken me in two. In the cell alone, I broke down. I didn't give a shit what they charged me with or that I was in a cell, I just felt so bloody hopeless. I felt I couldn't succeed whichever path I took. I was full of self-pity and I felt angry with myself. I forced myself to stop before the police returned to my cell. When I heard them coming, I lay face down on the hard wooden bench and pretended to be asleep. I had always done that to show the police that I wasn't concerned and I could sleep through their intrusions into my life.

The following morning, the cell door opened and the desk sergeant who had just come on shift took off my cuffs. He didn't say much, but his expression told me I looked a real mess. I was soaked in my own urine, I had dry blood caked all over my face and my clothing was torn. I was taken to the custody desk and the sergeant formally charged me with using abusive words, threatening behaviour and, after a calculated pause, assaulting a police officer. I now had two court cases to consider – the incident at Chelsea and this latest matter. I was fairly certain that if it all went against me I could end up behind bars.

Eleven days after being arrested for assaulting the police officer, I had to appear at West London Magistrates' in Hammersmith for assaulting the football steward at Chelsea.

In my eyes, I wasn't guilty. I had only retaliated after being slapped in the nose and grabbed by a couple of over-zealous hard men who thought they could flex their beer guts in front of children. I worked out the estimated cost of travelling and loss of income for a trial, which would surely happen if I pleaded not guilty. I decided a guilty would be preferable on the pocket – i.e. half a dozen 140-mile round trips to court, half a dozen days off work and only a 50–50 chance of a not guilty would prove more expensive than pleading guilty. I wasn't going to come out waving a flag though. I wanted enough mitigating circumstances to ensure I didn't get a custodial sentence.

My friend Benny, from south London, had gone to work in Japan so I sent him a typed letter which was supposedly written by him. The letter said that Benny was a businessman who regularly attended Chelsea matches and he had been appalled at the treatment I had received at the hands of the stewards. It said that after the incident he had taken my address and posted me this letter in case I should need a witness. Benny signed the letter and posted it back to me in England, the Japanese stamp and postmark making it appear authentic. When the contents of the letter were read out in court, the magistrate would not accept my guilty plea because the letter indicated I could be innocent. Instead, a not-guilty plea was entered despite my protests and the matter was set down for trial.

I wasn't quite sure how I was going to play it. The police had mustered six 'upstanding' stewards of impeccable good character as witnesses and the victim had been photographed bearing some pretty ugly injuries. I had the letter from my friend Benny in Japan, but there was a possibility they would rule that inadmissible as he wouldn't be able to attend and give evidence. It certainly didn't look good for me. When I arrived at the court I saw the stewards sitting with the detective who had arrested me so I sat on a chair immediately behind them. None of the stewards appeared to recognise me and they carried on talking, unaware I was able to hear every word they said. The steward I had head-butted was telling the detective that he wanted the magistrate to ban me from ever visiting Chelsea's ground again. 'In case I bump into him again,' he said. He then asked the detective what he should do if somebody didn't get 'their story straight'.

The detective said, 'Don't worry, it's a stipendiary magistrate today, she's a good old bird, she will guide you through it.' I stood up and turned around to face the detective and the stewards. 'Trying to get your story straight, are you? As a policeman, I'd have thought you would know better than to coach witnesses.'

I could see that they were shocked that I had been sitting listening to them so I added to their anguish by saying that I was going to complain to the stipendiary magistrate. 'You know the one officer, that good old bird.' I went to the court office and asked them to call the police as an attempt was being made to pervert the course of justice. At first the court official seemed keen to get some toerag locked up, but when I told him the instigator was a detective, his mood changed.

He said he would make the magistrate aware of what was going on and I would be informed what, if any, action was going to be taken. When I entered the court I was advised that I shouldn't make the complaint in open court but I could question the detective and the witnesses about matters 'which may or may not have occurred outside the court room'. When the witnesses entered the box I asked them what had been said outside; some were totally honest, some denied any conversation had taken place and others 'couldn't really remember'. The incident at the Chelsea ground became almost irrelevant as everybody could see that some of the witnesses were unreliable.

In less than half an hour the stipendiary magistrate dismissed the case against me. The detective and the stewards looked physically sick. On the stairs outside the court, the steward I had head-butted got rather upset and went for me, but his colleagues held him back. I smiled at him and walked off, thinking he shouldn't take matters so personally. His detective friend should have warned him that there is no justice any more.

11

A RIGHT CHARLIE

The Essex firm I had been part of was in tatters. Those who hadn't been murdered were either locked up, in hiding or facing some other distasteful dilemma. The remnants of our 1960s counterparts, the Kray firm, were not faring any better. Like our firm, gang members had defected after its leaders had embarked on an orgy of mindless violence against not only enemies, but their own friends. Further divided by deceit and betrayal, those not dead, imprisoned or in hiding were all waiting for their own personal tragedies to happen. On 14 May 1997, Charlie Kray sat in the dock at Belmarsh Crown Court with his head bowed. He had pleaded not guilty to a charge of supplying two kilos of cocaine. As his eyes roamed the public gallery looking for a friendly face, he must have felt both disappointment and relief. Disappointment because only two of the seats were taken up – one by a man who had written a book about Charlie's life and another by a female who had read that book and become a Kray fan. Absent were the legions of gang groupies that so publicly and vocally professed to be firm friends of the Kray family. It must have hurt Charlie to realise that so many of his friends were not friends at all. Now the shit had hit the fan, these friends were nowhere to be seen. Their loyalty, like the Kray legend, had been nothing more than romantic nonsense.

Charlie must have also felt relief because he had been spared the ordeal of having an audience hear the truth about him. For years he had basked in the infamy of his brothers, allowing people to believe that his family controlled some Mafia-type empire, awash with money. Nothing could have been further from the truth. Charlie squirmed uneasily in the dock as his defence barrister told the court that he was 'a pathetic, skint old fool who lives on handouts from his pals' and 'a charming but gullible old man that doesn't know his limitations.'

Charlie had been trapped in an elaborate sting by police officers keen to arrest the remaining free Kray. Had they been minded, the police could have gone on a prison visit and put Reggie in the frame as well. People were always putting hare-brained schemes to the Kray brothers, who always agreed to get involved.

They knew most proposals were nonsense, but the Krays had no capital, no business interests and no income to speak of, so they chose to take a chance on anything they were offered. To ensure the brothers would agree to a business proposal, they would be promised a high percentage of any profits without having to invest any of their own money. The person who had proposed the deal would then dash off to the nearest printers and have a wad of business cards and letterheads made which would proudly display their name alongside that of their heroes. These would then be dished out at every opportunity to friends, family, people down the pub and in the street and anywhere else these nobodies could pretend they were business partners with somebodies. The Krays rarely made money out of these ventures. What genuine entrepreneur would contemplate such a meaningless amalgamation? Reggie would justify getting involved with yet another loser by saying to me, 'You never know, one of them might make some decent money for us one day.' The trouble was, I did know, and Reggie was fooling himself. Just like Charlie had been fooling himself when he had unwittingly boasted to undercover police officers about being able to supply huge quantities of drugs.

Further shame and humiliation was heaped on Charlie as the details of his amateurish attempt to deal in drugs were revealed to the jury.

On 7 March 1996, Charlie Kray's son Gary died. He had been suffering from cancer. Charlie, who had an extremely close relationship with Gary, was, quite naturally, devastated. To add insult to injury, Charlie had to suffer the indignity of asking his brother Reggie for money because he couldn't afford to pay for Gary's funeral. When the funeral took place, the Home Office would not allow Reg to attend so an empty car was hired to follow the cortège. It was Reggie's way of saying that despite the fact he couldn't physically attend, he was there in spirit. One man who did attend was Patsy Manning.

Patsy was from Birmingham and I had met him on several occasions. He had been Reggie's co-author on the book *Slang* from which Reggie had originally pledged all proceeds to James Fallon, although neither he nor his family ever received anything. Patsy was a likeable man and had known the Krays all his life. He had spent time in prison with Reggie after clubbing a doorman with a hammer and almost killing him. I had attended Patsy's 60th birthday party in Birmingham at a club called the Elbow Rooms with my friend Stephen 'Boss-eye' Whiddon. Charlie Kray came along and we spent the entire weekend celebrating. Whilst at the Elbow Rooms, Charlie had called Stephen and me into a toilet cubicle where he was snorting cocaine with a £50 note. Giggling and unsteady on his feet, Charlie was urging everybody to share a few lines with him. Eventually, Stephen and I had to help Charlie back into the bar area as we thought he might collapse he was so drunk and drugged.

Patsy had attended Gary's funeral with another man called George, who had been kind enough to drive Patsy to London for the service in his Jaguar 'as a favour'.

Charlie always enjoyed a drink but following his son's death, he turned to the bottle for comfort. Instead of the drink making him the life and soul of the party, as it had done in the past, it now had the effect of making him extremely depressed and very emotional. Whether it was the alcohol or his state of mind, nobody knows, but Charlie certainly wasn't thinking straight in the months following his son's death.

Some time after Gary's funeral, Patsy rang Charlie to invite him to a party at the Elbow Rooms. Charlie told Patsy that he wouldn't be able to go, as he had no money. Patsy said that he had a friend in Birmingham who owned a hotel and Charlie would be welcome to stay there free of charge. Charlie didn't relish the thought of going back to the Elbow Rooms – on previous occasions he had gone there with Gary, so it would have been an emotional journey for him to return. However, his partner Judy encouraged Charlie to go, telling him that it would get his mind off things to be amongst friends and have a good time.

Charlie relented and travelled to Birmingham. After settling into his room, Charlie went to meet Patsy Manning who was waiting downstairs in the hotel bar. When he arrived, there were two men with Patsy who were introduced as George and Dino from Newcastle. George, it turned out, was the man who had driven Patsy down to Gary's funeral in his Jaguar. Shortly after Dino and George were introduced to Charlie, two more people entered the bar. One was a girl named Lisa and another was a man named Jack. George introduced them to Charlie as his friends. After a few minutes, Dino called out, 'Quiet for a moment.' He then presented Patsy with a present from himself, George, Jack and Lisa. When Patsy opened the small package, it contained a Simply Red CD. Feigning delight, Patsy thanked them all. However, Dino started laughing and said, 'That is only part of your present.' Then a very large package was brought into the room and given to Patsy.

When Patsy unwrapped it, he was pleasantly surprised. His 'friends' had bought him a top-of-the-range music centre. The 'generous' foursome spent the night plying Patsy and Charlie with alcohol and refused to let them buy a single drink in return. During the evening, Charlie gave Patsy a knowing look: he had noticed Jack had a Rolex watch on his wrist which was probably worth about £12,000. These new 'friends' had money, a fact which warmed Charlie to them. When Charlie went to the toilet, he got talking to Dino, who was also visiting the Gents. Charlie confessed to Dino that he didn't have the money to keep up with him or his friends, saying he was financially embarrassed. Dino laughed and gave Charlie £50. Smiling broadly, Charlie took the money and thanked him. He really thought he had landed on his feet with these people, but like the fools who approached the Krays with ludicrous schemes and business ideas, Charlie really had no idea who he was dealing with or what their motives were.

Once Charlie was suitably drunk and relaxed, Jack said to Charlie that he had been 'left a bit dry' after the guy he had been trading with was killed in Amsterdam. Instinctively, Charlie knew that Jack was talking about drugs and said he had a mate who could help out. The truth is Charlie was lying. Charlie was just doing what the Krays had always done. As soon as someone said anything that could lead to money, they would say, 'Yes, we can help you with that,' regardless of whether they could or couldn't. It was to be a grave mistake on Charlie's part.

A RIGHT CHARLIE

Over the next few weeks, Jack kept in touch with Charlie by telephone. Keen to keep Jack on board, Charlie told his 'friend' that he was having a charity event at a friend's pub in Kent to raise money for St Christopher's Hospice in Crystal Palace where his son Gary had died. Jack was his usual enthusiastic self, saying he would get a football signed by the Newcastle United team for Charlie to raffle.

He said he would 'pop down' with a pal of his named Ken and give it to Charlie personally. The men from Newcastle arrived for the event and stayed at a hotel near Charlie's home in Sanderstead, Surrey. They went to a couple of nightclubs together, where once again Jack would not let Charlie put his hand in his pocket. When Charlie was drunk, he put his Kray hat on and started to boast about his family's mythical criminal empire. Soon the subject turned to drugs. Jack and Ken asked Charlie about people who could supply them and Charlie, in a barely audible mumble, said he never went near drugs, he only put people together. 'Cause there's too many eyes on me,' he said.

The men were disappointed but not deterred. When Charlie told Jack that another friend of his was putting on a variety show at the Mermaid Theatre in Croydon in memory of Gary, he was as enthusiastic as he had been about the pub charity event. He told Charlie he would love to attend. 'It would be nice to show some support and meet some of your friends,' he said. Gullible Charlie thought it would be nice too. The event was a huge success. Three hundred people attended, amongst them the actor Bill Murray, Charlie's old friend Freddie Foreman and his actor son Jamie Foreman, all of whom Charlie introduced to his 'friends' from Newcastle. He also introduced them to two other friends, Ronnie Field, and a man named Bobbie Gould. Charlie had mentioned his 'friend's' interest in drugs to Gould and Field and they had said they might be able to help. A few days later, Jack telephoned Charlie and invited him and Ronnie Field to Newcastle, adding, 'We might be able to sort out some business.'

He told Charlie not to worry about his travelling expenses as he would send Charlie two airline tickets and meet him and Field at the airport. 'It's easier and quicker to fly,' he said. Charlie couldn't believe his luck and the words 'sort out some business' rang in his head. These weren't the sort of fools who had sat at the visiting table with Reggie and Ronnie, talking about security companies, one-armed bandits and dodgy car deals. These people had serious money, money that Charlie desperately needed.

Ronnie and Charlie flew to Newcastle and were picked up by Jack and Ken at the airport in a Range Rover and driven to a five-star hotel. Jack then introduced Ronnie and Charlie to Brian, another of his friends. As usual, Jack proved to be a faultless host, plying Charlie and Ronnie Field with drinks. Charlie couldn't remember the number of free Scotch and Cokes he drank. In his inebriated state he felt he had to live up to his gangster image and once more began to brag about his drug contacts. He said he and Field could supply Jack with five kilos of cocaine every two weeks for two years, adding that the first exchange would take place in Croydon the following week. The truth of the matter was he didn't have enough money in his back pocket for a shandy, let alone enough money to buy five kilos of quality cocaine.

The following few weeks were an emotional period for Charlie. It would have been his son's 45th birthday on 3 July and Charlie's 70th on the 9th. His friends in Birmingham insisted on having a party for him, but money was still an issue for Charlie and he didn't think he would be able to go. He didn't have a car, couldn't afford the train fare or even two £15 economy coach tickets for himself and his partner Judy. Jack rang him the Sunday before the party and Charlie asked him if he could borrow £500.

Jack told him that it wouldn't be a problem. He immediately put the money in a jiffy bag and sent it by registered post. The Geordie's generosity totally convinced Charlie that he was onto something good.

When Charlie and Judy arrived at the same hotel Charlie had previously stayed at, they were told the manager was aware of Charlie's financial situation and therefore there would be no charge. Charlie was surprised to find that Brian and Jack were also staying there. As usual, the champagne and drink flowed freely all night for Charlie. His 'friends' also presented him with a gold-plated cigarette lighter and Charlie appeared lost for words.

On Saturday, 20 July, Jack rang Charlie, asking him to tell Ronnie Field to contact him. Four days later, he rang again to tell Charlie that he would be in London the next day. He asked Charlie to book him into the Selsdon Park Hotel in Croydon. Without thinking, Charlie did so. Ronnie Field and Bobbie Gould were due to hand over two kilos of cocaine to the Geordies at the hotel in return for £63,000 and Charlie had just roped himself into the conspiracy by booking the room on their behalf. On the day Jack arrived, Charlie had been working on a book called *Me and My Brothers* at the home of Robin McGibbon, the co-author, near Bromley in Kent. Charlie received a telephone call from his partner, Judy, who told him that Jack wanted him to pop into the hotel and have a drink with him, Brian, Ronnie Field and Bobbie Gould.

Charlie didn't really want to go, but as he was passing the hotel anyway and the Geordies had been so good to him, he decided he would have a quick whisky. As had happened previously, Jack tried desperately to get Charlie to drink more but he insisted on having just a single whisky. Charlie explained that he couldn't stop as he wanted to get back to Judy and his children.

The exchange did not happen that night but the following Wednesday the deal was back on. Charlie was not present when the drugs were delivered, as he had driven to Kent again to work on his book and afterwards went to pick up Judy from work. Charlie was in good spirits and looking forward to the release of his book, which he thought might help ease his financial worries. At 7 p.m. that night, Judy had cooked dinner and Charlie settled down to watch television when there was a firm knock at the door.

Judy answered and came back into the lounge followed by four policemen – two uniformed and two plain-clothed detectives. As they came in, two other detectives came in through the patio doors. They gestured for Charlie to get up and then informed him that he was being arrested on drugs charges. Charlie was ordered upstairs and the police searched his bedroom. When the search was completed at 9 p.m., Charlie was asked if he wanted to change out of his tracksuit bottoms and into something more appropriate. Judy asked, 'Are they taking you away, Charlie?'

'Yes,' he said, 'they've arrested me.'

Charlie kissed her goodbye and then walked to the waiting police car. The car took him to Ilford police station in Essex where he was put in the cells.

At 10 p.m. that evening, Judy was allowed to see Charlie. She brought him fresh clothes as he had been warned that he would be appearing in court the following morning. Charlie asked if he could have a few moments alone with Judy and was told he could spend five minutes alone with her in an interview room. As Judy entered, Charlie stood up and put his arms around her. He said, 'I'm sorry, darling,' and, almost crying, whispered to her, 'That lovely guy, Jack, he's an undercover policeman. He's been tape-recording me talking about cocaine.'

It must have been obvious to the undercover policemen that Charlie Kray was no big-time drug dealer. In my view, it cannot be right that police officers can use a man's son's funeral to infiltrate his circle of friends. It is equally distasteful that police officers using taxpayers' money can spend large amounts of cash on presents, hotels, aeroplane flights, champagne and get you so drunk you would say anything they want. I felt deeply sorry for Charlie. The following morning, the deception in full was outlined to Charlie by his solicitor.

Charlie was told that Jack, George and Brian – his Geordie 'friends' – were all in fact undercover police officers and had been taping all the conversations that had taken place over a two-month period. Charlie knew that he had been snared by their elaborate trap as he had said incriminating things about drugs, not because he was able to supply them, but because he thought that these people would continue to buy him drinks and supply him with money so long as he acted out the part of Kray the Gangster. Later that day, Charlie appeared at Redbridge Magistrates' Court in Ilford. The shoes he was wearing as he stood in the dock had holes in them. He had a ten-pound watch on his wrist and not a penny in his pocket, yet, on the front page of *The Sun* was the headline 'Charlie Kray in £78 million cocaine sting'.

The police estimation of the value of the drugs he had promised to supply was a little more charitable. Charlie Kray, Ronnie Field and Bobbie Gould were each charged with conspiracy to supply three kilos of cocaine worth £63,000 and conspiracy to supply 520 kilos of cocaine. Charlie and Field were also accused of conspiracy to supply 1,000 Ecstasy tablets worth £20,000. The magistrate refused all three men bail.

Charlie, not surprisingly, was sent to Belmarsh, a top-security prison situated in Woolwich, south-east London. In case anyone missed the point that police had arrested one of the most dangerous gangsters in the country, armed police in flak jackets manned the rooftops of the magistrates court for the next hearing. Charlie Kray was driven there from Belmarsh Prison at high speed, with police motorcyclists riding ahead to clear the traffic. The only part of the circus that was missing was the deafening klaxons and the circling helicopters that accompanied him, his brothers and their so-called firm to the Old Bailey in 1969.

Charlie's trial was set for later that year but in the meantime, he was told he would have to remain in the high-security unit at Belmarsh with IRA hit men, PLO terrorists, Yardie killers and various other murderers. The notoriety of the name Kray had done Charlie many favours over the years, but he was soon to learn that it could be a burden too. The jurors who were to sit in judgement of Charlie were given round-the-clock protection as the judge felt they might be got at. If you are a juror attending a trial and armed police are assigned to protect you, it is reasonable to assume that the man in the dock is no angel. If you reach that conclusion, then you are possibly pre-judging the defendant, something that jurors are not supposed to do. With the odds already stacked against him, Charlie Kray began his trial at a distinct disadvantage.

Despite the damning tapes of him boasting about drugs, Charlie did have a defence. An undercover policeman had infiltrated his son's funeral in order to be introduced to Charlie so that he could subsequently be seduced into committing a crime. Believing the undercover police officers to be wealthy drug dealers, Charlie and Ronnie Field had agreed to pretend to be wealthy dealers themselves in order to get some money out of them. It wasn't the best of defences, but being a ponce, however distasteful, isn't illegal and the truth was the only defence Charlie had.

Charlie was defended by Jonathon Goldberg QC. In his opening address to the jury, Mr Goldberg said he was facing a unique difficulty in his career. He was defending someone called Kray before a jury under round-the-clock surveillance.

He told the jury not to fall into the trap of thinking the additional security measures being employed around the court were in place because the defendant was a top-class gangster, despite the fact the defendant had been held in prison under double-A security, the highest possible. He said the security measures being used concerning Kray were merely part of the hype surrounding the case.

> It is nothing other than the fact his name is Kray. Charlie Kray is nothing more than a pathetic, skint old fool who lives on handouts from pals. Because of the hand-to-mouth existence he has been forced to lead, he has become an expert at bull. He has been doing it all his life, it is the only way he has been able to

earn a living because nobody would give him a job. You'll hear that the defendant has never been a drug dealer in any way, shape or form. Have you ever heard of a drugs baron that lives like a pauper, cadging £50 here and £20 there? He doesn't even have a bank account. All you have in the dock is a charming but gullible old man that doesn't know his limitations, who does not recognise where his charm and bull ends and where the reality of life begins. The undercover officers should be ashamed of themselves for carrying out a deeply offensive operation.

With the help of a seemingly bottomless expense account, [the officers] acted as devious *agents provocateurs*, even using Gary Kray's death to infiltrate his father Charlie's circle of friends. No doubt it was a feather in the cap of several of the officers to have arrested the last of the Kray brothers. They targeted Charlie Kray. They lured a foolish and vulnerable old man with no money into a carefully prepared web; they made all the running.

The tapes you will hear of Kray talking about tonnes of cocaine and millions of pounds are nothing more than absurd exaggeration. The police must have realised that Kray was not a big-time criminal with wealth behind him, otherwise why would one of the undercover officers have given him £50 for nothing? If you genuinely believe someone is a drug baron, you don't insult him by giving him that sort of money.

During the trial it was revealed that undercover police work, although not the best-paid profession in the world, has its perks. Brian, one of the undercover police officers, was alleged to have spent the night with a woman named Michelle Hamdouchi at her home after Charlie's birthday party. It was also alleged that she turned up at the aptly named Swallow Hotel in the early hours, where she performed oral sex on him in his room. Whilst performing his public duty, Brian had allegedly kept asking Michelle if 'Charlie Kray could come up with the cocaine'. Nobody is certain what, if anything, came out of Hamdouchi's mouth. The undercover officer strenuously denied that he had been involved in any inappropriate behaviour with the lady.

Hamdouchi was understandably embarrassed, but she admitted she had performed a sex act on Brian at the Swallow Hotel. Brian and his colleague Jack did admit that whilst they were waiting for Michelle to come to the hotel (for whatever reason), they had been drinking champagne at the bar with Spice Girl, Victoria Adams (later Beckham), who coincidentally happened to be in the hotel. (And they say police work is tough!)

The trial dragged on for eight weeks and eventually the prosecutor rose to give his closing speech. 'The defence claim the police were cunning and devious and should be ashamed of themselves, but it was Kray's behaviour that was shameful. If Kray suspected that Jack's overture in Birmingham was all about drugs, all he had to say was, that's not my game, I'm going off to drink with my mates. But he didn't, he chose to remain and talk about drugs.'

Mr Goldberg, for Charlie, said in his final address to the jury:

> An elaborate and expensive operation has been launched by career-hungry police, who sought to put feathers in their caps by arresting this old man. The undercover officers who carried it out lived the life of Riley for two-and-a-half months at the taxpayers' expense. Bottle after bottle of champagne, £2,000 on booze from a cash and carry, £1,000 on air tickets and a loan to Kray. Rooms for five at a five-star hotel, birthday presents for Kray and Patsy Manning. They were spending money like crazy because they were Kray fishing. Other police officers might say, if this is undercover work, give us some any day of the week. Jack and his pals started to behave like the people they wanted to put away, but the detective screen they have hidden behind is a cloak for their unaccountability. Kray was on tape talking about tonnes of drugs, but where were the drugs?
>
> If the police genuinely believed Kray and Field were into drugs in a big way, why didn't the police put them under surveillance and catch others in their net too? The reason was that there were forces at work within the police to get Charlie Kray convicted. There was no surveillance because they knew he was bluffing.
>
> Why Kray was targeted for this elaborate set-up is not known because the undercover police are not obliged to say. Kray is in the dock only because he is a broken, shambolic figure, desperate for cash, who had to invent stories to keep up a front. If all the

stories he told the police on tape – losing one-and-a-quarter million pounds on a deal, contacts with the Israeli Secret Service and the rest – were accepted as rubbish, why weren't his statements about enormous quantities of drugs?

Mr Goldberg told the jury that they could be forgiven for thinking during the trial that they were in danger of being murdered in their beds. There was only one reason for them being under 24-hour surveillance for the past 5 weeks – the defendant's surname was Kray.

The police claim the jury protection was the court's decision, not theirs, but it is the police who have created the atmosphere you feel in this court. It suits their case for the hype surrounding the name Kray to stay in place. It was indeed a remarkable and unique case, the like of which we would not see again. A sad old-timer has been badly set-up.

The jury left the court to consider their verdict at 12.04 p.m. and returned the following day a few minutes before 3.30 p.m. When the jury foreman was asked if they had agreed on a verdict on count one, he replied, 'Yes.' He was asked, 'What is that verdict?' and replied, 'Guilty.'

When he was asked if they had reached a verdict on count two, which was the more serious charge, he said that they had not yet reached agreement on that verdict. Throughout the following day the jury deliberated and then just before 3 p.m., Charlie was called back into the dock. 'Have you reached a verdict on count two?' the jury foreman was asked. 'Yes,' he replied. 'What is that verdict?' 'Guilty,' he said.

Shortly before he was sentenced, Charlie said to the judge, 'All of my life I have advised people, particularly young people, never to be involved in drugs. I went along with the stories, as the officers did. But they are all untrue. It was only to get money. I swear on my son's grave that I have never handled drugs in my life.'

Charlie had either forgotten the night of Patsy Manning's 60th birthday party when he had snorted cocaine in the toilets of the Elbow Rooms in Birmingham or he was trying to fool the judge. I know Charlie lied about not touching drugs, but I will never believe he was a drug baron. He had played the Kray name game and lost.

You may think you're clever by immersing yourself in a gang and you may get away with fucking with the law for so long, but you're fooling nobody but yourself. One way or another, as Charlie found out to his cost, they will get you in the end.

Bobbie Gould was sentenced to five years' imprisonment and Ronnie Field to nine.

Turning to Charlie, the judge said

> Charles Kray, you have been found guilty on both counts by the jury on overwhelming evidence. You showed yourself ready, willing and able to lend yourself to any criminal enterprise which became known to you. There was never a real question of entrapment of you by these officers, but when caught, you cried foul. I am pleased that the jury saw through that hollow cry. Infiltration by officers is an important tool in society's fight against crime.
>
> Throughout this case, you professed your abhorrence against drugs, but the jury's verdict has shown your often repeated protestations to be hypocrisy. Those who deal in class 'A' drugs can expect justice from the courts with little mercy. Eight years on count one, twelve years on count two, to run concurrently.

As Charlie was led down the steps to begin his sentence, he knew that as a 70 year old, unless he could win an appeal he would never be a free man again. Like his brother Ron, he would die in custody.

Charlie was moved from Belmarsh Prison to Gartree Prison in Leicestershire, where his brother Reg had been 15 years earlier. Not long after being at Gartree, Charlie was moved to Parkhurst Prison on the Isle of Wight. He was the oldest man in Britain being kept under maximum-security conditions. Charlie was really too frail for that type of pressure and by now he also had a heart condition.

In March 2000, Charlie Kray was admitted to hospital. He only stayed a few days before he was returned to prison, but he continued to feel unwell. His brother Reggie requested a visit as he was concerned about Charlie's health. When Charlie was readmitted to the hospital a few days later, Reg was told he would be allowed to go and see him.

On 18 March, Reg Kray left Wayland Prison with four prison officers as escorts. When he arrived on the Isle of Wight he was taken to St

Mary's Hospital to see Charlie, who was sitting up in bed waiting for him. A prison officer had been assigned to remain by his bedside 24 hours a day. The brothers were allowed a 30-minute visit before Reg was taken to Parkhurst Prison where he was housed in Charlie's cell on C-Wing. Reg was permitted to visit Charlie on two further occasions, during which time a doctor told Reg that Charlie was getting progressively worse.

He was in a wheelchair, having to take regular oxygen and his legs had swollen to twice their normal size. The doctor said that Charlie had heart wastage, which could result in heart failure. Applications were made to the Home Secretary, Jack Straw, to give Charlie compassionate parole so he could spend whatever time remained of his life at home. This is normally granted when the inmate is terminally ill, but in Charlie's case, it was to no avail. Instead, the prison service and the Home Office talked about sending Charlie back to Parkhurst, either to the hospital wing or C-Wing. This really upset Charlie, as he thought it totally inconsiderate and inhumane.

On Monday, 3 April, Reg Kray was rushed to St Mary's hospital. Charlie's condition had deteriorated. When he reached his brother's bedside Charlie kept saying to Reg, 'I hope Diane gets here soon, please God, she gets here in time.' Diane was Charlie's regular girlfriend over the years and thankfully his prayers were answered. The following night Charlie died, holding Diane's hand. Reg was not present when Charlie passed away – three prison officers called at his cell to tell him that the remaining member of his family had died at 8.45 p.m.

On 19 April 2000, Reg was taken from prison to Bethnal Green police station to attend Charlie's funeral. There were 200 police officers and a motorcycle escort for the funeral procession and helicopters circling above. At the funeral parlour, Reg put a photograph of himself, Charlie and Ronnie inside Charlie's coffin. Charlie had told Kray family friend Wilf Pine that whatever happened, he didn't want a celebrity funeral like Ron's. He wanted his coffin to be taken to Diane's home, then to be buried quietly beside his parents and his son at Chingford. Above all, he wanted no fuss and no media circus. As usual, Charlie's wishes didn't count.

Nothing was going to be allowed to stop the Reg Kray roadshow. Too much depended on this funeral for Reg to waste it. He knew exactly what had to happen. Charlie, now lying safely in his coffin, was soon forgotten. As Reg walked from the funeral parlour, the crowds surged forward and bouncers and police had to join hands to hold them back. The crowd were cheering, 'Good old Reg' and 'Free Reg now'. Reg Kray was back amongst his people at last. There was no disguising the excitement and the affection of the crowd. There were brief handshakes and shouts of 'How you doing?' for those who were privileged to touch him, even some *Godfather*-style embraces for surviving old companions. Following the service at St Matthew's Church at Bethnal Green – where Ronnie's service had been held – the huge funeral cortège made its way to Chingford Cemetery.

The funeral was no longer about Charlie Kray, it was all about Reggie. But his greatest moment was yet to come.

Descending from the darkened people-carrier the prison service had brought him in, and surrounded by his many friends, Reg bore a wreath of a broken heart made up of red and white roses. But these roses were not for Charlie. Pausing by the grave of his long-dead first wife, Frances – with tears in his eyes – Reg laid them on the grass beneath her headstone. He then paid his last respects to his brother as the coffin was lowered into the ground. As this was happening, somebody shouted, 'Three cheers for Reg', and the cries rang out across the cemetery and with this, the show was over. The blue Renault with the darkened windows was already waiting for Reg. On this peak of high emotion, with the shouts of acclaim still ringing in his ears, Reg stepped aboard. As he did so, he raised his one free hand to the crowd and waved.

The door slammed shut and he was gone. Charlie could not possibly have had his final wish fulfilled and been allowed to go quietly, but his brother's funeral was to be Reggie Kray's grand finale as a living celebrity. Although he didn't know it yet, Reg Kray was a dying man.

12

REUNITED AT LAST

On 12 January 1998, I stood trial for breach of the peace, using threatening words and behaviour and assaulting the police officer who had stopped me whilst I was visiting my mother. Never have I come across police officers that were so honest or, as I thought at the time, so fucking stupid. The sergeant admitted he had walked over to chat with me earlier on in the evening and the officer I assaulted admitted he had pulled me over for no reason other than to ask me if I had been anywhere nice. I represented myself and found it wasn't too difficult to make the magistrates wonder why I had been stopped for no apparent reason on two separate occasions by two separate officers within the space of seven hours. I told the court I had only just arrived in the village after leaving my home in Essex because the police had told me a firearm had been brandished outside my house. This shooting 'incident' had occurred, police believe, because I had given evidence for them in a high-profile drug trial. As soon as I arrived in the village I was confronted by a sarcastic police officer and later that night by another. I was not by any stretch of the imagination intent on causing a breach of the peace, I was a man who had snapped under enormous pressure. I was found not guilty of using threatening words and behaviour and of causing a breach of the peace, but I was found guilty of assaulting the officer. The magistrate said that although it was a serious offence, given the circumstances in which it occurred I would only be given a two-year conditional discharge. All that meant was I had to stay out of trouble during that period or I could be brought before the courts for the same offence again.

The prosecution asked the magistrates to order that I pay £500 in costs, but they refused and said I would only have to pay £100.

Eight days after I had appeared in court, Mick Steele and Jack Whomes, the two men accused of murdering Tucker, Tate and Rolfe, were found guilty and sentenced to life imprisonment. Two more lives ruined, two more families torn apart by the events of 1995. Anybody who knows anything about the case knows that these two men should never have been found guilty and I am confident that one day their convictions will be overturned. Steele and Whomes will never be able to regain the time they have lost in prison and Tucker, Tate and Rolfe will remain dead, come what may. There are no winners in the end.

Although we appeared to be emerging from the fog the events of 1995 had shrouded my family and me in, the strain on us all was proving too much. Paul Betts had appeared on television calling me a bastard and saying I was responsible for the death of his daughter Leah. He based his allegations on the fact I had admitted I turned a blind eye to drug dealing in Raquels. The publicity his allegation created resulted in older children telling my children at school that their father was a murderer. How can you tell your tearful son or daughter to ignore such crap? What can you possibly say when he or she asks if it's true? In an effort to stop these ridiculous allegations, I wrote an open letter to Paul Betts which was printed in the press. I urged him to confront me on live TV so we could debate who was really responsible for Leah's death, but unsurprisingly he declined.

It was becoming apparent to me that staying with my children was causing them to be unfairly tarnished. They were suffering for something none of us had done.

Paul Betts' vile allegations were causing the children so much upset that Debra suggested, and I agreed, that we should part for their sake. Debra and I had to look at the situation in a cold clinical manner and do what was best for them and not what suited us. We sold our home in Mayland, Debra moved to a home near her mother and I returned to Basildon. I did not arrive in the best of moods. I was in turmoil over my family and I was tired of being blamed for causing the death of a girl who had been foolish enough to take drugs. I felt Paul Betts' allegations were as ridiculous as somebody blaming a pub landlord for getting them convicted of drunk driving. We all have choices in life and we all have to take responsibility for our actions. I was also sick of hearing about people who were supposed to want to kill me and of being advised where I should or should not go. So many people appeared to have fucking opinions on me, yet few knew me and none had ever had any dealings with me. If people didn't like me moving back to Basildon, that was a matter for them, not me. I had been driven out of one home, I was not going to be driven out of another. I started drinking in my old haunts. Most people I met droned on and on about the murders of Tucker, Tate and Rolfe as few in the town believe the men accused of the murders were guilty. In fact many believe I had been instrumental in luring the trio to their deaths.

Nobody said they had a problem with me personally and several had nothing but good memories of the trouble-free rave nights we had created at Raquels. The club had since closed down after the door team that had replaced us was unable to control the local villains who had swarmed back there after my departure.

A few months after moving back to Basildon, I bumped into a girl named Emma Turner, whom I had first met at Raquels. Emma and I had always got on well and we began to see each other quite regularly. Before too long I gave up the flat I had rented and moved in with her. Since the catalogue of court appearances had ended, I had been able to take on a full-time job driving a tipper lorry. Within a short period of time I was given a managerial position and offered a post in Peterborough, Cambridgeshire.

I didn't want to move away from the children as being able to see them every other day had lessened the trauma of being separated from them. Instead, I chose to drive to Peterborough every day, leaving the house at 4.30 a.m and returning at 8 p.m. Being straight was a real strain and the rewards were hardly endearing.

The small-time drug dealer who had bank-rolled Mark Murray after the police raid at Club UK in south London had been telling people in Essex that he was looking for me. John Rollinson, or 'Gaffer' as he liked to call himself, was apparently unhappy that I had named his drug-peddling friend Mark Murray at the Leah Betts trial.

Rollinson would have been well advised to keep quiet about the fact he had helped finance the batch of drugs which lead to Leah's death, but he wasn't the brightest of people. He was the type who tried to make himself seem important by having views and opinions on villains others looked up to. Only the gullible and naive took any notice of the likes of Rollinson. It had been a good friend of his that had told me he had been bad-mouthing me, but I was not too concerned. I had never done anything wrong to Rollinson and so I reasoned that he had no right to have a grievance with me. 'It's Gaffer trying to involve his name in a high-profile case,' I told his friend. 'You know what he's like, he just wants to feel important.'

One evening, Emma and I went for a drink over at the Festival Leisure Park in Basildon. This is a large entertainment complex consisting of bars, nightclubs, a bowling alley, cinema and fast-food restaurants. Some of the more witty locals refer to it as 'Bas Vegas'.

We had a drink in a couple of the bars and ended up in a nightclub called Jumping Jacks. When we entered the club, a small, thin, drug-ravished man started shouting 'fucking cunt' at me. He threw his baseball cap on the floor and repeatedly spat, each time repeating 'cunt, fucking cunt'. I thought the man may have been mentally challenged or was suffering from some sort of embarrassing disorder, so I decided it was best to ignore him.

Emma, not used to witnessing such alarming behaviour, clutched my arm and asked me who he was. It was only when the man started shouting about 'grassing Mark Murray up' that I took a closer look and realised it was Gaffer. I hadn't seen him since I had worked at Raquels and he had lost a lot of weight. He looked gaunt and thin – no doubt the result of a low-life existence, popping pills and feeding a cocaine habit.

When you are out with your partner for a drink, you don't really relish the thought of rolling round the floor with a drunk or loud-mouthed druggie. I apologised to Emma and told her we would have a drink at the other end of the bar, but if he continued to be abusive or offered violence, then I would have to give him a clip around the ear. Gaffer was not alone so his actions were despicable. What sort of man starts on another man who is out with his partner having a drink? No doubt Gaffer is another gangster who follows the criminal code – so much for showing women respect.

Throughout the evening, Gaffer kept glaring down the bar at me and tipping his hat like some amusing clown. 'Come on,' I said to Emma, 'I've had enough of this, let's go.' As I walked past Gaffer, the gutless coward squirted me in the eyes with ammonia. Gaffer had been telling everybody in Essex that he was after me. Now that I was temporarily blinded and standing in front of him he had the best chance he was ever going to get to do me.

My vision began to clear and so I made my way to the front of the club. Gaffer and his friend followed us outside, which frightened Emma, so I turned and confronted them. I knew Gaffer was not capable of fighting, so I was expecting him to pull out a weapon. To his friend's credit, he stepped back, making it obvious he wanted no part in any trouble. As Gaffer advanced, I grabbed his head and shoved him backwards.

I was not the slightest bit concerned about what he might try to do or do it with because I had a double-bladed 12-inch combat knife down the back of my trousers. If he got within striking distance of me with a weapon, I was more than prepared to bury the knife deep in his head. When I had shoved him backwards, his cap fell off. As he approached me again I could see in his eyes that he was unsure of himself. He pulled out a Jif Lemon container and, after lunging forward, squirted ammonia in my eyes again. The red mist rose and at that moment, I wanted to end his miserable and pointless life. I pulled out the knife and raised it. He saw it, screamed hysterically and ran back into the club. 'What the fuck am I doing?' I thought. 'How do I end up getting involved with these fools? I could end up serving a life sentence because some little nobody has chosen to attack me.'

The bouncer came out and told me the police had been called. 'You're on CCTV as well, Bernie,' he said. 'You had better make yourself scarce.' Emma and I tried to get in a taxi, but the driver refused to take us and the other taxis in the rank drove away empty. I could see Gaffer hiding in the club foyer behind the bouncers so I knew he wouldn't be troubling us again that night. We didn't live too far from the leisure park, so we decided to walk. We made our way across the car park to the main road, where two police cars pulled up.

My mind was racing. I had a certain prison sentence tucked down the back of my trousers and I didn't fancy being locked up for a loser like Gaffer. 'The knife, the knife . . . How the fuck can I explain away the knife?' I was thinking.

I knew everybody had seen it and the CCTV had recorded me brandishing it, so I knew it was pointless denying its existence. There was only one thing for it, I thought, I would have to bluff my way out of it. I pulled out the knife and approached the police officers. 'It's OK, officers,' I said, 'I've got the knife.'

'Drop the weapon! Drop the weapon!' they shouted.

I laughed and told them it was OK. 'It's not my weapon,' I said. 'I took it off a lunatic.'

I threw the knife on the ground. One of the police officers forced my hands behind my back and slapped a pair of handcuffs on. 'You're under arrest,' he said, 'for possessing an offensive weapon.' I asked the police to make sure Emma got home all right. They said they would. They then put me in the back of the car and took me to Basildon police station.

By this time, my eyes were becoming increasingly painful. They were red and swollen from the ammonia and now I had the handcuffs on, I was unable to wipe or try to clean them, so I asked the officers to remove the cuffs but they refused. At Basildon police station, I was put in front of the custody sergeant, whom I told I had been squirted with ammonia. I said I needed to wash my eyes out, but he said he wouldn't allow me to do anything until I had seen a doctor. An argument developed and the mood became pretty hostile. Eventually, they agreed to remove my cuffs so I could wipe my eyes. I was then bundled into a cell by the arresting officers and the door was slammed shut. A police officer later came and told me that he would have to investigate the matter further and I would be held in custody until those investigations were complete.

That night, a doctor did attend and after examining my eyes, told the police that I would have to go to hospital immediately. The two officers assigned the task of taking me there were the same two officers with whom I'd had the altercation earlier. On the way to the hospital they were making sarcastic remarks, until I told them both that they ought to be careful. 'What do you mean, be careful?' they asked.

I said, 'Just be fucking careful, because that uniform won't save you.'

From there on in, things deteriorated rapidly.

The accident and emergency department was full of people – not unusual around closing time in Basildon. The officers said they wouldn't let me into the hospital until they had handcuffed me for the safety of others. I told them it was fucking ludicrous and that I wasn't going to walk around in a public place with handcuffs on. They insisted that they wouldn't let me go into the hospital unless I was handcuffed. There was a brief struggle and eventually they managed to get them on me.

They then took me into the public waiting-room and I was told to sit down while they went to fetch a nurse. I was extremely embarrassed and continued to demand that the officers remove the handcuffs, but they refused. One officer went to talk to one of the nurses and when he returned he said we were going back to the police station. I reminded him that nobody had examined my eyes, which the doctor had insisted needed medical attention. The officers ignored me and repeated that we were going back to the police station. With my hands cuffed behind my back, there was little or nothing I could do. Half an hour after being sent to hospital, I was back in the cell. By this time, my eyes were extremely swollen and sore.

'Fuck them,' I thought. I decided I would lie down, close my burning eyes and hopefully sleep for the remainder of the night.

The following morning I used tea, which had been brought to me for breakfast, to wash my eyes out. It helped but they remained painful and my vision was impaired. At 3 p.m., a detective came to my cell to take me to the interview room. I had a rough idea of what I was going to say, but I was unaware of how much evidence the police had on me. I decided I would wait to hear what the detective had to say before telling my side of the story. The officer interviewing me told me a member of the staff at the club had called the police after a man had run inside screaming that I had brandished a knife outside the premises. He told me they had seized the CCTV footage and it clearly showed me lunging at this man with a large combat knife. I asked the officer if they had the video footage from inside the club, and he said he hadn't as the video inside the club had not been working.

As soon as he said that, I knew I was home and dry. I said to him that he only had half of the story.

'What do you mean?' he asked.

'That man attacked me inside the club, sprayed me with ammonia and pulled out a knife when we started to struggle,' I replied. 'When he tried to stab me, I took the knife off him and fearing for my safety, went outside. The man followed me outside and was asking me to give him back the knife. I didn't want to, as I thought he was going to stab me, so I refused. When he came towards me, I pushed him away, but then he attacked me with a container full of ammonia. Having been temporarily blinded, I feared for my safety, I pulled out his knife, which I had secreted down the back of my trousers, and he ran away screaming. I had pulled out his knife purely to defend myself. When he ran back into the club, I didn't run inside after him as the danger had passed.

'I stood outside for five or ten minutes. No taxis would take Emma and me home, so we walked across the car park where you arrested me approximately 15 minutes after the incident.

'If you ask the arresting officers, they will tell you I said, "It's OK, I've got the knife, I took it off a lunatic."'

'But that's not what other people are saying,' the interviewing officer said, 'they're saying it's your knife.'

'Well, you had better get these people to make statements, because it's not my knife. It belongs to the man who attacked me, he owns the knife,' I said.

The detective said he had spoken to Gaffer and he did not want to make a statement.

I knew Gaffer wouldn't give evidence against me so my defence was safe. I told the detective that Gaffer didn't want to make a statement because he had the knife in the first place and he was the one who attacked me. The officer insisted he had other witnesses and therefore I would be charged.

'Fair enough,' I said, 'fucking charge me.'

The detective said, 'OK,' and read the following charge to me: 'That without lawful authority or reasonable excuse, you had with you in a public place an offensive weapon, namely a knife.' He also alleged that I had used or threatened unlawful violence towards another, and my conduct was such as would cause a person of reasonable firmness present at the scene to fear for his or her personal safety.

I started laughing. 'How can you call a person reasonable when he's trying to blind you with ammonia?'

The officer just looked at me and said, 'Those are the charges, have you anything to say?' I did not reply, but the officer wrote on the charge sheet that I had replied, 'Guilty.' Fortunately for me, the interview was also being recorded on tape. I decided to say nothing about his error because I knew I would be able to use it against the police when the case was heard in court.

I was bailed to appear at Basildon Magistrates' Court and then released. It's hard to explain how depressing an incident like this can be.

You go out for a drink with your partner and you end up being locked up for the best part of 24 hours. After your release, you spend months agonising over whether or not you will receive a prison sentence.

And for what? For some drug-pedalling peasant who took it upon himself to try and attack you in the presence of your girlfriend and blind you with ammonia for no reason. His motive? You had assisted the police, who then lock you up and charge you for resisting the attack. Your attacker, meanwhile, walks free. It is absolutely sickening and I can fully understand why some people end up serving life-sentences for murdering this type of subhuman. The law tells you to turn your cheek and walk away from it, but what is the point of walking away when these low-lifes will just stab you in the back, cut you, maim you or try to blind you? It is pointless walking away. I should have left him lying in the gutter where he belonged. Once more, the never-ending trauma of going back and forth to court became part of my life.

The uncertainty of my future and the pressure of preparing for yet another trial left me marking time in complete misery.

In January 1999, a journalist from the *Observer* newspaper contacted me. He wanted to know what I thought about ex-Raquels doorman Mark Rothermel breaking out of custody in Congo–Brazzaville.

I was surprised Mark had been locked up in the Congo, but not surprised he had escaped. I had no idea where Mark had got to after the firm had self-destructed and so I asked the journalist what it was all about. He told me that Mark had been arrested in Brazzaville in November 1998 on suspicion of spying. He said that some time during the last week, Mark had escaped during a fierce gun battle from a police station where he was being held with 40 other people. The British Consul in Brazzaville was helping the local police search for him.

Mark had told friends that he had agreed to do voluntary work for Mission Aid, but checks with the Charity Commission had revealed that Mission Aid had ceased to exist two years previously. It also emerged that Mark had made a trip to the Congo two years earlier and had recently visited Russia and California, supposedly in connection with charity work. I thought the survival skills Mark had employed whilst hiding out in the woods after hacking off Bernie Burns's head and hands would be coming in useful now that he was trying to avoid the Brazzaville police. The journalist said he still had no idea of Mark's whereabouts or why he had been held without charge for two months. 'It's not very clear what is behind this,' he said. 'There is a civil war there and the authorities are very sensitive about people he may have had contact with.'

A few days later, Mark contacted the Foreign Office and told them he was alive and well, but he would not give them his location. It was later reported in the press that Mark had been sentenced to death in his absence by a court in the Congo. Wherever Mark was, I was sure he would not be hanging around there. Mark is an extremely adventurous, up-for-it man. Intelligent, fit and quick to spot an earner, many of his exploits seem somewhat eccentric to those who meet him.

In 1985, Mark had wanted to find a descendant of the dinosaurs called Mokele-mbembe, an African version of the Loch Ness monster, which is said to inhabit uncharted swamps. Together with another man, Bill Gibbons, he set up Operation Congo in the hope of gaining financial sponsorship. Mark did eventually go on the trip but failed to find the creature.

Bill Gibbons was greatly influenced by an American missionary couple he met, and according to a relative of another member of the expedition, he found God in the jungle. I suppose finding God is a better result than finding the African Loch Ness monster. Only Mark knows what he found in the jungle and why he chose to return there 14 years later. I have a sneaking suspicion it was not God or he would have brought him down to meet me at Raquels.

I heard nothing else of Mark until May 2001 when he and several other people were arrested for importing drugs onto a Suffolk beach by boat. Mark was named as the leader of the drugs gang, which aimed to import high-grade herbal cannabis and amphetamine from Holland. The plan was foiled when customs and excise officers, backed by armed police, intercepted the gang. Customs officers had observed Mark over a period of months carrying out checks on remote beaches on the east coast. Maps and notes giving marks out of ten for good landing spots were later found.

The notes, written in Mark's handwriting, gave Bawdsey Quay in Suffolk ten out of ten as the ideal site for landing drugs. Mark and another man had travelled from Dover to Zeebrugge and then on to the Netherlands, where they acquired 3.3 kilos of amphetamine and 40 kilos of 'skunk' cannabis with a street value of around £60,000. They loaded the drugs into a specially designed motorboat, which had arrived from Point Clear near Clacton. They then travelled back to the UK via the Channel Tunnel to await the return of the boat at Bawdsey Bay beach. A reception party of almost 100 customs officers, firearms officers from Essex, Norfolk, Suffolk and Kent police forces and a Suffolk police helicopter swooped as the boat landed at 8 a.m.

The trial was held at Woolwich Crown Court in south London. Alongside Mark in the dock stood Brian Richardson, a man I knew well from Dagenham; John McCann, another man I had met on the Essex scene; and Guy Clements, a doorman at a nightclub called The Venue in Ilford. I had heard of Clements – he had been involved with an Essex chapter of the Hell's Angels. Another man, Matthew Howes, had also worked as a nightclub doorman. Two females had also been arrested: Denise Smith, the manager of The Venue, and Bonnie Simon, who was a lap dancer at Stringfellows nightclub and tabloid topless model. Both females were acquitted. Richardson was sentenced to three-and-a-half years, Clements and Howes to three and Mark Rothermel was given five.

I had written to the Crown Prosecution Service after the first two court hearings concerning the knife incident with Gaffer and asked them to drop the charges, as there was little or no evidence to disprove my version of events and only a little to support theirs, but they refused. Changing tack, I made a lot of the fact that the detective had mistakenly recorded my reply to the charge, a point which would prove extremely embarrassing for Essex Police should it be aired in open court. Eventually, after a lot of haggling and mind-numbing games, they dropped both the charges.

The case had attracted publicity locally when the management at the Festival Leisure Park announced that they had decided to ban me from the complex for life. This meant I couldn't take my children to the cinema, Pizza Hut, McDonald's, bowling or any of the other normal activities children enjoy. To ensure I got the point, they even sent me an official certificate which carried my punishment of being cast out into the wilderness for life in fancy bold type. Choosing to ignore their petulance, I took my children into the drive-through at McDonald's a few weeks later. Within minutes, four police cars arrived and we were asked to leave. When I pointed out I hadn't been convicted of any wrongdoing, I was told it was not me the management were concerned about, it was other people having a go at me. 'You are being banned for your own safety,' the officer said with a wry smile. When I stopped laughing, I drove off.

I had been banned from working as a doorman for seven years, banned for life from setting foot in Bas Vegas and was being attacked by dope heads when I went for a drink with my girlfriend. For what? Apart from giving evidence in the Betts case, what had I done to warrant such treatment? I didn't need to be told it was time to move on.

I had expanded considerably the haulage business I managed in Cambridgeshire and it was now taking up more and more of my time. My working day was growing longer and this was affecting my relationship with Emma. Her mother had recently been killed in a tragic accident and Emma was feeling isolated and lonely when I wasn't there. The answer was staring me in the face, I had to leave Essex. Emma and I moved to a place called Stanground in Peterborough and soon settled in. It's hard to describe how I felt – it was as if the troubles of the world had been lifted from my shoulders. For the first time in years, I felt free.

As a parting shot, I had decided that I would make a complaint against the police officers who had not taken me for medical treatment and the officer who had written down 'guilty' on my charge sheet when, in actual fact, the tape-recording of my response to the charge clearly proved that I had made no reply whatsoever. I made these complaints against Essex Police on 9 June 1999. Two years and eight months after the incident with Gaffer, Essex Police finally managed to complete their investigation into my complaint. They had only spent six months investigating the murders of Tucker, Tate and Rolfe so why it took almost three years to investigate a simple complaint, which only involved myself and officers from the same force, I shall never know.

Out of eight separate complaints surrounding the incident, only one was found in my favour. This complaint had been that a detective had incorrectly recorded the reply I gave to him when charged. Fortunately, he could not dispute this as the written record and tape-recording of the interview had not been 'lost', as so many important items are these days in police stations.

In a letter to me, the Police Complaints Authority concluded:

The officer did record an incorrect reply to the caution following charge. It is the intention of the Force to have the officer seen by his Divisional Commander and advised with regard to the importance of accurately recording information. Advice is a form of police discipline, similar to an oral warning, and is neither given nor received lightly.

The officer had told his superiors that he had made an error because he was writing his reply from memory.

When a suspect makes no comment whatsoever and a police officer writes down the suspect has said he is guilty, I would suggest that the officer needs more than advice. With such a poor memory he certainly shouldn't be gathering evidence.

In October 1999, I heard that my good friend Darren Pearman (from the Epping Forest Country Club and a member of the Canning Town firm) had been having a bit of trouble with Ronnie Fuller, one of the doormen I had worked with at the Ministry of Sound. Ronnie was working on the door one evening at a venue in north London. Darren was in the club with the rest of the Canning Town firm and they had got into a row with somebody. It was said that Darren hit a man in the face with a beer bottle so Ronnie had no choice but to ask Darren to leave. Once outside, the threats started. People were telling each other they 'were dead', saying, 'We'll be back', and all the usual threats that are made outside nightclubs up and down the country every weekend.

Ronnie thought nothing of it as he'd heard these threats a thousand times. The only problem was, he hadn't heard them from Darren Pearman and the Canning Town firm. If they tell you they're coming back, be sure to expect them.

Not long afterwards, Darren, his brother and the rest of their firm were in the Epping Forest Country Club where I had worked and first met Darren and Ronnie. The Canning Town firm were in the Casino Bar enjoying themselves. Ronnie was working where I used to work – in the Atlantic Bar, where they played jungle music, and where most of the revellers went to dance. Later on in the evening, the Canning Town firm left the Casino Bar and went over to the bar where Ronnie was on the door.

Nobody was quite sure what happened next, but a scuffle turned into a massive brawl. During the chaos that ensued, Darren and his brother were both stabbed. Under no circumstances would members of the Canning Town firm call the police and calling an ambulance always results in alerting the police, so Darren was put into a taxi and rushed to hospital.

Sadly, Darren never made it. He died en route. He was 27 years old. Ronnie and two other men were arrested in connection with his murder but when the police sought witnesses, members of the Canning Town firm and others refused to assist. They told police they would sort out matters themselves. Eventually, because of lack of evidence, Ronnie and the other two men were released. If I had been Ronnie, I would have left the country, but Ronnie underestimated the friends of Darren Pearman. The Canning Town firm are without doubt, the real deal. You fuck with them at your peril. Ronnie did take some precautions – he moved approximately 20 miles from Loughton in Essex to Grays, also in Essex. It was never going to be far enough.

Throughout his endless years in prison, death was always going to be Reg Kray's biggest enemy. Release would have left Reg free to enjoy his notoriety and make the most of his celebrity status, but fame had rigged the odds in death's favour. With every book he published and every year that passed, the chance of him ever gaining freedom lessened.

Reg knew deep down that so long as he promoted the name Kray he would never be free, but he could never sit in prison and not enjoy his celebrity status. It was his name that kept him going, but time was closing in on him.

Had Reg played the game and served his sentence without the publicity, he would have been released in the spring of 1998, having served his full 30-year recommended sentence. He would also have been free to seek out whatever medical advice he needed and the cancer he didn't yet know he had would almost certainly have been discovered in its early stages. Instead, during those last two years, while the prison doctors were dismissing his complaints of agonising pain and chronic constipation, and prescribing milk of magnesia and yet more milk of magnesia, the cancer had been advancing in Reggie's body, moving from his bladder to his bowel. The crisis came in the second week of August 2000 when he suddenly vomited black bile and blood while in his cell.

An ambulance rushed him from Wayland Prison to a hospital in Norwich.

There the doctors took his medical condition more seriously and investigations confirmed a major intestinal blockage needing immediate surgery. During the four-hour operation, doctors discovered a tumour the size of a man's fist in his bowel and, at one point, thought he was dying from a heart attack. In fact, because of the loss of blood, Reggie's heart had faltered. When he came round from the operation, hope continued for some sort of recovery, but tests carried out soon made it clear that he was going to die. The cancer was aggressive and the blockage total. Reg couldn't eat or even drink. His only nourishment was through an intravenous drip. A drain was inserted in his kidneys; morphine controlled the pain.

Pressure grew on the Home Secretary to grant Reggie compassionate release. His lawyers had sent the Home Secretary a letter and then, after waiting year in and year out for the Home Secretary to recommend his release, it was granted so quickly that Reg found it hard to believe that he was finally free. The Home Office announced: 'As an act of mercy, under Section 31 of the Criminal Justice Act, Her Majesty's Secretary of State for Home Affairs has seen fit to grant Reg Kray his liberty.'

Now that Reg could hardly walk and was unable to feed himself, he was, for what it was worth, 'free'. Although he had the freedom he had craved for over 30 years, there was nowhere he could go. Despite the numerous books, newspaper articles and a film that had all helped him remain behind bars, Reggie Kray, king of the London underworld, was broke. The manager of the Town House Hotel on the outskirts of Norwich offered Reg his honeymoon suite with riverside views and a four-poster bed for £37.50 a night. Reggie accepted. Bill Curbishley, friend of the Kray family and wealthy manager of The Who, agreed to pay the hotel bill. The glamorous and celebrity-packed life Reg had talked about for decades was going to end in a low-budget room that he couldn't even afford.

Ten months had passed since the murder of Darren Pearman. Rather foolishly, people started to believe that his death was not to be avenged. What they didn't appreciate was that it takes time to organise an assassination. The assassins need to know where the target lives, works and when it is safest to carry out the hit. Darren Pearman's murder had far from been forgotten. His friends were as angry ten months on as they had been on the night he died.

On Bank Holiday Monday, 29 August, violence once more erupted at Epping Forest Country Club. About 3,000 people were thought to have been at the venue when, at 3 a.m., around 30 started fighting in the car park. The doormen ran out to try and break up the fight, but as they did so, a man took out a gun and shot two of them. One doorman was hit in the back, the other took a bullet in the stomach. Rumour and speculation were rife and everybody was saying that the shootings were connected to Darren's murder. Some thought this was the comeback everyone had been expecting, but they were wrong. This was just another Essex boy who didn't like doormen interfering in his business. Another Essex boy who would probably end up suffering an undignified death like his East End hero Reg Kray, who at the time was wasting away in a hotel.

At 7.45 a.m., less than five hours after the shootings at the Country Club, Ronnie Fuller left his home at Parkside, in Grays. Ronnie was on his way to work and was only yards from his gate when a man got off a motorcycle parked nearby and approached him. As he walked up to Ronnie he pulled out a 9mm pistol and shot Ronnie twice in the head and twice in the chest. The gunman turned and calmly walked away before riding off. Ronnie's wife Larissa ran screaming from the bungalow where they lived with their three-year-old son. Larissa held her blood-soaked husband until an ambulance came to take him away. Shortly after 8 a.m., Ronnie was pronounced dead at Basildon General Hospital. He was 30 years of age. Despite a huge police investigation, his killer has never been apprehended.

I was upset when I heard that Darren and Ronnnie had been murdered. My friend Chris Lombard had been murdered a few years earlier, and my friend Larry Johnston was serving a life sentence for murder. Four young men cut down in their prime and for what? A stupid argument in a tacky disco or pub. A stupid argument that had resulted in someone losing face, stupid arguments that had resulted in the waste of four young men's lives. Tell their mothers gangsters are fucking chic.

Reggie Kray, a man whom many young men aspire to be and who was in part responsible for the birth of gangster chic, had settled into his hotel and agreed to give a final interview for a television programme.

There were things he wanted to say, he said, things he wanted to share before he finally died. Paramount for him was the fact that he believed the road he had taken had been a terrible and painful one. He felt that if by speaking directly he could deter others from taking the same road, then perhaps something good could eventually come from it all. During the interview, Reg was extremely honest and extremely open. He did not want anybody to endure what he had been through. Reg knew only too well what he had lost and why he had lost it.

The majority of his life had been taken away and he knew it had been a tragic waste. His reputation and a place in history were not a fair exchange for 32 years in prison. He knew that respect was not more important than love. He knew that existing in legend did not make up for existing in real life. His brother Ronnie would disagree, because, for Ron, being a gangster was everything. Ron, however, had an excuse: he was mentally ill, his judgement clouded by paranoia.

Reg had learned too late that being a gangster meant nothing. Sadly, Reggie's words came too late for many of my dead friends, who saw the Krays as something of a criminal benchmark to match or surpass.

Throughout their lives, the Krays had been driven by publicity. As young boxers, the press had bestowed some essential meaning on their mundane lives. It was the press who had lifted them from the East End and onto the front pages of another world. Through boxing, street fights and teenage court appearances, it was the newspapers that evoked an unexpected and gratifying local respect.

That misguided respect gave them confidence and this confidence gradually inspired a very different kind of ambition. Success at any cost became imperative. Infamy and fame were two sides of the same coin. Like resentful partners, the Krays and the press fed off each other, each needing something only the other could provide.

Reg Kray died a free man on 1 October 2000, five weeks short of his sixty-seventh birthday. He died as he lived, in the midst of controversy. When it was announced who was to carry Reggie's coffin, Freddie Foreman and Tony Lambrianou insisted that they were going to boycott his funeral. A few days later, Reggie Kray's funeral took place. Unlike the earlier Kray funerals, Reggie's was ridiculed by the press. One headline read: 'He wanted a statesman's funeral but all he got was a freak-show full of has-beens.' The press seemed determined to bury the Kray myth along with the last family member.

WANNABE IN MY GANG?

Supposed 'celebrity' and underworld friends stayed away in droves after a row with Reggie's widow Roberta over the pallbearers. A pitiful collection of has-beens, wannabes and never-will-bes, looking more like the Blues Brothers than Reservoir Dogs, came to mourn their hero. Crowds of 50,000 were predicted, but the turn-out was a fraction of that, although, true to form, there were a few old grannies banging on about how the East End was safer when the Kray twins were running it. In a sleazy, undignified end, Reggie's coffin was carried out of the undertakers by six bearers, including boxer Adam Myhill, Kray solicitor Mark Goldstein, Bradley Allardyce and East 17 singer Tony Mortimer. The Kray firm must have misunderstood when they were told 'this lad is big in East 17'. They obviously thought this meant Tony Mortimer controlled Dalston, not that he mimed to shitty ballads from the '50s. The coffin was placed in a Victorian-style hearse, drawn by six black, plumed horses and driven by a Dickensian undertaker in a long black coat and top hat. The sides of the carriage bore the floral messages 'free at last' and 'respect'.

Behind came 16 black Volvo limousines, carrying friends and relatives. As expected, the cortège slowed in Vallence Road by the Krays' old house, then it drove to nearby St Matthew's Church. The mourners spilled from cars like so many clichés from ancient gangster films. A regiment of bull-necked security men with shaven heads, tiny earpieces on wires snaking into the collars of their black shirts, enjoyed their 15 minutes of fame. Despite the overcast weather they wore dark glasses to try and look the part.

While male mourners sporting chunky gold jewellery and ill-fitting suits tried to look hard, for the women it was clearly no effort. Many boasted bottle-blonde hair, perma-tans and tight tops. Miniskirts and high heels completed the look. It was a kind of pantomime of people too old, fat or brassy to make it as extras in *Lock, Stock and Two Smoking Barrels*.

The minders, probably fancying themselves as the new rulers of the East End streets, told the public where they could or could not stand. Bradley Allardyce, who had been Reggie's best man at his wedding to Roberta, told the congregation: 'I look for the words, but there are none.'

Reggie's coffin was carried out of church to the predictable strains of 'My Way', and then he was off to Chingford Cemetery to be buried alongside his first wife, Frances, his brothers, his father and his mother Violet.

Before Reggie's grave had been filled, his friends began to betray him. Bradley Allardyce decided to share some of his memories of Reg, in a BBC radio interview. He admitted to having a sexual relationship with Reg but added, 'It was against my will and he knew it was against my will.' Allardyce, who had written to me saying 'Reg was like a father, I love him very much', was claiming that Reggie Kray had raped him. I couldn't help thinking of what he had said at the funeral. He was certainly not stuck for words now.

If the rape allegation wasn't enough to rubbish the name of the man Allardyce had claimed 'nobody would cross', then Allardyce had prepared a second, equally heinous allegation. He went on to claim that one night, Reggie revealed the crime that haunted him the most: the apparent suicide of his first wife, Frances. Allardyce told Radio Four listeners that, 'He put his head on my shoulder and told me Ron killed Frances. He told Reg what he had done two days after he had murdered her. He claimed Ronnie had forced Frances to take the pills that had killed her.' The Kray gravy train had been derailed and the passengers who had lived off it for so long were clambering to salvage a bit of it to enhance their miserable lives.

Kray family 'friend', Maureen Flannagan, the page-three girl who took the bids at James Fallon's fundraising evening, also cashed in by auctioning off her personal letters via a Kray website. I have no doubt they were of great sentimental value to her.

The Kray family are all better off in Chingford Cemetery; amongst the living, they really had nobody. At least in death, they have each other.

As the crowds drifted away from Reggie's funeral, a teenager ran up to his friends and cried, 'I've just shaken Frankie Fraser's hand. I'm never going to wash this hand again.' It was a sad day in Bethnal Green when they buried the last of the Krays. A very, very sad day indeed.

13

PINKY AND PERKY

I believed that when Reg Kray was laid to rest, the gangster-chic industry that he and his twin had made flourish would be buried with him. Unfortunately, Kray fans saw it as an opportunity to promote themselves as heirs to their hero's vacant underworld throne by telling stories in 'true crime' books they thought would never be challenged. I was more than surprised when I heard that Leighton Frayne had published a book in 2003 called *The Frayne Brothers* with the sub-heading: 'Welcome to the terrifying world of the notorious Frayne brothers'.

I laughed so much when I saw the book, I was almost tempted to read it. However, the brief description of the terrifying world of the Frayne brothers on the cover proved too much for me. It described how the Fraynes had 'ruled their patch with a fair but firm hand'. It also claimed that the Fraynes were 'the brains and brawn behind one of the most ruthless and organised firms in the UK'. 'Violence and honour,' the cover blurb went on to say, 'are their watchwords' and 'they are more than ready to make sure that justice is maintained in the underworld'. Picking myself up off the bookshop floor, I wiped the tears from my eyes, caught my breath and stifled my laughter. Only three sentences I had read seemed to have a ring of truth about them and they had been saved until last: 'Much has been written about them. Little of it is based on fact. Now they tell their story.'

Like Lambrianou, the Fraynes have undoubtedly told 'their story' to anybody gullible enough not to question it. They will hope people will believe them and they can fulfil their dream and become gangland legends. As in Lambrianou's case, their story will have little to do with the truth.

The real Fraynes are a far cry from the gangland heavies they would like people to believe they are and I am quite certain that, like Lambrianou, the Fraynes will be bitterly disappointed that the truth is now being revealed. Not long after I had been banned from seeing Ronnie Kray at Broadmoor, brothers Lindsay and Leighton Frayne stepped into my vacant visiting shoes. The Fraynes were the Hale and Pace lookalikes from south Wales who had turned up at the boxing show in full Kray twin fancy dress. Meeting Ronnie sent their egos into overdrive and they began to really believe that they were the new Krays.

Everyone I spoke to was telling me about these two Kray wannabes who were trying to impress nobodies in the hope that they would be treated as somebodies. They began to make regular trips from their native Wales to London in order to try to form a gang based on the Kray model. They didn't immerse themselves in the underworld or associate with active criminals; instead, the Frayne gang lived a ridiculous copycat Kray lifestyle, intimidating people in their own circle, talking about 'big jobs' they were going to pull off, laying flowers on the Kray parents' graves, visiting their heroes' old haunts and propping up the bar in The Blind Beggar where Ron Kray had shot George Cornell through the head. In the evening they would head for the safety of the suburbs, drinking in pubs around Epping Forest where few, if any, of the wealthy residents had come into contact with the real Krays. The East End after dark was, after all, a dangerous place to be for two Welsh boyos from the valleys. Everybody was laughing at their antics. They would walk into pubs surrounded by as many as 15 minders all dressed in suits. Mark Bullen, one of the boys who used to fetch and carry for the DJ at Raquels, even managed to get into their gang.

In a desperate effort to be recognised and acknowledged, the Fraynes sought out publicity. They thought they had finally hit the big time when the *People* contacted them for an interview, but the subsequent article only poked fun at them.

PINKY AND PERKY

MEET THE KRAY TWINS' TWINS

East End Mobsters Recruit Lookalike Boyos From The Valleys

Jailed gangland killers the Krays have recruited clone twins as their right-hand men on the outside. Twins Ronnie and Reggie have formed an amazing bond with 30-year-old lookalike brothers Lindsay and Leighton Frayne.

Hard man Leighton, like Broadmoor inmate Ronnie, is the quieter of the two and likes to be known as 'the thinker'. Lindsay, like Reggie, looks younger, smoother and has the patter.

The Frayne twins dress like the Krays complete with slicked-back hair, Crombie coats, double-breasted designer suits and tie pins. They are inseparable and shared a prison cell after nearly killing a man over a family feud.

They were amateur boxers who learned to fight their way out of trouble as vicious street brawlers. Locals couldn't believe their eyes when they spotted the twins outside The Blind Beggar in Bethnal Green, where Ronnie Kray had blown away George Cornell.

The bizarre similarities only end when the Frayne twins open their mouths, for they are Welsh boyos from the Welsh valleys, and both insist they aren't involved in any villainy. 'We're no gangsters,' stressed 14-stone Leighton, 'we're businessmen. The Krays trust us to handle their merchandising affairs, we make money for them the legit way.'

I knew it wouldn't be long before Lindsay and Leighton were back in the news. I didn't expect it to be as contestants on *Mastermind* either. They were clearly desperate to follow in the Krays' footsteps and I was fairly confident that the way they were putting themselves about, they would succeed. It was not, after all, that difficult to get locked up in prison if you put your mind to it.

The curtain finally came down on the Fraynes' East End stage performance of pantomime gangsters when they were arrested for a £10,000 armed raid on a building society in their hometown of Newbridge, Gwent. They had planned to use their ill-gotten gains to finance their new crime empire in London, but the raid on the Halifax was badly bungled. An accomplice, Steve Cook, was apprehended trying to make his getaway on a bus after the getaway car had broken down.

The two women cashiers who were behind the counter that day were so badly traumatised by their ordeal that neither has worked since. It's a pity they didn't realise they were being confronted by fools. When the police began to look into the activities of the Frayne gang, they learned that they had also planned to kidnap soccer star Paul Gascoigne.

Paul Edwards was recruited as a minder by the Fraynes and he had been told that his job was to 'look mean' when they were out in public together. Seventeen-stone Edwards, a former SAS soldier, had been working as a chauffeur and bodyguard for Gascoigne when he had been playing for Tottenham Hotspur. It was claimed that the gang had suggested Edwards use his position to abduct the star, who was then playing for Lazio in Rome, and they would hold him for ransom. The kidnap plot was part of the fantasy world the Frayne gang had immersed itself in and so it never did happen.

Another witness told police that he was present when Edwards and the Fraynes discussed a plot to kidnap a Morecambe businessman until an underworld debt of £132,000 had been paid.

Leighton Frayne had been so desperate to be known as the new Ronnie Kray, he had even tried to copy Ronnie's schizophrenia-induced outbursts, exploding into theatrical violence without any obvious reason or warning. The Frayne entourage would embroider the facts when telling others about these tantrums. This boosted the Fraynes' egos and satisfied their craving for a reputation as violent gangsters.

One former associate told how a replica gun was rammed into his mouth during a row. What harm a replica gun could to do to him, only the replica Krays could know. A pub landlord almost laughed as he described how they had tried to start a protection racket in Newbridge. He told police that when the Fraynes approached him he said, 'Where do you think you are, Chicago? I told them to get out.'

The brothers even tried to silence witnesses as their heroes had done prior to their trial in 1969. Three ex-associates complained of menacing phone calls and letters warning them not to testify, and one potential witness beaten up by the Fraynes sold his home and vanished. He has still not been traced. One suspects that fleeing from the Fraynes has proven to be acutely embarrassing.

At their bungled-robbery trial, the Fraynes pleaded not guilty. After hearing the evidence, which often brought howls of laughter from the public gallery, and deliberating for 13 hours the jurors found them guilty of armed robbery, possession of an illegal weapon and conspiracy to deal in firearms. As they stood stony-faced in the dock at Newport Crown Court, Judge Michael Gibbon told the pair, 'You have to be deterred from committing armed robbery.' He then jailed them for a total of eight years.

Before their first bowl of prison porridge had gone cold, Tony Lambrianou was giving an interview to a tabloid newspaper about his meetings with the Kray clones. As I began to read the article, I was not surprised to learn that 'boxing promoter' James Campbell had been one of the Frayne brothers' entourage. The article described how he had introduced Lambrianou to the brothers whilst 'surrounded by seven burly minders'. From what I had seen of their minders, it was more likely their pantomime counterparts, the seven dwarfs, that had surrounded them.

Lambrianou told the reporter:

> The Fraynes didn't just want to know or be associated with the Krays, they wanted to be them. They told me they had a business in Wales and were hoping to make a film about the Krays in which they would play the twins.
>
> They said how much they admired the twins and said that Lindsay, the quiet one, was the Reg and Leighton, the slick one, was the Ron.
>
> As the evening wore on I realised they were obsessed, they even drank the same drinks. The 'Ron' drank light ale and the 'Reg' drank gin and tonic. It was unnerving. Those boys seemed to want to get inside the skin of Reg and Ron.
>
> They wanted to know every detail, where they bought their clothes, where they had their hair cut, who manicured their nails, what underwear they wore. I realised there was something warped about them. After 15 years in prison you have that sixth sense. Film research or not, they sent shivers up my spine. I sniffed that something wasn't right. It was like a *Fatal Attraction*-type thing, it really disturbed me.

Lambrianou's ability to sniff out a fake cannot be questioned, as he himself is in the top half of the counterfeit champions league.

When the cell door slammed shut on the Fraynes, I really believed they would wake up and realise just how foolish their fascination with two failed gangsters had been. I thought they would stop their ridiculous charade and get on with living their lives in the here and now. I was of course totally wrong. The Fraynes revelled in their new-found notoriety. It didn't matter that the tabloid press had poked fun at them after their trial.

One headline read, 'They thought they were the Krays but we called them "Pinky and Perky"'. The Fraynes told themselves that the press always had it in for Ron and Reg and so it was to be expected that they would be subjected to negative publicity too. Locking the Krays up had been the only way the government had been able to stop them from taking over London, or so the East End myth goes. So it was no surprise that the Fraynes began to claim they had been fitted up because the authorities were concerned about their activities.

In letters from prison, 'Ron the slick one' (or Leighton as his mother christened him) told a pen pal that despite the humiliating press reports they had endured following the trial, the Krays had not only stood by them, but supported them. Nothing, it seemed, was going to stop the Fraynes from living out their fantasy.

Prison had not only removed Leighton from society. It had distanced him even further from reality. One letter read:

> There is no rift with Reg and Ron. Some of the prosecution witnesses have asked Reg and Ron to print bad of us in return for money, but those people don't understand the close friendship and bond that Reg and Ron have with me and Lindsay. Reg and Ron are both fine. I received a letter off Reg yesterday as I do every week. Ron writes me when he's in the mood. Just like my brother, he doesn't like writing. I am like Reg, I write, for it pleases me and pleases the friends I write to.
>
> As for looking like Reggie and Ronnie, I have a difference of opinion. I see my brother looking like Reg and he says that he doesn't look like Reg but he sees me like Ron. But, yes, I do agree, it is uncanny. Even Reg and Ron see the likeness. It has been said that me and Lindsay have the deeds to Reggie and Ronnie's prime. I suppose that is true, but I wouldn't call it a firm.
>
> That's old fashioned. I would remould it on a machine; every little cog counts. All our minders had been sent by our elders.

Our personal friends seemed to take the roles of minders. There are four teams of minders, only two at one time are aware that they are active. The other two teams remain in the background. It all depends where we go. On some occasions in London there have to be 12 to 14 people at one time that you would be aware of. Some may get our drinks, watch the toilets. Sometimes the attention can get you down but I got used to it after a while. Yes, we have all the doors flung open for us. Never paid for drinks, yet offered all sorts of deals. What can you do when it is put in your lap?

When in London I feel it goes over the top, but people have jobs to do, they are classed as our minders. I am prepared to have my people way in the background as it can offend.

I was at Browns nightclub. Me and Lindsay had friends with us and some chap was making rude comments, and the older element didn't say nothing. I thought the doormen were very good, but they too had a stand-back approach, so I brought my people in. They had a word with the person in question and the night ended happily from my point of view. So, yes, the attention can get you down. I lose myself in the mountains and enjoy listening to the birds and the fresh air. I don't need minders when I'm in the mountains. It's where I grew up.

I sometimes think I am glad to be back in Wales, just to be myself. I don't think my life is like something out of James Bond. It can become very sexy if I so desired, but it's how you look at it. I like meeting new friends and believe there are good and bad in all walks of life; the police are more corrupt and more active than villains. That's my personal view. Please remember that I am not Ronnie, I am who I am. I really don't think I will end up like the Krays.

Rarely have I been known to praise the police but I must thank them for halting the rise of the Frayne gang, as we may have had to endure more of 'Ron the slick one's' ramblings had the robbery been a success. Stating that he didn't think he would end up like the Krays in a letter penned from his prison cell, just about sums up his grasp on reality. Leighton must have sat in his cell wondering what he could do next to enhance the Frayne brothers' rather dismal criminal reputation.

Few in prison would bother listening to him and so he decided he would turn to the public in the hope of gaining a fix of much-needed attention. Leighton decided that he would write the Frayne brothers' life story, which he believed would be turned into a film. Leighton assured his pen pal that this was not them writing a book just to copy the Krays, as the press would undoubtedly insinuate:

> My book is coming along fine. I won't rush it. I have been offered a deal for a film but I must think on it. The book won't be along the lines of *Our Story*, it will be an account of my life, the pain, the happiness, trouble, pleasure.
>
> So much has happened in my life and I felt that it should have been written later in my life, but I have been asked to put a book together from many companies, some of whom are dear friends of mine. I will write the text myself but can be put right with my spelling mistakes.
>
> All my fights I have had, which were some pretty violent fights, will be revealed in my book. I was stabbed very bad, through the lung, heart and spleen and seven other small wounds. Pretty bad ones, but that's life isn't it? I don't like bullshit. I am a man of my word. I have been to America several times but not as me, if you know what I mean? I enjoy my own company even though I am here for something I didn't do.
>
> It's a lot easier as I have no wife and no commitments to nobody, but who knows, I could meet a lady someday and settle down. If I were to have a firm, the people in the dock against me and Lindsay would be the last people I would have in any so-called firm.
>
> My publisher has given the book a name, which we agree with. It's called: *Guilty by Association: The Fraynes*. The book is planned to be published around our appeal date. It seems our solicitors are confident and our barristers.

Despite their solicitors and barristers being confident, the Fraynes lost their appeal against their conviction and the film was never made. No doubt Leighton didn't want Hollywood distorting the facts or damaging his image. It wasn't tinsel town that Leighton had to worry about rubbishing him though, it was the British Medical Association – I'm sure they would have questioned his ability to survive being stabbed 'through the heart, lung and spleen'. Then again, who would dare to ever doubt a man who claims he 'is a man of his word and hates bullshitters'?

As the Fraynes were being asked by 'many companies' to write their memoirs, it would indicate that they had a pretty extraordinary story to tell. When Leighton was asked to describe these 'extraordinary events' in his life, he told his prison pen pal:

> We have been asked to put our story together as when on remand we smashed a police station up. We have had interest of a production of a film based on that. What triggered me and Lindsay off in the police station was when we were shown disrespect by one of the sergeants. The sergeant also did that to my family. They didn't hurt me or Lindsay. Lindsay ripped his arm open by punching a cistern. We were just moved to different police stations. I went on a hunger and water strike for four days.

I couldn't imagine Quentin Tarantino entering into a bidding war for the rights to make the movie and even if he had, however much popcorn I chomped, I don't think I could sit through a film based on two failed Welsh gangsters attacking a toilet cistern in a police station. I, thankfully, wasn't thinking like Leighton. In his fertile mind the destruction of a toilet cistern could be no ordinary act of mindless vandalism if he and his brother had carried it out. Their violence, as Leighton loved to tell people, was always extreme and always extraordinary.

> I have been convicted for violence but all the convictions, I have felt, were unjust. I have always been set upon by more than one person, but I have always been able to defend myself. One sentence I did, I was given a beating by 14 Territorial Army blokes. I had to play dead, and when it all stopped I got to my feet and broke a few blokes' noses and broke arms, but I went to prison for it. Lindsay gets carried away. He once bit a bloke's ear off and ate it. The fight wasn't his fault.
>
> We were both boxers in our day. Lindsay, the boxer, me, the fighter, but to street fight we have no fears. We both have abnormal strength. We just seem to toy around but people's

bones are getting broke. But they are the ones seeking trouble and because they can't do what they're expected to do, they cry police. So that results in us getting a bad name. I was stabbed several years ago. I nearly lost my life. I was stabbed seven times, one which collapsed my lung. I paralysed the bloke that did this stabbing. It was only when I finished sorting him out that I fell to the floor with the wounds. At hospital, they lost me three times but I pulled through pretty quick. Strange things happened that day, but that's a different story. All will be revealed in my book.

'Ron the slick one' thought, unsurprisingly, that like his hero Ronnie Kray, he was misunderstood. He wasn't the hard man people believed he was, or the fool the press portrayed him as, he was, he said, 'thoughtful and generous'.

It's only other people that print the hard image. I never intended to look hard or be hard. If I could change time, I would never have fought back. I would like to consider myself kind, thoughtful and generous. I would give my last if I had it. I don't like seeing people hurt. I hate bullies. I don't like seeing children hurt, so as far as being hard, I don't know. I don't get messed about. I can be a very good friend, but a terrible enemy. I don't see that I talk bluntly about violence. I have never been the aggressor, but I don't have no mercy for my enemies. After all, why should I? They would do to me what I would do to them.

My brother and I are also artists and I would consider myself a master. I write poetry, I am also a great studier of the occult. I would consider me and Lindsay the best in all fields, such as pencil and paints. I have done a lot of work with models. I do the fantasy art side like women with tails and snakes and creatures in their hair. When I draw I feel I have turned out some nice work and have drawn pictures for judges, pop stars, etc.

I was going to get in touch with Pink Floyd to do the soundtrack for their second film, but unfortunately that can't be now. I have met many celebrities.

I have very good and genuine friends who are in the entertainment business in London, America, Australia and so on, besides underworld celebs . . . I am smiling now! I have met the old-time gangsters but I see them as people and very nice blokes.

I have met law lords, MPs. It makes you think what am I doing in here, doesn't it? Yes, I have met many stars of today. I am still in touch with many but, I keep my letters personal. That's the way I think it should be.

Like the Krays in the swinging '60s, he predictably claimed that he was well connected. Not only did he mingle with stars and celebrities, but announced he was heavily involved with the American Mafia:

Me and Lindsay have been to the core of the underworld, so as you must understand, you see nothing, you hear nothing and you say nothing. My world is fascinating, quite sexy and glamorous. I have been around the glamour, with sexy ladies. You get respect – that's nice – but I would prefer to earn respect as friends.

I can get on with most people, I speak my mind. If I don't like something, I say no. Lindsay does most of the talking on business deals. I take it all in. I work out if a person is on the level and not just wasting my time. There is plenty of mystery and tension but that is the case in all business, don't you think?

There are so many Mafia families, but we have met a man who is currently a Mafia godfather. It was his father that Ronnie met and became very good friends with, and me and Lindsay have met the son of the godfather Ronnie once knew. It is respect for Ronnie that keeps the Mafia out of the UK, but, yet again, there is nothing here to control. They have states bigger than London.

Al Capone passed the knowledge to Sophie Tucker. She passed it to Ronnie Kray and Ronnie Kray passed it to me and Lindsay. We have never told Reg and Ron our great-uncle was number-one advisor to Al Capone, but that's our secret. People seem to think that Reg and Ron gave us all our contacts abroad, but that isn't the case. Lindsay and I have been present at a lot of meetings in Wales and elsewhere. It goes deeper than what a lot of people realise, but I have to answer to my elders of which they are the cream. After all, they are never known and never will be known.

WANNABE IN MY GANG?

It would have been fun to have played a part in the Kray film. We were going to play Reg and Ron in a remake. Reg and Ron weren't happy with the first film so Ron revised his contacts with the Mafia for a second film to be made. The American actors were Al Pacino, Robert De Niro and Robert Duvall. They were going to play the Mafia bosses and some well-known British actors were going to play the British side. We were looking forward to that. Never mind, maybe later.

The reason why me and Lindsay did not attend for the major film parts in the first Kray film was we were doing a prison sentence of two years nine months.

Missing out on starring in the first Kray film because he was in jail must have been very disappointing for Leighton Frayne. I cannot begin to wonder how disappointed Pacino, De Niro and Duvall must have been to have missed out appearing alongside the Fraynes in the remake. However, that particular prison sentence was not all doom and gloom for Leighton.

When the prison officers thought that the dynamic duo were locked securely in their cell, Leighton was venturing out to distant planets, being abducted by aliens and discovering cures for a disease that has to date eluded the world of medicine:

It's a pity that the homosexuals have been hit with this Aids. I have the cure to Aids and have done so for a few years, and it is so simple. But the time is not right. I will give the cure when the time is right. It is no joke.

I am sincere in what I say. Me and Lindsay have checked, double-checked and treble-checked and it is the case. I have the cure. Freddie Mercury was to have my help, but it seems the people around him were full of shit. But it cost me nothing and I want no cash for it. I don't ask you to believe me on that; it makes no difference to me if I am believed or not. That's another story. I am not pulling your leg on the cure for Aids. I will give you a brief background on how, why and what to do. You may think it's a load of rubbish, but as you say, each to their own. It was on my last sentence and me and Lindsay did an experiment with regards to the occult and painted this circle on the floor.

This we carried out. After having a bit of a shock, I went to sleep.

Even though I am quite capable to astral travel, I had this dream that was so much like reality. I was on a modern craft, and there were ladies there with gold heads. Very pretty ladies. I watched them moving around from machine to machine and all was prepared for me. I was called over and asked to look into a microscope, and they explained what it was all about. Aids is a deliberate attempt to re-educate the population but it has got out of hand for the people who have so wrongly brought this disease to the surface.

I was on this craft for what seemed like a few days, being told this: how to give the cure and what was to be done with any money made of it, which would be a tremendous amount. I was briefed on all sorts of things – very interesting. I woke up and told Lindsay of this dream and Lindsay couldn't get over the biological talk I came out with. Being in prison, I wasn't in any position to pursue anything on this. When I was released, I made my studies and, believe it or not, I found a book well over 100 years old, and within the book it not only tells the cure, which I was told, but the name of the virus.

I could see why the Jehovah Witnesses were so funny about having people's blood. It's just they were about 80 years out. Cures have been given through dreams. Penicillin was given through a dream, so I must wait until the time is right. People have had Aids and have found themselves cured and I know why and how, and, believe me, it is so simple. It upsets me that children suffer with Aids, but I did try a major company and they were very interested, but I wouldn't give them the cure direct, unless they gave everyone a fair chance of a cure, rich, poor, everyone. But they seemed to decide that how can a bloke from Wales hold the cure, and I left it at that.

With Freddie Mercury, I felt so sorry for the bloke. I wrote a letter offering my help. I didn't want no payment, no publicity, but the letter was ignored. So much for his concern. It don't make any difference to me if he died or not. When you hold the key to life after death, life doesn't mean much. I would stake my life on the cure that I hold. That is how confident I am. People may laugh and scoff, it doesn't worry me.

So you see, that's it all in brief. Even with all the money off the cure, I would use it to give a gift of life to children that are hungry. To see a million little faces glowing with bellies full would surely be a gift in itself. Money means nothing to me.

By the time he had begun to babble in biological talk and the ladies with the golden heads had ushered him onto the spaceship, he had lost me.

Like Lambrianou, 'the gang boss', Leighton Frayne yearned to be linked to the name Kray. He became so desperate to achieve Kray status that he was prepared to gamble and lose his liberty. What Leighton failed to realise was that, like Lambrianou, his actions are a contradiction of the criminal code he and his heroes preached. Leighton wasn't behaving like the mythical criminals he yearned to emulate. He was behaving like a petty thug who really had no idea about decency, morals or ethics. Leighton told his pen pal: 'I don't believe in swearing in front of women. I will always be polite to women and never raise a hand to a woman. That's the way I've been brought up. I hope it's for good.'

But his admirable statement about being polite to women and never raising a hand to them had obviously been forgotten on the day he and his gang burst into a building society and threatened two innocent women with a gun. Perhaps the scheming police and vile press got it wrong, perhaps the Fraynes and their gang burst in and politely asked to make a large withdrawal?

As comical as they undoubtedly are, these blundering wannabe gangsters threatened, bullied and intimidated two women who were at their place of work. Like Lambrianou, Leighton Frayne is living a lie he has created, trying to portray himself as a well-mannered, firm-but-fair somebody, when in fact he is a terribly sad, third-rate nobody. When the luvvies in the media think about hyping up this failed gangster, they ought to spare a thought for the two women he terrified so much.

14

I'M A CELEBRITY? GET OUT OF HERE!

After Reggie's death, the Fraynes were not the only ones trying to salvage something from the wreckage of the fictitious Kray empire. Kate Howard, the housewife from Kent and former Mrs Kray, suddenly became an expert on the underworld and established herself as an author by publishing several books about various gangsters and murderers. Ms Kray then went on to present a television series based on one of her books, *Hard Bastards*, which purported to showcase Britain's hardest men. Unfortunately, by the time Ms Kray had got halfway through the series, the subject matter was failing to match up to the billing. In series two she was really scraping the barrel. Every wannabe and never-will-be who had been involved in a scuffle in the school playground was appearing on the show. As soon as the titles started rolling, subjects of the show would dash off to the nearest publishers, video of the programme in hand, insisting their lives as hard bastards were worthy of a book. Unfortunately for the British public, many were successful.

Tucker's old friend Carlton Leach appeared on the programme and subsequently wrote his autobiography, entitled *Muscle* (2002). On the cover of the book he boasted: 'I'm the deadliest bastard you'll ever meet.

WANNABE IN MY GANG?

If you cross me, I'll track you to the ends of the earth and destroy you.'

I knew when I picked it up I was in for a good read . . .

In a rather confusing ramble, Leach described trying to remember which 'events were significant' concerning the period leading up to the murders of his friends Tucker, Tate and Rolfe at Rettendon.

Leach said that there was one incident that kept coming to his mind, and that was when I had first met him at the Ministry of Sound:

> It was a meeting more dramatic than most – he turned up bleeding from a knife wound in his stomach. He was lying on the toilet floor writhing in agony. I suspected right away who might have done it, a mixed-race geezer who I'd banned once.

If such a meeting had taken place it would have been re-created for a comedy sketch rather than included in a true crime book. 'Hi, pleased to meet you, sorry I can't get up to shake your hand – it's the old stab wound, you know. You couldn't do me a favour and call me an ambulance?' I must admit, I laughed when I read it. Despite the fact Leach had never met me before, he claimed he instinctively knew who was responsible for stabbing me. He said that he then proceeded to bash my assailant's head in with an iron bar, which left the man requiring 56 stitches.

It is true that I was stabbed on a visit to the Ministry of Sound, but the incident took place in a shop doorway up the road from the club. My assailant and his accomplices ran away after the incident. I drove myself home to Essex and did not visit a doctor or a hospital until nearly a week later when the wound became infected.

Leach also claims in his book that whenever he was with Tucker, I would appear with a camera to take his photograph. I can only assume his memory has been damaged by drug abuse because I was only present on two occasions over a six-year period when photographs were taken in his company. The first occasion was at Tucker's birthday party when a man named Rod took three photos and the second was when boxer Nigel Benn opened the Academy Gym in Southend and photos of Benn, my son and Chris Wheatley's children were taken.

Chris Wheatley and I did not pose for the photograph because it was the children who had wanted their photo taken with Nigel Benn, not us. Tucker and Leach did stand next to Benn and the children – perhaps they thought they were also famous and the children would be impressed? They were not. When the photographs from Tucker's birthday party were developed, the only picture which included Leach was given to Tucker to give to him and Tucker and I had one each of the remaining two photos.

Hardly enough material for a gallery. Leach goes on:

> All these incidents were swirling around my head as I tried to fit the jigsaw together. I didn't know what was important, what wasn't. But I knew that somewhere there must be clues to the assassination of my pals.

Why Leach should link these harmless events to a triple murder only he knows. Surely he is not suggesting that I was somehow involved in the murders? Several people have suggested that I played a part in luring Tucker, Tate and Rolfe to their deaths. Even the police suspected me of being involved during the early stages of their investigation. I did drive to Rettendon around the same time as Tucker, Tate and Rolfe and our differences had not been resolved, but that proves nothing. The truth is I had no involvement in their deaths whatsoever and I had no idea they were going to get murdered that night.

I was disappointed when I read what Leach had written because I had always considered him to be a decent family man and, as far as I was concerned, we had never had reason to speak ill of one another. No doubt he has forgotten I fell out with his 'good friend' David Done because he was making him look a fool. After appearing on *Hard Bastards* and writing *Muscle*, Leach is probably a changed man from the one I knew.

Back then, he certainly wouldn't have put his name alongside such a ridiculous quote as the one on his book's jacket. Leach is welcome to track me to the end of the earth and he is welcome to try and destroy me, but I know he is an intelligent man and we both know that if I am in the right I don't roll over and what he has said about me is total bullshit.

The *Hard Bastards* programme, or 'Daft Bastards' as I preferred to call it, also featured John 'Gaffer' Rollinson, who went on to write a book with the ingenious title of *Gaffer* (2003). On the cover of his book

Gaffer warned: 'If you "diss" me, I swear I will never forget, never forgive and have my revenge.' Tame in comparison to Leach's outburst, but equally ridiculous. Reading his book, the hypocrisy of his self-penned epitaph struck me. How could a man who describes himself as 'a violent, selfish, lazy, pig-headed thug', whose idea of domestic bliss was 'to say goodbye on a Friday evening and turn up again on Monday morning, smashed out of my skull, with a load of drunken mates in tow, waking up the kids' talk about respect being a top priority?

As the tiresome story of how hard and how wonderful Gaffer is unfolds, I again come under strong criticism. The 'man' who attacked me when I was enjoying a night out with my partner describes me as a 'scumbag' and a 'bastard'. When writing about a man who is alleged to have attacked him in front of his wife, Gaffer says, 'Getting my wife Wendy involved in a really vicious brawl in the early hours of the morning was against every underworld code. These scum didn't play by any rules.' Continuing his rant, Gaffer says that he wants to kill me. Why he didn't do it at the Festival Leisure Park in Basildon when he had the chance, choosing instead to run away screaming, I shall never know.

His ego boosted by the fact he had recently ditched the mother of his children and started dating Tucker's teenage mistress, he boasts, 'When we did go into clubs, you'd see people nudging each other and saying, "That's the fella from *Hard Bastards* and she's the girlfriend of Tony Tucker, the drug baron who got murdered."'

Funnier still, he claims to be the most dangerous man in the country and legendary in the underworld. Not being the brightest of individuals, Gaffer goes on to say that I was a police witness in the Rettendon murder case, had sold photographs of the Rettendon murder victims in death to a newspaper and was making money out of a website which featured the Rettendon murder case. When I threatened to sue Gaffer and his publisher for these totally unfounded lies, they had to suffer the indignity of apologising unreservedly in two newspapers – one a national and the other Essex-based.

These people were only playing at telling half truths and lies, while the master was telling whoppers and making a good living out of it.

For many years Dave Courtney had yearned to be famous. With stars in his eyes he had signed up as a walk-on extra at the Central Casting agency in London and had appeared on TV and in film.

On 18 June 1991, Courtney appeared in a BBC documentary called *Wimps and Warriors* in which he was described as a 'Bermondsey boy', despite the fact he has no connections with the area. It depicted him going about his business as a small-time debt collector, bailiff and poorly paid bully. He was on trial at the time and was filmed bragging outside the court after he had been cleared of assault and affray. (Although he says in a book published later that it was malicious wounding, carrying an offensive weapon, attempted murder and possessing a sawn-off shotgun.)

In one scene, Courtney – draped in tacky gold chains and dressed in ludicrous cowboy boots, leather biker's jacket and dark glasses – is shown knocking on the door of a run-down council flat where a Mr Tommy Godson lives. Courtney and a sidekick demand £200 from Tommy, who is a frail elderly gentleman. Tommy tells the duo that he only owes £120 and he only has the money he got off the DHSS that morning to survive on.

With a cosh tucked in his back pocket for 'security', big Dave says to the trembling pensioner: 'Don't take advantage of your age because there's people here, or I will have a chat with you around the corner.' The pensioner tells Courtney he can't go short as he needs the money to live on, but he is told he is a liar and if he doesn't pay, something will be taken out of his house to cover the debt. A woman clutching a baby appears at the door and tells the old gentleman to give Courtney the money as she doesn't want anything taken from their home. The man hands over his DHSS money, a total of £165. Courtney tells him that he wants the balance the next day and walks off with his friend, laughing. It made me feel sick watching it.

The big break Courtney had longed for came when he supplied security guards for Ronnie Kray's funeral. He took every photo opportunity and ensured the press were given every chance to interview or quote him. On the back of the publicity created by the 'event', Courtney made every effort to be publicly recognised as Ronnie Kray's successor, or gangster number one. He appeared on numerous chat shows and in documentaries supposedly examining his activities. In reality, they were little more than showcases, designed to inflate the ego of the 'dodgy one', as he liked to call himself. Courtney, like his heroes the Krays, became a media junkie.

He needed his fix – to read his name in the papers, hear his voice on the radio and see his face on television. Because of Courtney's unquestionable ability to tell stories, he was given the task of writing a column for a men's magazine called *Front*. To show his new employer that he had newsworthy clout, Courtney asked Reg Kray if he could visit him with the magazine's editor, Piers Hernu. Reg was in Wayland Prison at the time and he agreed. When Courtney and Hernu arrived at the prison, they met Reggie's wife-to-be, Roberta. Whilst waiting to be allowed into the visiting-room, Courtney mentioned to Roberta that BBC2 were making a documentary about *Front* magazine and a camera crew were waiting outside the prison.

Courtney and Hernu didn't say too much more about it to Roberta and on the visit they gave Reg the impression that the proposed programme was no big deal. They were keen to point out, however, that if the programme did turn out to be damaging, it certainly had nothing to do with them. A year later, a documentary called *Between the Covers* was broadcast by the BBC. It told the sorry tale of Dave Courtney and Piers Hernu going into Wayland Prison to secretly interview Reg Kray. Undetectable recording devices and photographic gadgets had been secreted on the sneaky duo and they recorded Courtney and Hernu laughing and bragging as they passed through security into the visiting-room where the unsuspecting Reg Kray was waiting for them. After the visit, Courtney and Hernu were filmed celebrating their deceitful trick by cracking open a bottle of champagne on the bonnet of their car. They really thought what they had done was funny. They didn't care that it had a devastating affect on Courtney's 'friend', Reg Kray.

His parole hearing was only one month away and because Courtney was his visitor, the authorities believed Reg had colluded with him to break prison regulations by filming inside the jail.

The following morning, Reg was put in front of the prison governor and asked to explain himself, but he couldn't. Reg said he knew Courtney had arranged for him to visit but had no idea he was setting him up to be filmed. The governor chose to disbelieve Reg and concluded that if he had such bad judgement in prison, he would surely make even worse judgements outside. Reg couldn't possibly be considered for release under such circumstances. At his next parole hearing, when many thought he would be released, Reggie's application was refused. It was to be the last parole hearing Reg Kray would have before his death.

Having dispensed of Reg Kray's usefulness as a publicity tool, Courtney wrote his autobiography. Inevitably, he slagged me off in it and talked about trying to kill me.

This attempted murder was a reference to the knife incident on the boat in London and the invitation to a party afterwards when I had thrown his pal out of my car. If that was a genuine attempt to kill me, I am fairly confident I shall die of old age.

Courtney called his book *Stop the Ride, I Want to Get Off* (1999). It must have been a pretty fast ride because when he did get off I would suggest that he was still dizzy and disorientated when he sat down to begin writing. The book is not even on par with a comic; from beginning to end Courtney lies about himself and invents his involvement in events that have not even happened.

On Saturday, 31 December 1979, Courtney says that he and his friends were seeing in the New Year at a pub called The Railway Signal in Forest Hill, south-east London. Courtney's younger brother Patrick had left the pub just before midnight to go to a nearby Chinese restaurant to purchase a take-away meal.

According to Courtney there was some confusion when his brother ordered the food, because the waiters brought his order out on a plate rather than in a disposable tinfoil tray. Courtney's brother refused to accept the order and because of this, it is claimed that he was assaulted. Courtney says that he went to the restaurant when he heard about what had happened to his brother and a ferocious battle ensued.

One of them went to chop me. I grabbed his hand mid-air, pulled him towards me and butted him into next week. All the others are around me, hitting me when some of my mates turn up and run in fighting as well.

Then – get this – this geezer appears holding a sword, something like a sabre. I couldn't run so I went for him, dodged inside the blade on the back swing, chinned the geezer and took the sword off him. Now it's in my hand and they all jumped back. The bloke I've taken the sword off only jumped up on the counter.

Then he jumped down on me and landed right on the sword point. It went straight through him and I saw it come out of his back, smeared with blood. He slipped down off the blade and hit the deck. The waiters started going mental and grabbing knives off tables in the restaurant. They rushed at us and suddenly I was slashing and stabbing. I heard the kitchen door bang open and this fat Chef ran out screaming and carrying a wok full of steaming oil. I turned and whacked it with the sword, full belt, and spilt it everywhere. They rushed us again and we did one geezer and then another one who was rushing at me and Terry with two dinner knives in his hands and, again, it went right in deep. There was blood all over the tiles and everyone was screaming.

While all this was going on I followed the last guy into the kitchens, and he only went and got this massive chopper. We were squaring up to each other, out of the view of the others. He advanced and started swinging and I backed down the corridor until we came back out into the restaurant. He's just seen me stab most of his friends, remember – they're all wriggling on the floor in their own blood – and now he was trying to kill me. I am now in a real battle to the death. With swords. Me with mine and him with the steel chopper. The swords were clashing together, people in the street were at the window looking in, the restaurant diners were horrified. And then it happened . . .

He walked into the hot oil the other geezer had dropped, and cos he was only wearing little black slippers, he stopped for a second, and then started hopping about screaming. I saw my chance and took it. Ping! I did him. Last but not least the cocky bastard with the chopper got it.

Courtney claims it took the police a month to identify him, but despite the seriousness of the attack he was granted bail. Eighteen months later, Courtney says that he stood trial at a magistrates court where he faced charges of attempted murder (which were dropped), carrying an offensive weapon with intent, actual bodily harm, affray, resisting arrest and actual bodily harm to a police officer.

When I read this drivel I could imagine impressionable young wannabe gangsters squirming with glee at their brave swashbuckling hero's exploits. Most would be too naive to know a magistrate would not have the sentencing powers to deal with such a violent attack. If the details concerning the incident had been true, the matter would have been sent to a crown court to be dealt with.

Courtney claims he pleaded guilty and was sentenced to three-and-a-half years' imprisonment – quite remarkable when you consider the fact a magistrate would have only had the power to sentence him to a maximum of six months' imprisonment on each charge.

It would seem Dave's pen was mightier than his imaginary sword. Courtney says he served 18 months of his prison sentence before being released. The dodgy one then found employment as a dustman before applying to become a fireman. Courtney then claimed he appeared in court because he had accumulated 'enough unpaid parking tickets and speeding fines to sink a battleship'. He set up a kind of criminal employment agency which earned him the title, 'The Yellow Pages of Crime'; he worked as a DJ, became a professional boxer, fighting five bouts before 'retiring' (although he doesn't appear to have been registered with any of the boxing authorities), fought 17 bouts as an unlicensed fighter and was arrested after:

> I went down to Crystal Palace stadium. There was a massive athletics track event going on. I saw that the 1,500 metres was coming up to the last lap, with Olympic champion, Daley Thompson, leading. I dropped my pants so I was in my shorts and T-shirt. Then I jumped the barrier, ran out on to the track just as Daley was taking the bend, overtook him (cos he was shagged) and won the race. I ran off back into the crowd.

Courtney says disgruntled athletics fans remonstrated with him and he ended up assaulting one of them. For this, he says, he was convicted of grievous bodily and given probation. Quite a busy schedule by anybody's standards, but Courtney's most bizarre, almost miraculous stunt came at the end of that year.

> It was the end of the year, though, which gave me the best result of my life. Tracey [his partner] had got pregnant as soon as I got out. No shock there really, we'd had a lot of making up to do, and on the 18 of December 1982 she gave birth to my boy. She was 48 hours in labour!

I am surprised Courtney was not shocked that his partner had fallen pregnant and had then given birth to their son in December 1982. The medical world would have been astounded and called it a miracle. Courtney had said that the incident in the Chinese restaurant had happened on 'Saturday, 31 December 1979' (which was in fact a Monday). He says that he was arrested a month later and bailed (end of January 1980).

Then, 18 months later (July 1981), he claims he was sentenced to three-and-a-half years' imprisonment. After 18 months, Courtney says that he was released. This 18-month stint inside would have taken him up to January 1983.

Courtney's claim that he fathered a child born in December 1982 and prior to that had managed to work as a dustman, DJ, professional boxer, unlicensed fighter, head a criminal employment 'agency', apply for the fire service, accumulate numerous parking and speeding tickets and be put on probation for GBH, is, despite the dodgy one's lack of surprise, simply unbelievable – he would have still been serving his prison sentence.

Then again, everything dodgy Dave Courtney writes about in his book is extremely unbelievable.

One evening in the late 1980s the dodgy one says he was in a pub called The Foresters in south London, celebrating a victory in a prize fight he had fought earlier that day. 'I was really buzzing in the pub and buying everyone drinks and champagne and generally having a laugh celebrating. Loads of pals were coming up to congratulate me, slapping me on the back and rubbing my head, that kind of thing.'

According to Dave, there was a professional hit-man in the pub watching the gaiety and he didn't like Dave being the centre of attention. No doubt he would have preferred everyone to recognise him and say, 'Hello, aren't you that well-known murderous hit-man? Can I get you a drink?' Dave says that he went to use the telephone and the hit-man started putting money in the juke box which was adjacent to it.

Dave said, 'Do you mind not putting that on for a second while I make a quick call?' The hit-man just looked at Courtney and continued pressing the buttons before walking off. According to Dave, Status Quo started blaring out of the speakers and so he unplugged the juke box. When Dave did this, the hit-man ran over and started shouting, 'I'm going to fucking do you! I don't care who you think you are, I'm going to kill you. I'll fucking kill you!' Any man prepared to kill for Status Quo should not be feared, he should be reported as he is obviously not well.

But this was happening in Dave's world where strangeness appears to be the norm.

Courtney said he had heard similar threats many times before, but this time he knew the man meant it. The hit-man was led away from Dave (by a very brave man from the sound of it), but later that night Dave received several phone calls warning him that the hit-man was trying to find out where he lived. Dave knew what he had to do – and it wasn't buy the hit-man Status Quo's *Greatest Hits*.

Dave decided he had to shoot him.

> On the chosen night, I visited a certain nightclub. I knew I'd be filmed on the security cameras going in. After a while I left by the fire exit, drove round to this guy's, shot him before he shot me, and went back to the club. At the end of the night I left by the front entrance.
>
> Eight the next morning, the police came round and arrested me (probably the shortest murder inquiry in British history). It was common knowledge what the guy had been saying. The police have one of the biggest grapevines in the world, next to the underworld's. There was no evidence against me. It was all down to whether I grassed myself up or not. Well, that was a big 'not' in my book. And because I said 'no comment' to everything, they charged me. I did some time on remand. I didn't tell them what proof I had.
>
> When I went to court I just produced the video from the club which showed the date and time and me entering and leaving, and the witnesses that saw me in there.

No doubt the judge didn't object to witnesses appearing midway through the trial like in Perry Mason movies. No doubt nobody asked why the dodgy one's defence team were setting up television monitors for the judge and jurors pre-trial when no video evidence had been disclosed. No doubt the judge allowed the case to continue despite the fact the prosecution would have had difficulty giving their opening address and presenting their case to the jury because, according to Dave, they had no evidence.

Against all the odds, our hero was tried and found not guilty, but it didn't end there. Courtney says:

When I came out there were loads of reporters there waiting for me. I was quite high profile and fair game for the press. The reporters all crowded 'round and asked me if I did it. I couldn't resist.

'Yeah, 'course I done it,' I said. That little admittance was a bit of a bombshell, to say the least. Talk about hold the front page. They had a fucking field day with that one. I was even more high profile now.

What sort of deranged social misfit would confess to a murder which never took place is a question for the psychiatrists, I'm afraid. I certainly cannot answer it. I do know that the murder did not take place and I do know David Courtney has never murdered anybody, never been charged with murder, never stood trial for murder and never been found not guilty of murder. Whatever evidence is produced to disprove Courtney's disturbing claims will be rubbished by him as he has probably convinced himself that he is a serious criminal by now. But I know the surest way to make a monkey of a man is to quote him.

Courtney says in his book that around the time of his acquittal for murder he got 'into the acting game' as an extra in TV and films. 'I was in *Chicago Joe and the Showgirl*, *Bullseye!*, *Hamlet*, *Henry V*, *Robin Hood: Prince of Thieves*, *The Krays* and *Batman*,' he explains.

The TV work Courtney talked about was when he had appeared in the series *The Paradise Club* which ran from 19 September 1989 to 21 November 1989 and then a second series from 25 September 1990 until 27 November 1990. *Henry V* was screened in 1989, *Hamlet* in 1990, *Chicago Joe and the Showgirl* in 1990, *The Krays* in 1990, *Bullseye!* in 1991 and *Robin Hood* in 1991. Naturally, the programmes and films had to be made before they could be screened on these dates and so Courtney must have been at large in the early part of 1988 and up until the end of 1990.

Despite Courtney's unbelievable claim that the police solved the murder within hours, Courtney would still have had to spend the best part of a year on remand awaiting trial. If he got 'into the acting game' after his acquittal, as he claims, that meant he would have stood trial in 1987 or 1988 and the murder would have happened in 1986 or 1987.

The dodgy one will undoubtedly have an explanation for his young naive wannabe followers which will help his murder story fit in somewhere between these dates, but even that will not survive scrutiny when his other activities are considered.

Courtney states that his son was born in December 1982 and then goes on to describe his 'activities' in detail up until the time he says he married in 1984.

Following his marriage, he claims he worked as a doorman at The Queens, The Yacht Club, Tattershall Castle, Dexter's, The Vibe Rooms, The Hippodrome, Equinox, Maxims, Heaven, Limelight, The Astoria, Stringfellows, The Gass Club, The Park in Kensington and EC1 in Farringdon. Courtney and his wife had two other children together, one born around 1986 and the other around 1987. Courtney says that he continued to work as a doorman and then from March 1988 until Tuesday, 22 August 1989, was running a club in south London called The Arches. Add his film career on to the back of his nightclub security empire and his story of murder becomes totally ludicrous, as he was by his own admission otherwise engaged from 1982 until at least 1990.

Courtney's book was serialised by a national newspaper and received rave reviews from the critics. One such critic named Craig Brown, working for the *Mail on Sunday*, nominated it as their book of the week and described it as:

> An extraordinary read, scary, eye-poppingly horrible, and yet funny at the same time. Dave is as hard on himself as on anyone else (well . . . most of the time, anyway) and you do get to see a savagely honest self-portrait. But it's a terrific read and you'll not regret buying this one. And if you like it, Dave's 'sequel' comes out this autumn!

Review after review heaped praise on Courtney and the book became a bestseller. It is a pity none of the numerous investigative reporters in the media bothered to check out his 'savagely honest' tales of mayhem and murder. I thought that the Metropolitan Police, who had set up a murder review group to look at unsolved murders, would question him about his murder confession in the book but even they didn't trouble him. Then again, they had access to his criminal record and would have known it was all bullshit. Courtney claims in his book that he committed another murder, this time in Holland. To ensure nobody doubted him, Dave named his victim, a man called Blondie, who had a friend called Mr Tan.

Fortunately our underworld hero wasn't apprehended by the authorities and the murder was never reported. What a guy!

Courtney became so popular, a fan club was set up for him. For £20 his fans are given a signed photo and a monthly newsletter, plus four times a year their names are put into a hat and the lucky winner is promised 'a night out with Dave'. Courtney also tours the country doing 'an audience with Dave Courtney' shows in clubs and theatres. He was invited to speak to graduates at Oxford University and appears on countless radio and television programmes bragging about his underworld muscle and murderous deeds.

On various sites on the Internet, his fans are invited to hire Dave to attend their parties and open supermarkets, or to purchase Dave Courtney merchandise. On offer are:

A superb figurine of Dave Courtney standing 10 inches high. This is a must-have for any DC aficionado and we've seen them going for £120 in auctions. It is available in two different materials: Welsh Coal, mined at Tower Colliery (the last deep mine in Wales). Welsh Slate (over 500 million years old), beautifully highlighted in copper. £39.99 + £5.50 carriage (insured) £44.99 + £5.99 carriage (insured).

A life-size cast of Dave's fist, with Dave's trademark knuckleduster and bejewelled ring is the product of a live casting. It's a must-have for every fan. Mounted on a plinth and with an engraved plate, it will be the centre of attention on your mantelpiece. £39.99 + £5.50 carriage (insured).

A full-scale bejewelled replica of Dave's trademark knuckleduster is a must-have for every fan. Mounted on a plinth and with an engraved plate, it will sit very proudly on your desk. (Not to be used as an offensive weapon.) £24.99 + £5.50 carriage (insured).

A presentation set consisting of a 10cl bottle of superb brandy liqueur and a specially engraved miniature brandy glass in a sumptuous black satin lined box. Of course, we don't expect you to actually drink the brandy, because this is a one off limited edition presentation set that we expect to grow in value once all the sets are sold. But, if you DO decide to drink it, then you are in for a superb drinking experience.

Due to the amount of e-mails we have received requesting a Dave Courtney Clock, we are proud to launch 'The Dave Courtney Knuckle Duster Wall/Mantle Clock'. Using the very latest Laser Technology, we produced this clock from 2mm stainless steel (brass will follow soon). It measures 6' x 10' and currently comes in 3 finished effects: Antique Pewter, Polished Aluminium and Matt Black. Each one comes embellished with 15 of the finest Austrian Crystals and the highest quality German Quartz Movement and is backed by a 12 month guarantee, all for only £25.00. It has a wall fixing as standard but a stand is available for £1.50 which converts it to a mantle clock.

Dave Courtney lighters, which are described as standard disposable lighters transformed from a lump of tacky coloured plastic into a stylish fashion statement. There are also key rings. Well, not quite 'just' key rings. Both carry Dave's knuckleduster logo and signature in gold. One is on leather and the other's a bottle opener.

One can only imagine how jealous Gaffer and the other wannabe underworld kings must feel as they look on at the master of bullshit in awe. Periodically, they surface to try and snatch some limelight but inevitably they soon fade back into oblivion.

During the Iraq conflict Gaffer appeared in the *Basildon Evening Echo* newspaper claiming Prime Minister Tony Blair had telephoned him to thank him for his support after he had written to the PM backing his stance on the need for war. Gaffer said, 'The voice said, "Is that John Rollinson?" And I said, "I don't know, mate, you rang me." When he started speaking I knew who it was.'

Gaffer refused to discuss the confidential conversation he had with Mr Blair but he did say he mentioned his criminal history later on in their conversation. He said: 'I told him to buy my book, and once he reads that, he won't ring again.' I cannot say whether or not Gaffer is telling the truth about this story, although I am sure there will be one or two in Essex who will think it was an attempt to get his book some much-needed publicity.

However, I am confident that Mr Blair will not be buying Gaffer's book and he will not be ringing him again, regardless. It is a missed opportunity for the PM because in Gaffer, Mr Blair has a true admirer.

Gaffer told the reporter that, 'Tony Blair is a man of England and has stood by his beliefs and I admire him for that. He does stand to lose his job, but I think he will win the next election. He has the support of the underworld.'

It would undoubtedly be an interesting partnership, the king of spin united with the masters of bullshit. One suspects it's a marriage that will never take place.

15

THE RIDE BREAKS DOWN
AND THE JESTER IS UNMASKED

Almost 15 years after the brutal murder of a private investigator named Daniel Morgan, a chain of events was set in motion that was to expose Dave Courtney as a registered police informant, the very thing he himself has repeatedly said he despises. In 1987 Morgan was found slumped in a south London pub car park with an axe embedded in his skull. Not only was £1,000 left in the dead man's pocket, but sticking plaster had been wound around the axe handle to ensure no fingerprints were left behind.

Equally intriguing were the startling allegations made in the aftermath of his brutal murder. It was claimed that Morgan had been about to expose police wrongdoing or corruption and that officers may have been involved in his killing. No evidence came to light to support these claims. Morgan had run a company called Southern Investigations; his partner, Jonathon Rees, was charged with his murder, but the case against him was dropped by the Director of Public Prosecutions because of lack of evidence. Despite the collapse of the case, the police remained determined to solve the murder, not least because it had cast a shadow over their integrity.

In 1987, around the same time as Daniel Morgan had been

murdered, Dave Courtney says that he was approached by a detective constable named Austin Warnes, who told him that he was a corrupt officer and was prepared to help Courtney if needed. Dodgy Dave claims that Warnes was 'a bit of a villain groupie who loved to hang about with the criminal fraternity'.

> I was living in East Dulwich at this time and I had an interest in a number of nightclubs in the Old Kent Road, Peckham, Woolwich, Abbey Wood and the West End. Not long after I first met Warnes he saw me at a nightclub.
>
> On that same night, funnily enough, there was a geezer there called Tony Thompson, who was working on a book called *Gangland Britain*. Anyway, Thompson was stood next to me when Warnes approached me, said he'd heard about me, and made it clear that he was a bent copper and that he had information that some of my friends were being looked at.

Courtney says he decided to use DC Warnes to obtain information about police activity concerning himself and his associates, but in order to do so he had to become what he now calls a fake informant. Being a fake was nothing new for Courtney but being an informant brought him closer to DC Warnes and the two shared a fairly active social life together. These were certainly not nights out dancing at the policeman's ball. The unlikely duo would go to fetish clubs, snort cocaine together and visit sordid private sex parties hosted by perverted sexual deviants for the benefit of other perverted sexual deviants. Wife swapping, sadomasochism, bondage and gay sex were all put on offer for the fake police informant and his bent police handler.

Courtney's story about not being a real informant began to lack credibility when he alleged that not only DC Warnes but police officers nationwide were involved in fake informant scams. Dodgy Dave claimed that police officers were filling in informant contact sheets with false information, presenting them to their superiors and then getting their fake informant to pick up '20, 30 or 40 grand in cash' as a reward for information that had simply been made up.

According to Courtney, fake informants are people who have registered as police informants but they do not ever tell the police anything that will get anybody into trouble.

THE RIDE BREAKS DOWN AND THE JESTER IS UNMASKED

All the fake informant does is milk the police for information, escape prosecution for motoring offences, avoid paying parking fines, give false information about non-existent criminals and collect hundreds or thousands of pounds in rewards from the police. I have always known why lottery winners choose not to be identified and if Courtney is to be believed, I now know why police informants ask to remain anonymous also.

This kind of get-rich-quick, no-questions-asked scheme may happen in Dave's mind, but it cannot happen in the real world. The police usually recruit informants from those under investigation or facing prosecution. Police tell would-be informants that they can make life easier for them if they would be prepared to make life easier for the police and help with their enquiries. If people agree to give information to the police, that information has to be tested before any other information gleaned from them is used. If the information proves to be genuine and arrests are made, then the officer who has the relationship with the informant will go back to him or her for more. The information has to be of good quality and concern crimes of a more serious nature. The police neither have the resources nor the will to meet informants who are only prepared to tell them that Billy Smith drops litter and Mary Evans swears in public. If informants deliver regular, reliable, good-quality information, their handlers will put them forward to their superiors to become registered police informants. The informant, handler and a senior officer then have to meet and the pros and cons of becoming a registered police informant are explained to the informant. If everybody is happy, the informant signs a registered informant agreement and is given a pseudonym to use for whenever he or she contacts the handler.

This is done so people do not overhear the informant giving his or her name during telephone conversations or see the informant's name on contact sheets which must be completed every time the police handler meets the registered informant. Dave Courtney was given the pseudonym 'Tommy Mack'.

When an informant gives information which results in an arrest he or she is usually paid a few hundred pounds, not 20, 30 or 40 grand. There have been rare cases when an informant has been paid thousands of pounds, but these instances are very few and far between.

In order to physically collect the reward, the informant picks one of several high-street banks offered by the police and is told to go in and ask for the chief cashier. He or she then gives the chief cashier a prearranged name and is paid, over the counter, in cash. For Dave Courtney to suggest that the police have no control over the money paid to informants is beyond belief.

In 1999, the police anti-corruption unit CIB3 launched Operation Nigeria, which was an investigation set up to target the murdered private investigator Daniel Morgan's former associates. With the backing of the Metropolitan Police's then commissioner, Sir (now Lord) Paul Condon, warrants were obtained for the planting of listening devices in the offices of Morgan's private investigations agency in Thornton Heath, south-west London. Operation Nigeria's aim was two-fold: to pursue the unsolved murder of Morgan and to gather evidence about allegations that his investigations agency was involved with corrupt police officers and former detectives who had allegedly supplied confidential information and assisted with 'other favours'.

One of CIB3's principal targets was Jonathon Rees, who had continued to run the investigations agency after the murder charge against him had been dropped.

When the police planted the listening devices in the offices they were warned not to leave any sign whatsoever that anyone had been inside the premises, let alone planted a bug. 'They are alert, cunning and devious individuals who have current knowledge of investigative methods and techniques which may be used against them,' said an internal police report. 'Such is their level of access to individuals within the police, through professional and social contacts, that the threat of compromise to any conventional investigation against them is constant and very real.'

Almost immediately, the various bugging devices began to reap rewards for the police. Visitors to the premises had asked Rees to obtain blank police charge sheets, he had agreed to pervert the course of justice over a theft, and he was waiting for police contacts to give him information about the desecration of the street memorial to the murdered black teenager, Stephen Lawrence. One police progress report stated:

> Rees and [others] have for a number of years been involved in
> the long-term penetration of police intelligence sources. They
> have ensured that they have live sources within the Metropolitan

Police Service and have sought to recruit sources within other
police forces. Their thirst for knowledge is driven by profit to be
accrued from the media . . .

Examples of those media contacts and live sources within the
Metropolitan Police were revealed during the following weeks. Rees was
heard expressing concern over CIB3's arrest of a long-time associate, ex-
Detective Constable Duncan Hanrahan, who ran his own private
investigation company, Hanrahan Associates, with another former DC,
Martin King, who was later jailed for corruption.

Although Hanrahan had turned supergrass, giving information about
others, including King and Rees, he was jailed for 9 years after
confessing to a string of corruption and conspiracy charges, including
his involvement in a plan to rob a courier bringing £1,000,000 in cash
through Heathrow airport.

In one recorded conversation, Rees appears to be explaining to
someone over the phone that Hanrahan was passing information to
him about CIB3's enquiries. According to the transcript, Rees says:
'Hanrahan said what CIB3 want to do is fuck us all. He said they keep
talking about the fucking Morgan murder every time they see me.'

Later in the same taped conversation, Rees also talks about having
sold a story to a reporter about Kenneth Noye, the notorious criminal
then being held at Belmarsh top-security prison, following extradition
from Spain to face trial for the M25 road rage murder of Stephen
Cameron. Rees says he provided information about how GCHQ was
involved in tracking down Noye. He also claims to have given a reporter
information about what he calls personal services being provided to
Noye in Belmarsh.

In another recorded telephone call, Rees was heard calling 'a source'
and asking: 'How are you getting on with that story?' The ensuing
conversation is summarised in a CIB3 transcript as having included
mention of David Copeland, the neo-Nazi London nail bomber, then in
Belmarsh Prison awaiting trial.

Copeland was said to be in a cell next to a black prisoner. The pair hated
each other. Rees told the caller if he 'can find out more about Copeland and
the messages he's receiving from God, that would be brilliant.'

A serving police officer was recorded passing information to Rees
about the Yorkshire Ripper, Peter Sutcliffe.

A CIB3 report stated:

> Rees and [others] are actively pursuing contacts with the police and business community to identify potential newsworthy stories. They then sell the information to the national media. The investigation has so far identified a serving police officer who has supplied confidential information and private investigators who can supply phone and bank account details of any person.

At nearby Bexleyheath police station where Courtney's handler DC Austin Warnes was stationed, more mundane, less exciting police work was being carried out. Detective Inspector Michael Latham was the officer at Bexleyheath who was responsible for 'controlling informants and the informants register'.

On 24 May 1999, DI Latham had sent an email to all 'handlers of police informants' in Bexleyheath. DI Latham had asked the officers if they could obtain information from their informants about burglars and those that handle their stolen goods because the police were launching Operation Bumblebee, which they hoped was going to reduce the numbers of these types of offences in the area.

One of the police handlers who received an email from DI Latham was DC Warnes. His read:

> 'Tommy Mack'
> Re: The above source;
>   Please contact him or her, to task with obtaining intelligence information on burglaries and handlers for a forthcoming Bumblebee. All replies, positive or negative, to me by 7 June.

Whilst DI Latham, DC Warnes and Dave 'Tommy Mack' Courtney were busy trying to snare the burglars of Bexleyheath, the CIB3 surveillance operation continued to reap rewards against bent policemen and their criminal associates.

On 25 May 1999, into their trap fell a serving police officer called DC Tom Kingston, who was with the elite South East Regional Crime Squad. At that time he was suspended, awaiting trial with other corrupt officers over the theft of two kilos of amphetamine powder from a drug dealer. Later found guilty, he was sent to prison.

Kingston was recorded in Jonathon Rees's offices talking about a Scotland Yard contact who was keeping 'his eyes and ears open' for information. He boasted that this officer could do vehicle checks for him on the police national computer.

The death of TV presenter Jill Dando was discussed by Rees in a phone call which was recorded on 4 June. Rees said he knew how one newspaper was obtaining information about the police investigation into her murder and explained that he was trying to do the same.

> There's big stories . . . nearly every day with good information on the Jill Dando murder. We found out one of our bestest friends is also on that fucking murder squad, but he ain't told us nothing.
>
> We only found out yesterday after that torrent of abuse we initially gave him. He's going to phone us today.

Kim James was an attractive, likeable young mother, who, like many 'ordinary' people, was oblivious to the double dealing, corruption and criminality which went on amongst some members of the police force. Kim, a former model, who had been dated by the likes of soccer star Stan Collymore, should on the face of things have had everything going for her, but she had been enduring a pretty miserable time of late. She had met her husband Simon James in 1994, married him in June 1995 and divorced him in April 1999 when their son was aged two. The couple then became embroiled in a bitter custody battle. Simon had decided to discredit his ex-wife prior to any court proceedings, so she would lose custody of her child.

Initially, Simon had asked private investigator Jonathon Rees for help in obtaining damaging evidence against his wife. Unknown to Simon or Rees, their conversation was being recorded by the devices left by CIB3 in Rees's office. Officers heard Simon James describe Kim as a drug dealer, a loose woman and an unfit mother. The truth was, Kim James was a very hard-working mother, employed as an aerobics and nursery teacher. Kim had no blemish on her character whatsoever, in fact the only mistake she had made in her life was when she married her twisted husband.

Rees agreed to help Simon, but at their second meeting, the CIB3 officers who were monitoring the conversation recorded Rees saying:

One of our surveillance team is a police motorcyclist on the drugs squad, and he works for us on the side. It's a couple of years before he retires from the squad. He did a check on her, but there's nothing on the files. She doesn't come up associated with any drugs dealers.

Undeterred by the fact his ex-wife had nothing to do with drugs, Simon agreed to pay Rees £8,000 after he offered to plant 15 wraps of cocaine in Kim's car.

Rees was in no doubt that once he had ensured the police had been made aware of the drugs and they had been found, Kim would be sent to prison and Simon would win the custody battle.

Rees recruited DC Austin Warnes to do this dirty work.

CIB3 officers, realising they now had hard evidence of Rees conspiring to commit a very serious crime, employed extra resources to monitor not only Rees, but Simon James, Austin Warnes and anybody else who may be involved in the conspiracy.

On 9 June, DC Warnes filled out an informant contact sheet which stated that his informant 'Tommy Mack' had told him in a telephone conversation on 8 June that Kim James and another girl named Lauren Manning were dealing in cocaine.

The address of Kim James was given and the make, type and registration of her car. DC Warnes also wrote that 'Tommy Mack' had told him: 'Kim deals on Fridays and Saturdays with her friend Lauren Manning, she is due to receive a large consignment of cocaine and would be dealing this Saturday.'

On Thursday, 10 June, DI Latham found an envelope on his desk which DC Warnes had left. The envelope was addressed to DI Latham and contained two police 5020D forms – records of police officers' contacts with their registered informants.

The 5020D forms said that Kim James and Lauren Manning were 'going up to London on Fridays and Saturdays and dealing in cocaine'.

The forms also stated that not only were the women drug dealers, but they were currently in possession of a large quantity of cocaine.

DI Latham, who was at this stage unaware of any wrongdoing, contacted DC Warnes about the information concerning the two women and asked him to 'input it onto the police criminal intelligence system', which is a computer system for information management. That afternoon, Detective Superintendent Quick of CIB3 contacted DI Latham and briefed him about the conspiracy concerning DC Warnes, Jonathon Rees, Kim James and Lauren Manning.

A few days later Rees contacted a friend of his named James Cook, who was given the task of breaking into Kim's car and 'planting the gear'. Unfortunately for him and his co-conspirators, officers from CIB3, already had Kim's car under surveillance. They filmed Cook breaking into the vehicle and planting 'the gear'. Having allowed Cook to 'escape', officers broke into Kim's car themselves and replaced the wraps of cocaine with wraps of harmless white powder.

The wraps Cook had planted were then sent off for analysis to see if they were indeed cocaine. Pretending to 'act' on the information which DC Warnes had said had come from 'Tommy Mack', police officers attended Kim James's home on 15 June. After 'searching' the property and her car, police 'discovered' the packages and Kim was arrested and taken to Wimbledon police station.

Nobody was allowed to tell the terrified young woman that they knew she was totally innocent. Senior officers had agreed to allow her to be arrested and accused of being a drug dealer to guarantee they could gather all of the evidence they needed to prosecute the scum who were involved in such a disgraceful plot.

On 16 June 1999, the unsuspecting DC Warnes made himself busy putting the paperwork in order that he hoped would condemn an innocent mother to several years' imprisonment. Another informant contact sheet was completed by DC Warnes which said that 'Tommy Mack' had told him in a telephone conversation on Sunday, 13 June, that Kim James and Lauren Manning were now in possession of a quantity of cocaine and would be dealing all week. 'Kim may have it in her silver Punto motor vehicle.'

On 17 June, DI Latham found another envelope on his desk from DC Warnes which contained information relating to the fact that search warrants had been used to search the home of Kim James. The same day DC Warnes, undoubtedly pleased by his vile handiwork, treated himself to a holiday and jetted off to Portugal. Simon James, meanwhile, informed social services of his wife's arrest and was recorded by CIB3 officers agreeing to make a final payment to Rees for a job well done.

Before the payment could be made, Simon discovered that his wife had not been charged with any offence and the police wanted to talk to him as she was claiming that he had set her up. In a blind panic, Simon fled to Wales with his son, but he was soon apprehended.

Courtney says that at that time he was trying to distance himself from DC Warnes because he believed DC Warnes was going to set him up, but for what, he fails to mention.

I would have thought a corrupt, cocaine-snorting, sexual deviant in the Metropolitan Police would have had great difficulty in pointing the finger at his informant and friend, but if Courtney claims it's true, then it must be true.

Courtney says that he had a rather unusual visit from DC Warnes at 3 a.m. He says that he heard a noise outside and when he went to investigate he found DC Warnes skulking about. When Courtney asked the detective what he was up to, DC Warnes is alleged to have said that he was looking at a mural on the side of Courtney's house. (A three-storey-high tacky painting of Courtney on horseback, supposedly looking like King Arthur with his partner Jenny as Guinevere.) Courtney says he feared he would upset DC Warnes if he challenged his explanation, so he chose instead to pretend to believe him. The dodgy one says that when DC Warnes left he suspected he was being set up, so he decided he would have to find some form of insurance policy against him. That opportunity, according to Courtney, presented itself when Detective Constable Warnes returned from his holiday in Portugal.

Whilst DC Warnes had been lounging in the sun, his police colleagues were busy gathering evidence against him. DI Latham was contacted by officers from CIB3 who asked him to arrange a meeting with DC Warnes and his informant 'Tommy Mack'.

DI Latham rang DC Warnes and said: 'Right, the lady who has been arrested has really been kicking up a stink, saying the stuff that was found by the tactical support group in the car was something that was not hers. It was her husband's. It has all been planted because it's due . . . it is all over a custody argument with the kid. There has been a couple of High Court cases already this week up at the Strand in front of the judge to try and get the kid back. I am going to have to do a Public Interest Immunity hearing on the source of the information.'

DI Latham said he needed to speak to 'Tommy Mack' directly so that he could 'ascertain his knowledge of the information' and so be in a position to answer any questions asked of him by the judge presiding over the custody battle in the High Court.

Unknown to DC Warnes, officers from CIB3 had planted listening devices in his car whilst it had been parked at the airport when he had gone on holiday to Portugal; everything DC Warnes was saying was being recorded.

Some time later, DC Warnes telephoned DI Latham and said, 'Hello, it is Austin, Governor. I needed time. I saw him this morning. He is ever so nervous about meeting but, I mean, he said . . . I mean, he has got no choice but to meet you, but I said that I cleared with you a time and then arranged to meet. We can do it anywhere really as long as it is not the nick. Yeah, Plumstead Comminish. Right. Do you want to meet me first and then we will drive to it? Is that a big job to do then? Right. OK. Well, I will get him to come to us, if you would like. That will probably be easier out of his own area. So, if you want to meet down the Jacobean, we can meet down there.'

DI Latham suggested to DC Warnes that they meet up at about midday and DC Warnes replied, 'Have you got that form he needs to sign?'

The form DC Warnes referred to was part of a contract between the police and their informants which had recently come into existence. Its purpose was to assure informants that the police would discontinue criminal cases which had arisen from informants' tip-offs rather than reveal who their source of information was.

Courtney had never been given such assurances before because as DI Latham explained later, '"Tommy Mack" had been registered for quite some time and there had not been an opportunity to do it since they were introduced.'

DC Warnes telephoned Courtney in a blind panic and pleaded with Courtney to meet him as soon as possible. The pair met at 10 a.m. on Plumstead Common, just up the road from Courtney's house. DC Warnes wrote on his informant contact sheet that this meeting was to discuss 'signature of terms and conditions regarding information concerning Kim James'.

DC Warnes explained to Courtney that he had been crediting information to 'Tommy Mack', which was in fact false. Because Courtney had been registered as his informant for some time, DC Warnes didn't think the reliability of any information received from him would be questioned. Now that it had, DC Warnes said DI Latham wanted to meet Courtney to check how he had come across the information so he could tell the judge presiding over Simon and Kim's custody battle that procedure had been followed and everything appeared to be above board. Courtney was understandably furious – DC Warnes was putting him in danger of being exposed as a police informant. Courtney knew that if he didn't agree to say he had given DC Warnes the information, DC Warnes would be charged with corruption and he would be dragged into a court case that would undoubtedly reveal his double life. If he met DI Latham, agreed the information was genuine and agreed it had come from him, the judge in the custody battle would believe the police and Kim James would lose her son and her liberty, but then things could carry on as normal. Unfortunately for him and DC Warnes, the police knew Kim had been set up and were just trying to find out who was involved in the conspiracy.

Courtney agreed to meet DI Latham and confirm the information had come from him. Because Courtney knew it was false information, he told DC Warnes he would only go through with it if he had some form of insurance policy.

Courtney told DC Warnes that he wanted to record him saying he had nothing to do with the information concerning Kim James and was only meeting DI Latham to help DC Warnes out. Realising his career as a policeman could be over and he might be joining the criminal fraternity he allegedly admired so much, DC Warnes knew he was in no position to haggle the cost of a lifeline, so he agreed to do the tape for Courtney.

Courtney rushed home to get a tape-recorder and camera. When he arrived he asked his partner Jenny and friend Brendan to accompany him to Plumstead Common. Courtney and Jenny rode back to DC Warnes on a motorbike and Brendan followed at a discreet distance in his car. When Courtney and Jenny arrived at the common, they found DC Warnes sitting waiting for them on a bench.

As DC Warnes spoke into the tape-recorder Courtney's partner Jenny took a photograph to confirm it was indeed DC Warnes making the recording.

> Austin Warnes: I am sitting here on Plumstead Common with Dave Courtney and Jenny. I've asked him to get me out of a bit of bother.

> Dave Courtney: I know nothing about it though, do I?
>
> AW: Dave knows nothing about this, no.
>
> DC: What's the information? What do you want me to say?
>
> AW: Just to say that Kim James and her friend were dealing cocaine and that the information was passed to me by you.
>
> DC: That is right . . . just in case this tape ever comes to light, this is fuck all to do with me. It's to help my fucking pal, all right? Thank you very much.

Pleased he had now covered himself, Courtney declared he was prepared to meet DI Latham and confirm he had supplied the information which could send an innocent mother to jail. A seemingly small sacrifice to ensure his secret life as a police informant would never be unearthed.

At 11.15 a.m., DC Warnes telephoned DI Latham on his mobile and asked him if he would meet him at 'the Jacobean Barn at the bottom of Gravel Hill near Bexleyheath'.

At 12.37 a.m., Courtney and DC Warnes arrived and DI Latham got into the back of DC Warnes's car. Introducing himself to Courtney, DI Latham explained that he was the officer 'who controls all the people who help us like yourself'. He continued: 'First off, can I say thank you for meeting me at such short notice.' DI Latham told Courtney that when they found the drugs in Kim's car, 'she denied all knowledge of it, and said it's down to someone else, down to her husband. But everyone makes allegations when they're in it.'

Courtney replied, 'Yes, I know, absolutely.'

DI Latham asked Courtney about the information DC Warnes had said he had supplied. Courtney, fearing Kim and Simon's High Court child custody case involving information he was saying he had supplied could expose him, said to DI Latham, 'All of this is a little bit more than I expected would happen out of this.'

Trying to reassure Courtney, DI Latham replied, 'My primary concern, as in all these situations, is about your security. I will tell you, at the end of the day, you will remain anonymous. You will always be 'Tommy Mack'. Should anything ever arise which requires you to go to court for a case, we drop the court case rather than go ahead.' Despite concerns he claims he had, Courtney signed the agreement concerning the information DC Warnes had credited to him and the measures the police were prepared to take to protect him.

When pressed about the information produced regarding Kim James, Courtney told DI Latham:

> It's just a little problem I had in a club. I own the place. Park Royal in Mitcham. I also supply doormen. Not that I am running the drugs myself, but because I have been at it a long time and I know how to stop the problem. People I have been catching in my club have been putting up the names of the people they have been working for. At least two different people I have caught selling gear in the past.
>
> The person they got the gear from, not that they were actually doing it for them but, as their supplier, you know, I would actually rather get rid of the supplier, then the dealers do not come. Them I will deal with myself. The two girls, I'm fucked. These are the people I have caught in the Park Royal in Mitcham High Street.

Courtney then named Kim James and Lauren Manning as the 'two girls he has caught' and says he can't remember their addresses but 'I have got them at home on a piece of paper'.

The conversation ended prematurely when DI Latham thought DC Warnes and Courtney suspected he was on to them. As DI Latham stepped out of earshot, a motorbike drove past and Courtney and DC Warnes feared they were about to be arrested. DC Warnes was recorded saying, 'I swear to God he was a fucking 4-2-4-2 driver [police motorcyclist]. What the fuck are they doing around here?'

Courtney replied, 'They are looking at me and you, mate.'

DC Warnes said, 'They are looking at me. They are not looking at you.'

Despite their fears, nothing happened. Months passed and it appeared as if DC Warnes had got away with fitting up Kim James and Courtney had got away with supplying DI Latham with false information. Then, in September 1999, officers from CIB3 swooped on Jonathon Rees, Austin Warnes, Simon James, Dave Courtney and James Cook.

All were charged with offences relating to the conspiracy surrounding Kim James and in November 2000 the case was sent to the Old Bailey for trial. DC Austin Warnes pleaded guilty and was sentenced to four years' imprisonment, which was later extended to five years when he appealed. Jonathon Rees and Simon James were both found guilty and were sentenced to six years' imprisonment, later extended to seven when they appealed.

James Cook told the jury when he was asked to plant 'the gear' in Kim James's car by Rees he believed 'the gear' was surveillance equipment and not drugs. The jurors chose to believe Cook and he was found not guilty. Courtney was quite rightly found not guilty of conspiring to pervert the course of justice by supplying DC Warnes with false information concerning Kim James. DC Warnes admitted he credited the false information to his informant Dave Courtney and Courtney knew nothing of the initial plot to set up Kim James. The fact still remains that Dave 'Tommy Mack' Courtney was a registered police informant long before the matter concerning Kim James ever arose and he did tell DI Latham that the false information which could have sent a young mother to prison was genuine. However, since the case ended Courtney has refused to face reality, choosing instead to make up ridiculous stories about fake informants. The dodgy one has also claimed that the 'not-guilty verdict was both for the charge I faced and the accusation I was a grass. I have never been an informer'. Sadly for 'Tommy Mack', we in the real world know he wasn't on trial for being a police informant as it is not illegal to be one.

Now I've written this book I must prepare myself for the backlash. I have no doubt whatsoever it will come. To be honest, I couldn't care less what these so-called hard men say or do. They can see me or sue me, I don't give a fuck, because the facts cannot be denied. I now live in the real world where hard cases are people who fight adversity, sickness and disease, where respect is earned and not given to some drugged-up bully because he carries a knife or a gun. Here people are judged by their deeds rather than their ability to intimidate people with threatening words and behaviour. Dave Courtney managed to turn the words of intimidation and violence he had gleaned from crime books and films into a lucrative industry, but like so many of his underworld cronies in this book, those words have returned to haunt him.

In *Stop the Ride, I Want to Get Off*, he wrote:

Fifteen years ago, if someone was a grass he would have had the shit kicked out of him when he was in prison. Now you go to prison you have whole wing-loads of grasses. If the first supergrass had been shot, like he fucking should have been, it would never have become a trend.

And now everyone's at it. If you had told me 15 years ago that there would be a programme on prime-time telly for grasses, I'd never have believed it. But you watch *Crimewatch* and they say, 'If you know anyone who's done anything, give us a call and we'll nick them and give you loads of money.' For people like me, it's like trying to imagine that in 15 years there will be a programme just for paedophiles, that's how disgusting it is.

Courtney wouldn't have known at the time that his admirable underworld spiel was going to unmask him as a hypocritical fake. The strange thing is, the impressionable young people who read the drivel the media publish about the dodgy one refuse to accept the fact he is an odd, disturbed character who lives in a fantasy world.

In Manchester recently, his gullible fans were invited to fork out up to £190 to hear him talk about his life of crime. Included in the price were accommodation, tickets, T-shirts, a signed photo and a bottle of champagne. Those in the media who hype this man and others as successful criminals should take a long hard look at themselves and hope none of their children ever meet the Dave Courtney wannabes of this world created by their irresponsible reporting. They should be reporting the facts and not the fiction, highlighting the plight of victims of crime and not glamorising the attention-seeking idiots who think they are gangsters. A life of crime is in reality a life of fucking misery; trust me, I know, I've been there. If you don't believe me, visit the Essex graveyards littered with the debris of our firm's reign or talk to the mothers who have lost their sons and daughters through the drugs my associates imported. Seek out the maimed and emotionally scarred young men whose lives were left in ruins because they were deemed guilty by some power-crazy bully of committing some alleged, petty misdemeanour. Visit the prisons awash with my former friends and so-called enemies and then ask yourself: Do you still wannabe in my gang?

EPILOGUE

Nobody can say for certain what the future holds. I would like to think that my problems with the law are over, but since moving to Peterborough I have been arrested, clubbed by overzealous policemen with batons, locked up overnight and then released in the morning without charge. In an effort to 'escape' before things got out of hand, I moved to a place where I thought nobody would bother me.

One Sunday afternoon, I was sitting in my own home watching football on the TV when the phone rang. The caller said he was a policeman and asked me if everything was OK as they had received a report of a disturbance. I laughed and said, 'It's a wind up, isn't it?', but the policeman was adamant.

He asked if anybody else was in the house and I told him Emma was asleep upstairs as we had both been out late the night before. The policeman insisted on talking to her, so I called up to Emma and she picked up the phone in the bedroom and confirmed to the police that there was no problem or disturbance in or around our home. The policeman said OK and put the phone down.

Ten minutes later there was a loud knock at the door. I had ordered a pizza and assumed it was the delivery boy, so I sorted out some money and went to the front door. When I opened it, approximately eight police officers were standing there looking very, very agitated. Three of them took their extendable batons out and flicked them open.

A WPC said she wanted to come into my home and when I asked why, she said, 'There's been a disturbance.'

I laughed and said, 'We've just had your people on the phone saying the same thing. My partner's in bed, I'm watching a good game of football on the TV and waiting for a pizza. What is disturbing about that?'

The WPC tried to push her way in and I told her that she was not welcome in my home and as she had no warrant she wasn't getting in. I shut the door. Somewhat bewildered, I walked back towards the lounge. Moments later, there was an extremely loud crash. I guessed it wasn't the pizza delivery boy and turned to see that the police had kicked my front door off its hinges. They ran up the hallway towards me and without saying a word sprayed me several times full in the face with CS spray.

I was pushed to the floor, handcuffed and four officers then sat on me. One of them struck me across the ribs with his extendable metal baton despite the fact I had not said a word or offered any form of resistance. Emma came downstairs and asked what was going on. The police said that they had been told I had assaulted somebody and I was under arrest for it. At no stage had they asked my name, but they certainly knew it.

Emma was in shock. She repeatedly told them they were talking total nonsense, that she had been in bed since the early hours of the morning and nobody had fallen out, let alone been assaulted. Fearful of their true intentions, Emma plugged in a cassette recorder and taped herself, telling the officers they were talking rubbish, but their only response was to radio their headquarters and inform control that they were being recorded. After 15 minutes of being sat on by four burly officers who were not quite sure what to do next, I was frogmarched out into the street where five police vehicles and one ambulance were parked with their blue lights flashing. I was put in a van, taken to a police station 15 miles away (there's one half a mile from my home), locked up until 3 a.m. and then released without charge. When I left Peterborough, I didn't move to Iraq or Palestine – this diabolical incident occurred in sleepy Lincolnshire.

I am not saying I am a saint and that I deserve to be treated well, I am just saying this is the way you are treated if you have behaved like a bastard all of your life.

EPILOGUE

I have spoken to a senior police officer since and I have emphasised the fact that my past is in the past and there is no need for 'extra vigilance' where I am concerned. Only time will tell if he was listening.

One evening I was sitting in the local pub with Emma when two young musicians walked in, set up their equipment and began to play. I could not believe what I was hearing. I have loved music all of my life and have seen most, if not all, of the major artists play live, but these boys were something else. I asked the landlord who they were and he said the guitarist and vocalist was Adam Mezzatesta, and the keyboard player was a guy named Anthony Shiels. 'They call themselves Mesh 29,' he said. When they were packing up their equipment, I introduced myself to them and said I thought they were wasting their talent playing in village pubs in front of a dozen or so people. I offered to manage them free of charge for a year and if at the end of that period we were not getting anywhere we could go our separate ways. Adam and Shielsie said that they would 'give it a go'. We shook hands and from that moment on I threw myself into getting them as much exposure as possible. Within weeks they had performed at The Cavern in Liverpool, The Rock Garden and The Borderline in London and supported ex-Carter USM star Jim Bob at The Shed in Leicester. An American record company has shown an interest in the band and two German TV stations have featured them in programmes. I know it is only a matter of time before somebody offers them a recording contract. It is extremely rewarding to see my efforts helping two decent young men fulfil their dream.

Listening to them talk about the future with such hope and excitement makes me realise the true cost of my wasted years. I can never take back the pain and misery I have caused those I love, those I thought I hated, or myself. I can only try to make amends.

How can anybody who has joined me on this journey say that crime is glamorous or gangster equals chic? If being a gangster is all about being clever and streetwise, why do so many of them end up living their entire life in the gutter?

The men and women who write these books about events they have made up or who lie to show themselves in a better light are inadequate social misfits crying out for attention. They are sad, lonely individuals who want people to admire them, like them and think they are somebodies. They surround themselves with fools they publicly call 'a firm' and privately call friends, but they know deep down nobody really gives a shit about them.

That is not a criticism, it is a fact. When the individuals in this book have finished telling people they are going to shoot, stab or murder me for what I have said, they will go home, reflect and know everything I have said is true. I have no doubt their loved ones will have been telling them the same thing for years, so it shouldn't come as that much of a shock to them.

When they sat down to write an account of their lives they may have thought that they were producing a book which people would admire them for. They were obviously so ashamed of telling the truth they turned to fantasy for inspiration. Stuck for genuine material, they probably believe that their lives have only been worthy of filling one book, but if they were prepared to unburden themselves of this gangster, I'm-so-fucking-hard nonsense, they would have another, more useful and important story to tell.

Tony Lambrianou, always keen to point out that he can walk around with his head held high, may be able to really walk tall if he knew that by being honest he had prevented an impressionable young man from spending his life in jail. If he told young people how he had been treated by the Krays, that gangs are no good, that the Krays were selfish, seedy bullies and there can never be loyalty amongst people who have devoted their lives to breaking rules and laws, he may be able to look at himself with pride. These days, the former 'Kray gang boss' must wonder what side of the mirror he is really on.

I am sure Gaffer, who I know endured the misery of spending an unhappy childhood in a home through no fault of his own, could give a boy in a similar situation hope and a will to make something of his life. Instead of writing a book about how hard he is, he could write about how much pain his anger, stupidity and recklessness have caused him and those he loves.

As for the Frayne brothers and Dave Courtney . . . Well, I suppose everybody is entitled to dream.